THE CHURCH OF IRELAND AND THE THIRD HOME RULE BILL

New Directions in Irish History is a series initiated by the Royal Irish Academy National Committee for History, which showcases the work of new scholars in Irish history. The series reflects the most up-to-date research, inclusive of all historical periods and with a broad inter-disciplinary approach.

FIRST TITLES IN THIS SERIES

Seán MacEntee
A Political Life
Tom Feeney

The Glory of Being Britons
Civic Unionism in Nineteenth-Century Belfast
John Bew

Faith and Patronage
The Political Career of Flaithrí Ó Maolchonaire c. 1560–1629
Benjamin Hazard

THE CHURCH OF IRELAND AND THE THIRD HOME RULE BILL

ANDREW SCHOLES

IRISH ACADEMIC PRESS

DUBLIN • PORTLAND, OR

First published in 2010 by Irish Academic Press

2 Brookside,
Dundrum Road,
Dublin 14, Ireland

920 NE 58th Avenue, Suite 300
Portland, Oregon,
97213-3786, USA

www.iap.ie

British Library Cataloguing-in-Publication Data
An entry can be found on request

978 0 7165 3052 7 (cloth)

Library of Congress Cataloging-in-Publication Data
An entry can be found on request

Printed in Great Britain by the MPG Books Group, Bodmin and King's Lynn

Contents

Acknowledgements

This book is the result of the Ph.D. thesis I completed at Queen's University Belfast. I owe a great deal to many people at Queen's, past and present. Professor Alvin Jackson first stimulated my interest in Unionism and the third Home Rule period, and set me on my way on my Ph.D. Professor David Hayton, among his many other duties, supervised me for a short time, a brief period during which I learnt a lot about being an historian. Dr Fearghal McGarry, Dr Marie Coleman, Robert Blair and Professor Sean Connolly provided valuable advice and support, as did Professor John Wolffe. My greatest thanks here goes to Professor Peter Gray, my supervisor for the best part of three years. He generously provided great guidance, advice, criticism and encouragement. For any errors of fact or judgement, I am, of course, solely responsible.

Financially, I am grateful to the Department of Education and Learning, for their generous grant towards my tuition and living expenses.

At Irish Academic Press the staff dealt with my manuscript with professionalism and enthusiasm. I would particularly like to thank Lisa Hyde for her help in patiently guiding a first-time author through the process of publication.

I owe a great deal of gratitude to the staff of the various libraries and record offices I used in the course of my research. The baulk of my research was undertaken at the Public Record Office of Northern Ireland (PRONI). Thanks here also go to the Ulster Unionist Council, for permission to view their archive, and to Gordon Lucy for his help in facilitating this. Elsewhere, staff at Belfast Central Newspaper Library, the Robinson Library in Armagh, the Representative Church Body library, Trinity College Dublin, the National Library Ireland, the British Library, Lambeth Palace, the House of Lords, the National Archives, Kew and the Plunkett Foundation provided assistance in a professional and helpful manner. Particular thanks must go to the select vestries of those parish churches that granted me access to their church records, and to the many unpaid volunteers who gave up their time to allow me to view the records.

Finally, I would like to thank my parents for their support and encouragement, and for providing an environment where reading and education were a valued part of growing up. Most importantly, my greatest thanks goes to my wife, Gillian, for her support and encouragement, and for patiently enduring the first year of her marriage to a Ph.D. student trying to turn his thesis into a book.

Introduction
Defending the Walls of Jericho:
The Church of Ireland and Irish Politics, 1910–18

> Religion has been woven into the very fabric of Irish identity and culture
> … religion has been inextricably bound up with political, intellectual,
> economic and social developments.[1]

> The history of modern Ireland can scarcely be written without frequent
> allusion to the established or erstwhile established church – a remarkable
> state of affairs given its size.[2]

Despite the apparent importance of religion and of the Church of Ireland in particular in Irish history, the Church's involvement in the events surrounding the third Home Rule Bill has been largely overlooked by historians. However, the period covered in this work – from the general elections of 1910 to the December 1918 general election (a period which will be referred to as the third Home Rule Bill period) – offers fertile ground for an historian of the Church of Ireland.

Home rule was an idea that had a 'very high level of brand recognition' among Irish voters.[3] Central to the demand for home rule was the abolition of the 1801 Act of union and the granting of some degree of Irish legislative autonomy. Isaac Butt, a Protestant, was an early advocate of some form of home rule, but it was during the 1880s, with the leadership of Charles Stewart Parnell (also a Protestant), that home rule became a viable force in British politics. Parnell harnessed the twin forces of fenianism and agrarianism, as well as the support of the Catholic Church, in driving forward home rule.[4] However, like Butt before him, Parnell found a precise definition for home rule elusive and maintained he was not a separatist, and promised that the 'Queen would be our Queen'. Instead, it was the Liberal premier, William Gladstone, who gave home rule 'reasonably finite form' in the 1886 Government of Ireland Bill.[5] Gladstone's bill was not especially radical. It allowed for the creation of a legislative body in Dublin dealing with Irish affairs as distinct from imperial affairs, but Westminster remained the supreme legislative authority for Ireland and retained control over matters of defence, the crown, and foreign affairs. The Irish executive was to be relatively powerless: the lord-lieutenant, acting for the Crown, was not required to choose ministers from the majority party in the Irish parliament and was responsible for summoning and dissolving the parliament.

However, despite such legislative moderation with regard to the constitutional link Ireland would retain with the rest of the United Kingdom, the first Home Rule Bill was defeated on the second reading by a combination of Tory opposition and the votes of disaffected Liberals in the Commons, led by Joseph Chamberlain. The subsequent general election demonstrated that while the majority in Ireland was committed to home rule, the majority in Britain remained opposed to such a measure, as a Conservative, unionist administration led by Lord Salisbury replaced Gladstone's. A second Home Rule Bill, brought forward in 1893, passed the Commons but was vetoed by the House of Lords. The parliamentary forces arrayed against home rule in 1886 and 1893 were mirrored in Ireland by the intense opposition aroused among those (mainly Protestants) who wanted to preserve the union. The events of 1886 and 1893 poured Irish politics into a 'mould which could not, apparently, be broken – a mould of "Home Rule verses Unionism"'.[6]

The story of Irish unionist opposition to home rule, in its party political, leadership and ideological aspects, has been comprehensively told. Patrick Buckland's work on the southern Irish element of unionism remains largely definitive;[7] Alvin Jackson's *The Ulster Party* and Graham Walker's *A History of the Ulster Unionist Party* trace the emergence of Ulster Unionist Party organisation and militancy.[8] Jackson has also contributed to the growing literature on Edward Carson, the leader of Ulster unionist opposition to the third Home Rule Bill.[9] Paul Bew's *Ideology and the Irish Question* deals with the third home rule period in terms of the competing ideologies of the nationalist and unionist protagonists.[10]

However, the role of the Protestant Churches in unionist opposition to home rule has been largely overlooked. This is surprising given that the religious element of unionism was held to be central in generating a political community capable of mounting credible resistance.[11] The Protestant Churches in Ireland believed home rule would mean 'Rome Rule': it was feared that by granting the majority Catholic population their desire for an Irish parliament, the civil and religious liberties of the Protestant minority would be threatened. The introduction of a third Home Rule Bill in 1912 once again aroused unionist opposition; after the constitutional changes of 1911, with the curtailment of the House of Lords' right to veto legislation, 'the time had come, it seemed, for the trumpet to sound, and the walls of Jericho would fall down of their accord'.[12] The Church of Ireland formed an important element of the opposition mobilised by the threat of home rule. The walls of Jericho may have been breached; the Church aimed to ensure that they would remain standing.

The third home rule period was rich in dramatic and controversial events, including the Ulster Covenant, the Larne gun-running, the First World War and the Easter Rising. The Church of Ireland, in various capacities and to differing degrees, was involved in these key events. Two essays, Finlay Holmes's 'Ulster will fight and Ulster will be right: the Protestant churches and Ulster's resistance to Home Rule, 1912–14' and Alan Megahey's '"God will defend the right": the Protestant churches and opposition to Home Rule' offer an overview of ecclesiastical involvement in unionist politics and support for Ulster unionist militancy.[13] Graham Walker's 'The Irish Presbyterian anti-Home Rule convention of 1912' details the response of the Presbyterian Church in Ulster to the imminent introduction of the third Home Rule Bill.[14] However, there are no extended and detailed works on the Protestant Churches comparable to those covering the role of the Catholic Church in Irish politics in a similar period, such as David Miller's *Church, State and Nation in Ireland, 1898–1921* or Jérôme aan de Wiel's *The Catholic Church in Ireland: 1914–1918*.[15]

This work seeks to rectify the relative anonymity of the Church of Ireland in accounts of the third Home Rule Bill period. It analyses the importance of the Church of Ireland to the various manifestations of Irish unionist resistance to the bill, and to what extent the Church actively influenced Irish politics as opposed to merely reflecting, at an ecclesiastical level, the differing (and at times competing) elements of Irish unionism. Within 'secular' Irish unionism, the period was marked by growing divisions between Ulster unionism and southern unionism, especially over partition. The extent to which these tensions were reproduced within the Church of Ireland is a theme of the work, and contributes to answering whether the third Home Rule Bill period changed the Church of Ireland – both in terms of its self-perception and how it viewed its role in Irish politics and its relationship with 'secular' Irish unionism. As part of this, the Church's response to the First World War, perhaps the main catalyst for change in Irish politics in the period, is analysed. An attempt is also made to answer how far the possibility of home rule contributed to a sense of pan-Protestantism in Ireland, and how the Church of Ireland's political involvement was a reflection of wider cultural trends also exhibited by the Church of England.

I

Kenneth Milne has asserted that since disestablishment the Church of Ireland has had to 'account for its stewardship, and needs the scrutiny of the historian to help with the audit'.[16] However, the Church has on the whole been short-changed by historical accounts of its role in the third Home Rule Bill period. Early works displayed a confessional approach, more concerned with defending the Church of Ireland's position in the new Irish Free State than with explaining the Church's role in the third Home Rule Bill crisis. Archdeacon H.E. Patton's *Fifty Years of Disestablishment: A Sketch*, published in 1922, drew attention to *Ne Temere*, a decree 'that had come to stay, and was calculated to raise further trouble for many years to come'.[17] Patton focused on the role of bishops and synods in the home rule dispute, and adopted an uncritical interpretation of the Church's support for unionism. The Church's involvement in the First World War was venerated. Having rallied to the empire's call, the Church of Ireland had 'honoured the splendid chivalry of the sons whom she had nurtured ... in many a remote district, in south and west, where churchmen were but few, there would be the thrill of a proud remembrance "that he was born there"'.[18] Patton avoided any reference to the Church of Ireland's involvement in militant Ulster unionism. Perhaps for his audience of southern Anglicans, the sacrifices of the war offered a more useful narrative than accounts of bishops and clergy blessing loyalist resistance, by placing the Church of Ireland, then in an apparently precarious position in the Free State, firmly in a tradition of loyalty to Britain.

Patton's concern with *Ne Temere* was repeated in the first comprehensive history of the Church of Ireland written after the third Home Rule Bill period, W.A. Phillips's *History of the Church of Ireland from the Earliest Times to the Present Day*. Phillips's work was commissioned by the General Synod to 'constitute a "measure of defence against hostile propaganda"'.[19] *Ne Temere* was but one example of 'Roman aggression' 'injurious' to the interests of the Church of Ireland.[20] Treatment of the pro-unionist role of the Church of Ireland during the third Home Rule Bill period was given less space than the Church's opposition to the aggressiveness of the Catholic Church, and even to disputes over canons and rubrics for worship in a number of dioceses. Like Patton, the contributor to Phillips's work focused heavily on the effect the war had had on the Church of Ireland. While 'morally strengthened by the deeds of heroism and self-sacrifices inspired by her teaching', the Church had, he observed, emerged from the period of the Great War materially weakened in comparison with her rivals.[21] In retrospect, the war provided a glorious story and a more appealing form of sacrifice than that which the covenanters of Ulster may have been prepared to undertake in defence of Ulster. The war dead, so soon after the war had ended, appeared to be more deserving of remembrance than those who actively resisted home rule.

The southern focus of the early post-home rule literature reflects the political preoccupations of southern Anglicanism as it came to terms with no longer being part of the 'union'. This southern orientation may have been due to the fact that the machinery of Church of Ireland government and administration was based in Dublin, as was the training college for prospective ministers. It should also be noted that members of the Church of Ireland in the Free State continued to regard the end of British rule in the twenty-six counties with apprehension.[22] However, T.J. Johnston and colleagues' *A History of the Church of Ireland* (1953)[23] failed to mention home rule at all, perhaps reflecting the Church of Ireland's official acceptance of the newly constituted Irish Republic. Johnston's work did not rectify the lack of attention paid to the Church's role in Irish politics, and was flawed in failing to take account of the transformation in Irish historiography already evident by the early 1950s.[24]

A beginning was made in establishing a more impartial, academic approach to the history of the Church of Ireland by R.B. McDowell in his *The Church of Ireland, 1869–1969*. McDowell, as a product of the *Irish Historical Studies* school of history (which sought to correct overly partisan interpretations of the Irish past), adopted a professional and 'scientific' approach to the history of the Church of Ireland. He utilised a wider range of sources (such as the papers of John Henry Bernard, archbishop of Dublin) than earlier scholars in his work on the Church of Ireland; he also began to scratch the surface of the tensions within the Church over how to respond to the threat of home rule, drawing attention to the disputes between the northern and southern bishops concerning the Ulster Covenant and partition.[25] McDowell was sympathetic to the Church of Ireland, although he was at times critical and adopted a 'detached' tone rarely seen in the earlier confessional accounts. However, like Phillips's work, *The Church of Ireland, 1869–1969* was written to satisfy a need within the Church – McDowell (an Anglican himself) had been asked by Archbishop Simms to provide an account of the Church of Ireland in the century since disestablishment. McDowell's work is a good introduction to the Church of Ireland and the third Home Rule Bill period, but is no more than that. This work enlarges on McDowell's account of the Church's role beyond that played by the bishops and synods, to take into account the involvement of lower clergy and parish vestries. This deeper approach allows a greater exploration than that offered by McDowell of the Church's importance – or otherwise – to Irish unionism. McDowell's account of the political participation of the episcopate is also expanded beyond his focus upon John Henry Bernard. His assumption that Bernard was a figure who attempted to preserve unity will be questioned, and it will be suggested that Bernard's particular brand of southern unionism was indicative of the internal divisions within the Church raised by the threat of partition.

McDowell's work is one of the few examples, in the period since the Troubles began in Northern Ireland, of a history that refers to the Church of Ireland's role in the third Home Rule Bill period.[26] Alan Megahey's 1969

Queen's University doctoral thesis offers a brief but valuable insight into the Church of Ireland's mindset towards home rule, while his *The Irish Protestant Churches in the Twentieth Century* is a useful survey work.[27] Alan Acheson's *A History of the Church of Ireland, 1691–1996* devotes only two pages to the third Home Rule Bill, perhaps unsurprising in a work that covers over 300 years.[28] Acheson, like McDowell, was sympathetic to the Church of Ireland, having been a member of various committees of the General Synod for over thirty years. The 'insider' nature of Acheson's work was emphasised by a glowing introduction from Harold Millar, bishop of Down, and the fact that it was published by APCK, an Anglican publishing house.

A short corrective to the various histories of the Church of Ireland and home rule written by those sympathetic to the Church was provided by Thomas P. O'Neill in an essay included in *Irish Anglicanism: 1896–1969*. This was a collection of essays written by non-Anglican commentators and historians; O'Neill's account focuses on the nationalist or home rule figures in the Church of Ireland, such as Rev. James Owen Hannay, Erskine Childers and W.B. Yeats.[29] However, while interesting and valuable in demonstrating that there were dissenting voices against the Church's anti-home rule stand, O'Neill's essay serves principally to illustrate the necessity for a more comprehensive, balanced work on the subject. Clearly, the majority of the members of the Church of Ireland were against home rule – what is needed is a history that deals with this opposition as well as taking account of the dissenters and those unhappy with the political stand the Church was taking.

While the majority of works that refer to the Church of Ireland and home rule do so at the episcopal and synodical level, there is a dearth of autobiographies and biographies of leading Church of Ireland figures of the period.[30] The only notable exceptions are Charles Frederick D'Arcy's autobiography, *The Adventures of a Bishop*, and biographies of John Henry Bernard and John Gregg. D'Arcy was the stridently Ulster unionist bishop of Down during the third Home Rule Bill period, and his autobiography, described as 'lamentably inadequate as a self-portrait' by Gregg's biographer, tends to obscure more than illuminate.[31] Unsurprisingly, considering he was primate when writing *Adventures*, D'Arcy made no reference to the tension caused within the episcopate by the covenant and threat of partition. In other ways, *Adventures* is what would be expected from a conservative unionist bishop of a northern diocese – D'Arcy was effusive in his praise of Ulster Day and the wider anti-home rule movement.[32] R.H. Murray's rather hagiographical biography of John Henry Bernard, alongside the fact Murray was a clergyman, made his work part of the wider confessional literature on the Church of Ireland. However, his account of Bernard's career is none-the-less useful in explaining his subject's attitude to partition and involvement in the Irish Convention.[33] George Seaver's biography of Gregg (bishop of Ossory from 1915) is of most value to the historian of the third home rule period. Gregg was one of three Church of Ireland bishops who joined with seventeen of his Catholic counterparts in issuing a manifesto against partition in 1917. Seaver drew upon the newspaper record and the private correspondence of D'Arcy and John Baptist Crozier (archbishop of Armagh) in order to piece together the tension caused within the Church of Ireland by the manifesto.[34]

II

The Church of Ireland is a hierarchical church, and at the time under investigation a thirteen-man House of Bishops formed the apex of that hierarchy, presided over by archbishops for the two provinces of Armagh and Dublin. The archbishop of Armagh was primate of all Ireland. Although the House of Bishops remained largely unaccountable, voting privately and meeting 'behind closed doors',[35] they were not autonomous actors. Bishops shared authority with the General Synod, which in turn was a partially elected body, having at its base the parish system.

Given the partly representative nature of the Church's structure, the episcopal focus of much Church of Ireland historiography of the third Home Rule Bill period is flawed in tending to overlook the important role played by parochial clergy and the laity. To achieve a balanced perspective, this work does not jettison a hierarchical or 'vertical' perspective, but instead incorporates it within a 'horizontal' one. This combination allows a study of the church at the 'high political' level of the bishops and synod alongside reaction at a local parish level. Vertical ecclesiastical history is concerned with the role of a church hierarchy in a church with a traditional episcopal structure. Various sources are used to piece together the role played by the episcopacy. Speeches, sermons, articles in journals and letters to the press were public ways for bishops to influence opinion. While only the archbishop of Dublin, John Henry Bernard, left a collection of papers, private correspondence between bishops and politicians is preserved in the papers of various unionist figures. The minutes of the House of Bishops and the Standing Committee of the General Synod, closed to contemporaries but now held by the Representative Church Body of the Church of Ireland, lend some insight into the importance of political issues for the Church of Ireland hierarchy.

Horizontal ecclesiastical history focuses on the laity in a given church or parish, with what they actually believed 'and what they have done with that belief'.[36] Patrick Collinson's definition of what comes under the terms of a horizontal approach is modified slightly by including the parochial clergy, who have been overshadowed in Church of Ireland historiography by their episcopal superiors. To explore what was happening at a parish level during the third Home Rule Bill period, some often-overlooked primary sources are utilised. Parish records, including select and general vestry minutes, church magazines and preacher books provide valuable insights into activity at a local level. Minutes reveal that select vestries were often concerned with 'the three f's' – finance, fabric and furnishings – of a church. However, occasionally vestries expressed opinions on political issues, such as home rule or the impact of war. At the annual general vestry meeting, when it was common for the minister to give an address on the state of the parish, the subject of home rule was often raised. It is fair to assume that an anti-home rule general vestry address was reflective not only of the rector's views, but also of the views of the majority of parishioners. It is unlikely that a clergyman would have used the opportunity of his 'keynote' speech, more often than not an opportunity to pat the congregation on the back for a successful year and bask in the reflected glory or to rebuke them for the poor state of the church finances or low attendance at holy communion, to express controversial political opinions. Parish magazines normally included a letter from the rector, addressed to the parish. These magazines were often used as vehicles to express the political opinions of the clergy. For example, during the war, rectors' letters were largely focused on encouraging involvement in war work. Preacher books recorded the officiating clergy and attendance at each church service, and often included details on everything from the weather to the nature of a particular service. Preacher books are useful in ascertaining the popularity of 'unionist' services – those attended by local unionist clubs or the UVF.

Provincial newspapers are valuable in demonstrating how active local parish churches were in opposing home rule or participating in the war effort. In addition, the Church of Ireland was covered by two Church newspapers – the national *Church of Ireland Gazette* and the more Ulster-focused *Irish Churchman*. The differing political stands of these papers provide fertile ground for the historian in tracing the emergence of discord within the Church of Ireland over partition.

III

In 1911 the Church of Ireland was the largest Protestant church in Ireland, and through its parish system was the only Protestant church to cover the whole of the country. Adherents to the Anglican Church made up 13 per cent of the population, compared to the 10 per cent who were Presbyterian. These figures disguise regional variations. The Presbyterian Church was largest in Ulster (covering 26 per cent of the population in the nine counties), but barely registered in southern provinces. The Church of Ireland, still claiming a sizeable proportion of Protestants in Ulster (23 per cent of the population in the province), was also the church of most Protestants in the south and west of Ireland, making up almost 7 per cent of the population in the three southern provinces.[37] Indeed, it is not too much of a generalisation to view the history of southern unionism as the history of the 'political experience of the Church of Ireland population'.[38]

Disestablishment, in 1869–70, had turned the Church of Ireland from a state church to a self-governing voluntary body, substantially altering the Church's administrative and governmental structures. Church government became representative in nature and parliamentary in style.[39] The organisational triad of parish–diocese–province operated under the 'supreme legislative authority' of the General Synod.[40] The General Synod, modelled on the Westminster parliament (as it existed in 1870), met annually and was composed of an upper house (the House of Bishops) and a lower house (the House of Representatives) made up of two lay members for each clerical member.[41] The synod discussed and voted on amendments to the Church's constitution, changes in doctrine, articles, rites and rubrics, and considered the reports of the various committees and boards elected by the synod.[42] Day-to-day administration of Church business was carried out by the Standing Committee of the General Synod (composed of the bishops and one lay and one clerical member from each diocese, plus co-opted members). The standing committee was also charged with taking into account any legislation brought forward by parliament that could affect the interests of the Church of Ireland, and to take such action as might be deemed necessary.[43] At each level of Church government, elections were held, bringing accountability in its administration for the first time.[44]

Beneath the General Synod in the governmental structure were diocesan synods (essentially regional versions of the General Synod), which elected members to the House of Representatives of the General Synod on a triennial basis. Diocesan synod members were elected by parish general vestries, again on a triennial basis. General vestries were composed of men who had registered as members (or general vestrymen) of their parish church. An additional layer of government was provided by select vestries, which were involved in the management of the Church at a parish level. Select vestry members were elected at the annual meeting of the general vestry, usually held shortly after Easter. In an article on Church government published in 1918, the *Church of Ireland Gazette* termed the annual general vestry meeting the 'general election' of the Church, allowing an opportunity to vote for 'fit and proper persons to represent the parish or congregation'.[45]

The 1910 Church of Ireland Conference, held in Belfast, provided evidence of the Church's self-perception on the eve of the third Home Rule Bill period. The conference was an opportunity to discuss various issues of concern and importance, and brought together members of the Church from across Ireland, as well as representatives from other churches. The archbishop of Dublin, Joseph Peacocke, addressed the conference in a debate entitled 'the Church's positions and problems'. Peacocke reasserted a commonly held view among Irish Anglicans that the Church's 'claim to be descended from the ancient Church of Ireland, and to be its present representative in this land, is fully justified on historical grounds'.[46] The episcopal character of the Church of Ireland linked it with St Patrick, while it also followed the 'ancient Irish Church' in accepting the ancient creeds on the basis of the 'most certain warrants of Holy Scripture'. Peacocke also drew attention to the Church's parochial system, through which 'she occupies the whole country with her organisation'. The Church would 'hope and pray' that this position would continue, 'even under difficulties, throughout the land, from North to South and from East to West'. This belief that the Church of Ireland was in essence a 'national Church' was reinforced by Canon Flewett, who told the conference that 'we are Irishmen, our Church is the Church of Ireland, and we are very proud of the fact'.[47]

The Church of Ireland's self-definition as an 'Irish Church' with links stretching back to St Patrick did not, however, encourage it, corporately, to identify with cultural nationalism. Despite the involvement in the Gaelic League of a number of prominent Church of Ireland members and clergymen (such as Rev. James Owen Hannay and Douglas Hyde, the son of a County Roscommon rector), the Standing Committee of the General Synod refused a request from the League to make the teaching of the Irish language compulsory in Church of Ireland schools. In a letter to the standing committee, the Gaelic League claimed it had not met much 'sympathy and assistance from the general body of the Church of Ireland ... as a whole your people have hitherto held aloof'. The standing committee *did* appoint a sub-committee to consider a response to the Gaelic League. However, its outcome was largely predetermined by Bishop Crozier's belief that while the Church should support the teaching of Irish as well as English in Irish-speaking parts of the country, at a wider level 'we would be doing an injustice to our children by compelling them to learn a language which would be of no practical value to many of them afterwards'.[48]

It would be a mistake to doubt the genuineness of the theological or historical convictions motivating the Church of Ireland's perceived status as an Irish and national church. However, for a church representing a small (although relatively prosperous) minority, the sense of a deep rootedness in the Irish ecclesiastical past granted a degree of legitimacy and confidence. The refusal to patronise the Gaelic League hinted at the underlying utility of this belief. The defence of the 'Irish' character of the Church of Ireland became a main feature of the Church's opposition to the third Home Rule Bill, characterised by refutations of the competing claim of the Catholic Church and a fear that a home rule government would allow the Catholic Church to confiscate the cathedrals and other material endowments of the Church of Ireland.

The Church of Ireland's national status rested partly on the fact that it integrated Anglicans in Ulster with those in the rest of Ireland into one institutional structure. Despite prophecies of 'schism between north and south' as a result of disestablishment from, among others, William Magee (the Irish-born bishop of Peterborough and scion of an influential Irish ecclesiastical family), there was no division within the Church.[49] There were some signs of tension – complaints were raised in 1909 at the unbalanced nature of the Church of Ireland's representative structures, which gave the less populous southern province of the Church a disproportionate influence at the General Synod.[50] However, it is possible that the all-Ireland nature of the General Synod actually served to develop closer links between northern and southern churchmen by bringing them together annually to debate and vote on issues of importance for the Church. The essential theological unity of the Church of Ireland should also be noted. McDowell attributes the lack of dispute over doctrinal issues after disestablishment, especially when compared with the Church of England, to two factors: the 'cautious distaste for extremes' of the Dublin divinity school, which provided a common intellectual background for clergy, and the legislation passed in the early 1870s which left ritualists little opportunity to depart from established usage – and deprived anti-ritualists of satisfactory targets.[51] The unity of the Church of Ireland pre-1910 was demonstrated at the outset of the third Home Rule Bill period with a repudiation of any abandonment of their southern brethren from Ulster-based clergy. However, ultimately the threat of home rule, and the related possibility of partition, served to bring Magee's prophecy of 'schism' close to fruition.

The Church of Ireland's Irish and national character, established pre-1910, was an important element of its response to the third Home Rule Bill. In addition, the Church's links with other Protestant churches played a role in how home rule was opposed. The Church of Ireland, due to its erstwhile status as an established church and geographical proximity to England, was strongly influenced by its relationship with the Church of England. Clearly, disestablishment had altered, although not greatly impaired, this relationship. The constitutional link with the Church of England had been broken – as the archbishop of Dublin pointed out at the Church conference, disestablishment had 'cut the bonds that tied us to the state'. The Church of Ireland was now 'autonomous' but had remained in 'full communion' with the Church of England.[52] While 'autonomous', the Church of Ireland was influenced by its sister church in England. McDowell points out that the Irish Church derived most of its 'intellectual subsistence' from the Church of England, with the result that the moderate 'central churchmanship' imbibed from English theological scholarship 'was bound to have considerable influence over the Church of Ireland'.[53] The relatively close ties between the two episcopal churches were confirmed at the Church of Ireland Conference. The bishop of Durham, Handley Moule, preached the conference's opening sermon in Belfast Cathedral, claiming 'no tongue could tell how much English Christianity in the primeval days owed to Ireland'. Moule's presence, along with that of the head of the Episcopal Church in Scotland and other leading Church of England clergymen, was seen as evidence of the 'interest and sympathy' in England and Scotland for the work of the Church of Ireland.[54]

While the Church of Ireland on the eve of the third Home Rule Bill period had relatively close links with the Church of England, of more importance in a study of the Church's political role was its relationship with the Presbyterian Church in Ireland. In 1911 objections to Protestant ecumenism were raised by Bishop Elliot of Kilmore, who believed 'Home Reunion' was more dangerous to the Church of Ireland than home rule. It was a waste of the Church of Ireland's time to pursue reunion, as nonconformist churches were divisive and tended to 'disintegrate', while English nonconformists supported home rule. The existence of different Protestant denominations allowed diverse religious thought and 'afforded a safety valve' for freedom of thought.[55] However, Elliot was a minority voice who went against the trend for closer denominational co-operation under way by 1911. In 1905 the General Synod had established a committee to consider how best to pursue the 'spiritual and organic' union of the various Protestant denominations in Ireland, 'which have so much of belief and interest in common'.[56] While the committee later reported that its work was 'mainly one of quiet observation',[57] its existence at least pointed to the growing links between the Church of Ireland and the Presbyterian Church. In 1910 and 1911 the committee pointed to education as an issue on which co-operation was possible;[58] to this could be added the temperance campaign, led largely by the 'Catch-my-pal' movement, which was established by a Presbyterian clergyman but supported by many in the Church of Ireland. The Presbyterian moderator was accorded a warm welcome at the 1910 Church of Ireland Conference, and in a speech devoid of references to the political situation, welcomed how the two Churches were 'drawing closer together'.[59]

Disestablishment altered the social complexion of the Church of Ireland clergy and episcopacy. After the death in 1885 of Marcus Beresford (archbishop of Armagh) and in 1897 of William Plunkett (archbishop of Dublin), few bishops came from the ranks of the landed gentry.[60] Plunkett believed that disestablishment had produced ministers who 'socially and intellectually' fell short 'of the standard of the past'.[61] This may have been an exaggeration – Megahey points out that many clergy ordained after disestablishment had attended the Irish equivalent of public schools, and were largely drawn from the wealthy middle class.[62] In 1914 there were 1,483 clergy, of whom 1,310 were graduates. Trinity College Dublin (TCD) was the preferred university for those seeking holy orders: 81 per cent of ordained clergy had studied at Trinity, whereas only 6 per cent were graduates of the Queen's colleges of Belfast, Cork and Galway.[63]

Occupationally, in the forty years following disestablishment the Church of Ireland had lost its commanding position in the professional world. However, it still had a disproportionate share of barristers, doctors, bankers and civil engineers.[64] In one area – farmers and farm labourers – the Church of Ireland had been weakened since disestablishment: in 1911 fewer than 8 per cent of farmers were members of the Church.[65] Membership of the Church of Ireland covered a broad social spectrum, from the majority of the aristocracy to a high proportion of the labouring classes.[66] As with lay governance in the Presbyterian and Methodist Churches, the upper middle class composed the majority of the Church of Ireland's representatives. Such members were generally educated, wealthy (and therefore shouldered the burden for the upkeep of the Church) and perhaps equally significantly were able to afford time off work to attend meetings of the General Synod or diocesan synods.[67]

A theme running throughout this work is the attitude of three key bishops towards the various events of the period. John Baptist Crozier, Charles Frederick

D'Arcy and John Henry Bernard exerted the greatest influence within the Church of Ireland. From 1911 Crozier was primate and D'Arcy, having replaced Crozier, was bishop of Down and Connor and Dromore, the most populous Church of Ireland diocese. Bernard replaced D'Arcy as bishop of Ossory in 1911, and in 1915 was elevated to the archbishopric of Dublin.

Born in Cavan in 1853, and ordained in 1876, John Baptist Crozier was rector of Holywood for seventeen years (1880–97). In 1907 he was elected bishop of Down and in 1911 became primate. His long incumbency of an Ulster parish, allied to his Ulster roots and his four years as bishop of Down (1907–11) on the eve of the Ulster crisis, made Crozier sympathetic to Ulster unionism. However, it is likely Crozier's Cavan upbringing may have led him to doubt the possibility of a 'clean cut' of the six north-eastern counties of Ulster, while his position as primate of Ireland led him to question any form of Ulster exclusion, fearing partition could split the Church of Ireland. Crozier has been unfairly ignored in histories of the Church of Ireland. This is probably largely due to the fact he produced no written work of note during his career and left no collection of private papers or correspondence. However, as primate, he set the tone of the Church's opposition to home rule and support for the war through his speeches at the General Synod. Crozier is also deserving of study as he was at the centre of the partition dispute within the Church, and took part, along with Bernard, in the Irish Convention (1917–18). In addition, he corresponded with many leading unionists – he was in close contact with the Londonderrys and was well enough acquainted with Edward Carson to address him as 'My dear Ned'.[68] In the eyes of contemporaries, Crozier was an important figure. The historian H.E. Patton believed the Church of Ireland never had 'a more watchful pilot ... none more sensitive to every ripple on the waters, none more keen to detect a coming storm, none more ready to meet it when it comes'.[69] However, it is Crozier's uncertain reaction to the 'coming storm' of partition that makes him of particular interest.

While Crozier occupied a middle ground between Ulster and southern unionism, John Henry Bernard came strongly to oppose Ulster exclusion. Bernard was politically conservative and was a strong critic of home rule who publicised the potential threat posed to Church of Ireland property by the Catholic Church under self-government. Theologically, however, Bernard held high-church views and was suspected of 'having sympathy with Ritualism'.[70] Like Crozier, Bernard's position on home rule was modified during the period. At the Irish Convention Bernard followed the lead of Lord Midleton and supported a home rule settlement that did not exclude Ulster. Unlike Crozier, Bernard plays a leading role in accounts of the Church of Ireland's involvement in the third Home Rule Bill. It was largely down to his role in the convention that Bernard has been described as 'undoubtedly the greatest ecclesiastical statesman in the Church of Ireland – perhaps in Ireland'.[71]

Charles Frederick D'Arcy travelled the least distance in his political views during the third home rule period, remaining a staunch Ulster unionist throughout. He was the firmest supporter of the Ulster Covenant and UVF among the episcopate and put pressure on Crozier at the Irish Convention to support the Ulster unionist delegation. Born in Dublin in 1859 to middle-class parents, D'Arcy was a talented scholar, and it was a desire to reconcile science and the 'new and wonderful thought of the age' with Christianity that he recalled had attracted him to the ministry.[72] D'Arcy's spell as bishop of Down and Connor and Dromore (which covered counties Antrim and Down) placed him at the heart of

Ulster unionist resistance to home rule. With such a unionist colouration to his core constituency, it is perhaps not surprising that D'Arcy was such a firm advocate of Ulster unionism. However, according to his autobiography, *Adventures of a Bishop*, D'Arcy did not need persuading in his political beliefs. His view of history made him a natural unionist. For D'Arcy, nineteenth-century Ireland appeared to represent an Arcadian paradise. He believed landlords had received unfair opprobrium and the Church of Ireland 'was not the wicked vampire that her enemies declared'.[73] The Ulster Protestant had an innate right to possession of the land – 'the Ulster of today belongs to the Ulsterman, because he made it'.[74] Observing an Orange Order parade in Belfast in 1886, D'Arcy realised the Ulsterman was opposed 'in unalterable resolution to the threatened revolution'.[75] However, like Bernard, D'Arcy's theological views did not mirror his political conservatism. D'Arcy described himself as being 'very broad' in his theological views. Emotionally, he was in sympathy with the evangelical wing, but believed it too 'narrow and rigid'. However, he was equally averse to the 'Catholic' school, associating it with a 'theological or ecclesiastical system which bound upon men an elaborate system of dogmatic constructions and of regulations for the religious life' which infringed upon 'intellectual liberty'. To D'Arcy, the 'via-media' seemed the 'way of truth and wisdom'.[76]

IV

Heal Not Lightly is a recent treatment of the Church of Ireland's involvement in Ulster unionist resistance to the third Home Rule Bill. Written by Harry Smith, a member of the 'Christian Renewal Centre' based in Kilbroney, County Down, and published by New Wine ministries, a charismatic grouping within the Anglican Church, *Heal Not Lightly* criticises the Church of Ireland's involvement in the third home rule period in general, and the Ulster Covenant in particular. Smith believes the Church used fear to communicate the errors of the Catholic Church, and that it supported the Ulster Covenant to avoid losing political power. By supporting the Covenant, the Church of Ireland had given Satan power, the baleful results of which were demonstrated in the sectarian divisions of Northern Ireland.[77] In a dream, Smith claimed he had seen a 'very vivid, full-colour movie picture of a beaver's dam'. People were attempting to dismantle the dam, but to no avail, as at its foundation the dam was supported by a large log bearing the words 'The Ulster Covenant'. Smith heard a voice telling him 'if you want to see this water flow out across the land, then you must remove the log in the foundation of this dam.' The 'you' apparently carried a personal and 'wider, corporate' dimension.[78] Smith interpreted his dream as meaning God longed for the current leaders of the Church of Ireland to atone for the sins of their forefathers, who had supported the Covenant. The current leadership should dismantle the Covenant, through repentance, 'thus enabling a mighty torrent of the Holy Spirit to flow'.[79]

   Heal Not Lightly was reviewed by Johnston McMaster, lecturer at the Irish School of Ecumenics, in *Search*, a theologically liberal-inclined Church of Ireland journal. Although welcoming *Heal Not Lightly* for bringing to wider attention a defining event in establishing Ulster unionist identity, McMaster criticised Smith's interpretation of the Bible. Despite asserting 'all readings of the Bible are perspectival', McMaster believed Smith's highly spiritualised and literalised reading was flawed, leading to a 'proof-text' approach to scripture.[80] However,

McMaster's review of *Heal Not Lightly* revealed his own presuppositions concerning the Ulster Covenant. He believed Smith's analysis was flawed for containing no analysis of the 'deep-rooted anti-Catholicism at the heart of historical evangelical religion', which helped explain the sectarianism inherent in the Ulster Covenant.[81]

Smith's book and McMaster's review reveal some of the perils and pitfalls of the third Home Rule Bill period for an historian of the Church of Ireland. *Heal Not Lightly* demonstrates the danger of reading present-day theological or political concerns into the history of religion in this period. Smith, by not adequately explaining or taking into account the motivations and prejudices of the Church of Ireland in 1912, has produced a fundamentally ahistorical interpretation of the Ulster Covenant. His application of charismatic presuppositions heavily influences his judgement to the extent that the Covenant is not seen in terms that would be recognisable to members of the Church of Ireland in 1912. McMaster's belief that the Church of Ireland's support of the Covenant can be understood as the outworking of evangelical beliefs is also flawed. While undoubtedly an important element in explaining Protestant fear of home rule, a reliance on evangelicalism as an explanation over-simplifies the complex mixture of religious and political beliefs that motivated opposition to home rule. In addition, a number of leading members of the Church of Ireland who supported the covenant in 1912 would not have described themselves as evangelical.

While it may not be possible for historians to make their own beliefs 'simply and literally irrelevant in understanding' the people they study, 'imperfect self-restraint is better than none'.[82] It is hoped this work will avoid the traps of historicism and reductionism. Once the danger of prejudice and the necessity for self-awareness is recognised,[83] it is possible to be guided, as far as possible, by an understanding of what religious – and political – beliefs meant for members of the Church of Ireland in relation to the third Home Rule Bill.

NOTES

1. A. Ford, 'Standing one's ground: Religion, polemic and Irish history since the Reformation', in A. Ford, J. McGuire and K. Milne (eds), *As by Law Established: The Church of Ireland since the Reformation* (Dublin, 1995), p.13.
2. K. Milne, '1870–1992', in K. Milne (ed.), *A Church of Ireland Bibliography* (Dublin, 2005), p.49.
3. A. Jackson, *Ireland 1798–1998: Politics and War* (Oxford, 1999), p.110.
4. A. Jackson, *Home Rule: An Irish History, 1800–2000* (London, 2003), p.39.
5. A. O'Day, *Home Rule: 1867–1921* (Manchester, 1998), p.10.
6. D.G. Boyce, *The Irish Question and British Politics, 1868–1986* (London, 1988), p.32.
7. P. Buckland, *Irish Unionism I: The Anglo-Irish and the New Ireland, 1885–1922* (Dublin, 1972).
8. A. Jackson, *The Ulster Party: Irish Unionists in the House of Commons, 1884–1911* (Oxford, 1989); G. Walker, *A History of the Ulster Unionist Party: Protest, Pragmatism, and Pessimism* (Manchester, 2004). Jackson subsequently placed unionist opposition to home rule in the wider context of attempts to solve the 'Irish question' in *Home Rule: An Irish History, 1800–2000* (London, 2003).
9. A. Jackson, *Sir Edward Carson* (Dublin, 1993); for Carson, see also A. Gailey, 'King Carson: an essay on the invention of leadership', *Irish Historical Studies*, vol. 30 (1996).
10. P. Bew, *Ideology and the Irish Question* (Oxford, 1994).
11. See C. Townsend, *Ireland: The Twentieth Century* (London, 1998), p.59.
12. A.T.Q. Stewart, *The Ulster Crisis* (London, 1967), p.25.
13. F. Holmes, 'Ulster will fight and Ulster will be right: the Protestant churches and Ulster's resistance to Home Rule, 1912–14', *Studies in Church History*, vol. 20 (1983); A. Megahey, '"God will defend the right": the Protestant Churches and opposition to Home Rule', in D.G. Boyce and A. O'Day (eds), *Defenders of the Union: A Survey of British and Irish Unionism since 1801* (London, 2001).
14. G. Walker, 'The Irish Presbyterian anti-Home Rule convention of 1912', *Studies: An Irish Quarterly Review*, vol. 86 (1997), pp.71–7.

15. D.W. Miller, *Church, State and Nation in Ireland, 1898–1921* (Dublin, 1973); J. aan de Wiel, *The Catholic Church in Ireland: 1914–1918* (Dublin, 2004).
16. Milne, '1870–1992', p.49.
17. H.E. Patton, *Fifty Years of Disestablishment: A Sketch* (Dublin, 1922), p.264; for the third Home Rule bill and after, see pp.260–4.
18. Ibid., pp.271–2.
19. Milne, '1870–1992', p.41; see also Marie-Claire Considere-Charon, 'The Church of Ireland: continuity and change', *Studies: An Irish Quarterly Review*, 87, 346 (Summer 1998), p.110.
20. Rev. C.A. Webster, 'The Church since Disestablishment', in W.A. Phillips (ed.), *History of the Church of Ireland from the Earliest Times to the Present Day*, 3 vols (Oxford, 1933), vol iii., p.399. See below pp.19–22 for a discussion of *Ne Temere*.
21. Ibid., p.412.
22. J.H. Whyte, 'Political life in the South', in Michael Hurley (ed.), *Irish Anglicanism: 1869–1969* (Dublin, 1970), p.143.
23. T.J. Johnston, J.L. Robinson and R.W. Jackson, *A History of the Church of Ireland* (Dublin, 1953).
24. Milne, '1870–1992', p.41.
25. R.B. McDowell, *The Church of Ireland, 1869–1969* (London, 1975), pp.104, 108.
26. Martin Maguire has produced a number of articles of a socio-economic bent focussing on the Church of Ireland and the Dublin working class. See 'The Church of Ireland and the problem of the Protestant working-class of Dublin, 1870s–1930s', in Ford *et al.* (eds), *As by Law Established*, pp.195–203; '"Our people": the Church of Ireland and the culture of community in Dublin since disestablishment', in R. Gillespie and W.G. Neely, *The Laity and the Church of Ireland, 1000–2000: All Sorts and Conditions* (Dublin, 2002), pp.277–303.
27. A. Megahey, 'The Irish Protestant churches and social and political issues, 1870–1914' (Queen's University Belfast, unpublished Ph.D. thesis, 1969), ch. 2; A. Megahey, *The Irish Protestant Churches in the Twentieth Century* (London, 2000), pp.7–12, 23–43.
28. A. Acheson, *A History of the Church of Ireland, 1691–1996* (Dublin, 1997), pp.225–6.
29. T.P. O'Neill, 'Political life, 1870–1921', in Hurley (ed.), *Irish Anglicanism: 1869–1969*, pp.101–9.
30. Milne, '1870–1992', p.46.
31. George Seaver, *John Allen Fitzgerald Gregg: Archbishop* (Dublin, 1963), p.34.
32. C.F. D'Arcy, *The Adventures of a Bishop* (London, 1934), p.190.
33. R.H. Murray, *Archbishop Bernard: Professor, Prelate, and Provost* (London, 1931), pp.315–29.
34. Seaver, *Gregg: Archbishop*, pp.85–92.
35. Raymond Refaussé, *Church of Ireland Records* (2nd edition, Dublin, 2006), p.45.
36. P. Collinson, 'The vertical and the horizontal in religious history: internal and external integration of the subject', in Ford *et al.* (eds), *As by Law Established*, pp.19–21.
37. See Megahey, ' Irish Protestant churches and social and political issues', pp.52–6.
38. Milne, '1870–1992', p.44.
39. Refausse, *Church of Ireland Records*, p.44.
40. Daithí Ó Corráin, *Rendering to God and Caesar: The Irish Churches and the Two States in Ireland, 1949–73* (Manchester, 2006), p.8; J.L.B. Deane, *Church of Ireland Handbook: A Guide to the Organisation of the Church* (Dublin, 1962), p.146.
41. Ó Corráin, *Rendering to God and Caesar*, p.8.
42. Ibid.
43. Deane, *Church of Ireland Handbook*, p.154.
44. Refausse, *Church of Ireland Records*, p.44.
45. *Church of Ireland Gazette*, 22 March 1918.
46. John Henry Bernard expressed similar sentiments in 1903 in a paper entitled 'The present position of the Irish Church' (see A. Megahey, 'William Connor Magee, the Church of England and the Church of Ireland', in T.C. Barnard and W.G. Neely (eds), *The Clergy of the Church of Ireland, 1000–2000: Messengers, Watchmen and Stewards* (Dublin, 2006), p.186.
47. *Belfast Newsletter*, 12 October 1910.
48. Minutes of the Standing Committee of the General Synod, 19 May 1910 (Representative Church Body (RCB) Library, Dublin).
49. Megahey, 'William Connor Magee, the Church of England and the Church of Ireland', p.192.
50. Ibid., pp.192–3.
51. McDowell, *Church of Ireland*, p.88.
52. *Belfast Newsletter*, 12 October 1910.
53. McDowell, *Church of Ireland*, p.89.
54. *Belfast Newsletter*, 10 October 1910.
55. *Irish Times*, 15 September 1911.

56. Report of the 'Home Reunion Committee of the General Synod' 1910, *Journal of the General Synod* (1910).
57. McDowell, *Church of Ireland*, p.91.
58. Report of the 'Home Reunion Committee of the General Synod', *Journal of the General Synod* (1910–11).
59. *Belfast Newsletter*, 12 October 1910.
60. Marcus Tanner, *Ireland's Holy Wars: The Struggle for a Nation's Soul, 1500–2000* (New Haven, 2001), p.229.
61. Ibid.
62. Megahey, 'Irish Protestant churches and social and political issues', p.27.
63. Ibid.; Megahey, *Irish Protestant Churches in the Twentieth Century*, p.16.
64. McDowell, *Church of Ireland*, pp.121–2.
65. Ibid., p.122.
66. Megahey, 'Irish Protestant churches and social and political issues', p.21.
67. Ibid., p.37.
68. For example, see John Baptist Crozier to Lady Londonderry, 13 December 1911 (Public Record Office of Northern Ireland (PRONI), Lady Londonderry papers, D/2846/2/27/19); Crozier to Edward Carson, 7 May 1916 (PRONI, Carson papers, D/1507/A/16/11).
69. Patton, *Fifty Years of Disestablishment*, p.260.
70. N.J.D. White, *John Henry Bernard, Archbishop of Dublin: Provost of Trinity College, Dublin. A Short Memoir* (Dublin, 1928), p.11.
71. McDowell, *Church of Ireland*, p.108.
72. C.F. D'Arcy, *The Adventures of a Bishop*, p.67.
73. Ibid., pp.37–8.
74. Ibid., p.85.
75. Ibid., p.88.
76. Ibid., p.77. See Chapter 1 in this volume.
77. Harry Smith, *Heal Not Lightly* (Chichester, 2006), pp.64, 16.
78. Ibid., p.14.
79. Ibid., p.15.
80. Johnston McMaster, review of *Heal Not Lightly*, *Search*, 30, 1 (Spring 2007), pp.77–8.
81. Ibid., p.79.
82. Brad S. Gregory, 'The other confessional history: on secular bias in the study of religion', *History and Theory*, vol. 45 (December 2006), p.147.
83. Alan Ford, 'Standing one's ground', in Ford *et al.* (eds), *As by Law Established*, p.14.

1

'Life and death importance': The Church of Ireland and Irish Unionism, 1910–11

With the zeal of a prophet, Dr Alfred Elliot, bishop of Kilmore, lamented the state of Ireland in his diocesan synod speech of 1909. To counter the lawlessness in the country, Elliot urged his audience to pray for unionism and teach the political creed to their children. The bishop was subsequently commended by the organ of Ulster Anglicanism, *The Warden*, for making unionism 'not a matter of politics, but of life and death importance'.[1] Prayer in aid of unionism became ever more necessary ahead of the general election of January 1910. The election was called in response to the rejection by the House of Lords of David Lloyd George's 'People's budget'. The result was inconclusive and a second election was held in December 1910. The Liberal party, led by Herbert Asquith, was returned to power after both elections, but was reliant upon the support of Labour and John Redmond's Irish Nationalists for a parliamentary majority.

Two important, and related, developments followed the January 1910 election. Due largely to the increased importance of the Irish Nationalists in Westminster, home rule for Ireland returned to the political agenda, as had been predicted by British and Irish unionists during the election campaigns. In addition, the Liberal party fought the elections promising to curb the House of Lords' power to veto legislation. The 1911 Parliament Act restricted the House of Lords' veto to three parliamentary sessions, after which time bills would become law without the consent of the upper house. The combination of a neutered House of Lords and an Irish Nationalist party holding the balance of power in Westminster made the passing of some measure of home rule for Ireland a real possibility.

Church of Ireland clergy reacted to events in Westminster in a similar manner to the majority of Irish Protestants – by opposing any possible Home Rule Bill and mobilising in support of Irish unionism. The clergy's position as public figures offered them a sometimes leading role in grassroots unionist politics – chairing election meetings or holding positions of leadership in newly revived unionist clubs. Two elements were crucial in motivating and sustaining the unionism of Church of Ireland clergy. Anti-Catholicism (given added potency by the 'McCann case') and a strong sense of 'imperial' identity (articulated at the coronation of George V) were long-standing tropes used by Anglican clergy against home rule that remained resilient throughout the third home rule crisis, particularly in Ulster.[2] However, the all-Ireland brand of unionism exhibited by the Church of Ireland in 1910–11 was challenged as early as 1912 by the controversy surrounding the Ulster Covenant. Such elements of continuity and imminent change make 1910 and 1911 an interesting prologue to the Church of Ireland's involvement in the more dramatic events of the 'Ulster crisis' later in the decade.

THE FORTRESS UNDER ATTACK: THE 1910 GENERAL ELECTIONS

The 1910 general elections were not fought purely over home rule. Other issues, such as tariff reform, the budget and House of Lords reform were prominent, especially in England and Scotland. However, there is little doubt that the main issue animating the Church of Ireland was home rule. At both elections, *The Warden* identified home rule as the major issue. In January the paper claimed 'the coming election will decide whether Ireland is to be managed by a Roman Catholic Nationalist Parliament in Dublin or not. The Protestants of Ulster are as firm in opposition as ever they were.'[3] In November the newly launched *Irish Churchman* (a replacement for *The Warden*) realised the need to 'open the eyes' of voters to the danger of home rule, claiming 'in the midst of all the prominent questions which will have to be answered by every intelligent voter is the question of Home Rule for Ireland.'[4] Although the House of Lords was the 'ostensible' target, the 'Unionism of the Kingdom is the fortress which is the ultimate object of attack'.[5] The 'veto question' was a 'mask', which when removed revealed Home Rule 'in all its ugliness … no longer is it a "bogey". It is a vital issue which the British electorate must face.'[6]

Canon William Pounden's role in the campaigns of James and Charles Craig was indicative of the role played by Church of Ireland clergy in the 1910 election campaigns.[7] Pounden, rector of Lisburn Cathedral since 1884, was the elder statesman of Lisburn unionism – he sent James Craig a telegram after Craig's victory in East Down in January, stating 'Lisburn and I rejoice at your success.'[8] When C.C. Craig held a victory parade in Lisburn ('one of the largest and most representative known in the town') after his victory in South Antrim, the procession stopped outside the rectory and 'heartily cheered' Pounden.[9] Such a display endorsed Pounden's prominent role in the January election. Lisburn bordered two constituencies, East Down and South Antrim, contested by James Craig and Charles Craig respectively for the unionists. Pounden spoke at unionist association meetings, Orange Order gatherings and unionist rallies extolling the virtues of both unionism and the Craig brothers and lamenting the effect of home rule on Ireland.[10] Pounden had a long history of opposing home rule. In 1893 he was authorised by the select vestry of Lisburn Cathedral to sign a protest 'from this parish against the passing of the Home Rule Bill presently before Parliament'.[11] His position in the Orange Order and unionist association, allied to the longevity of his standing as a public figure in Lisburn, lent Pounden an influence within local unionism that rectors in other parts of Ulster may have lacked. A figure such as Pounden had a higher profile and greater involvement in the electoral campaigns than most clergy did.

However, when clergy did get involved in the campaigns, they did so in a style similar to Pounden, making speeches, moving resolutions of confidence in parliamentary candidates, chairing meetings or moving votes of thanks. For example, Canon Harding of Willowfield parish in east Belfast, hoped that 'all over Ulster people would see to it that the candidate returned was pledged to oppose Home Rule'.[12] At an election meeting for John Gordon, unionist candidate for South Derry, the rector of Kilrea proposed a resolution expressing 'an unalterable determination to resist Home Rule in any shape or form',[13] while the rector of Drumbo, County Down claimed that the Liberals had put home rule on the 'forefront' of their banner and that 'the whole election turned on the issue of Home Rule'. He was in no doubt that the main danger of home rule was religious, meaning 'slavery for themselves and the end of Protestantism in this country'.[14] At an election meeting in December, the rector of Saintfield, after supporting a vote of confidence in James Craig, pointed out that it was clear to any 'thoughtful man' that the election was not being fought on the House of Lords veto, but on home rule.[15] In Dublin, a number of Anglican clergy supported the candidature of Bryan Cooper, who took South Dublin for the unionists in January, only to lose it in December.[16]

Church of Ireland clerical involvement in the 1910 general elections continued the Church's opposition to home rule from the introduction of the first bill in 1886. The first and second Home Rule Bills were denounced by archbishops, bishops and laymen from the floor of the General Synod. Bishop Reeves thought it better for Protestants to 'rest in a patriot's grave than to live a living death, stripped of their rights and liberties, and robbed of their faith'; Primate Knox claimed the second Home Rule Bill was an attempt 'to subjugate this country to papal dictation'.[17] The extent of clerical involvement in politics followed a series of peaks – when home rule was perceived as a threat – and troughs, when the union appeared secure. The pattern of clerical participation in the 1906 general election mirrored, to a lesser degree, that of 1910. The devolution crisis coloured the 1906 general election, especially in Ulster, to the extent that Rev. J.E. Browne suggested the only issue was home rule.[18] However, the general election of 1900, when home rule was off the political agenda, witnessed relatively little Anglican clerical participation in Ireland.

While the 1910 general elections represented a continuation of the clergy's role in unionist politics, the events of 1910 also served as a prelude to the Church of Ireland's involvement in Irish unionism throughout the third Home Rule Bill period. Traditional vehicles of involvement in grassroots unionist politics continued. For example, clergy often played a leading role at the meetings, demonstrations and church services of the Orange Order. The annual 12 July celebrations were an ideal opportunity for Orangemen to demonstrate the vitality and popularity of Protestant opposition to home rule. In 1911 the *Irish Churchman* asserted that 'never in the history of the organisation were there so large celebrations or such straight speaking'. Orangemen were determined to 'thwart the nefarious schemes of designing Jesuits, and to uphold the cause of civil and religious liberty which had been purchased for them by the blood of their forefathers'.[19] An example of such 'straight speaking' came at the 1911 demonstration in Lisburn from the rector of Hillsborough, who claimed that 'Roman Catholics, once they got power' would 'expunge Protestant liberties'.[20] In County Londonderry, the rector of Desertmartin called for Orangemen to pray from their hearts: 'God save Ireland from Rome.'[21] 'Orange' church services were generally better attended than ordinary services. For example, in Down parish church, where the average attendance was 180–200, the 12 July anniversary services in 1911 and 1912 were attended by 431 and 500 respectively.[22] In Armoy, County Antrim the average attendance was around 70–80; the 12 July service in 1912 attracted 127, while 147 attended in 1913.[23] Orange services in Willowfield (east Belfast) almost trebled the average attendance. In 1910, 1,400 attended; in 1911, 1,500 attended, and in 1912, 1,700 attended.[24]

The revival in 1911 of unionist clubs offered Church of Ireland clergy another means of exercising political influence. These clubs, in suspension since 1895, were started again in 1911 in response to the campaign for home rule. Through the clubs, the unionist leadership hoped to produce a degree of formality and discipline among unionists tempted to indulge in 'belligerent' opposition to home rule.[25] Unionist clubs aimed to defend the legislative union and render assistance to their members and others in carrying out that policy.[26] The *Irish Churchman* welcomed the revival of unionist clubs, and urged members not to 'slacken in their efforts to bring home to the British electorate the folly of sacrificing the loyal section of the communion to the Fenian American dollar-paid Irish Nationalist party'.[27] In 1912 the Ulster Unionist Council (UUC) produced a booklet listing the name, president and secretary of each of the 331 unionist clubs in Ireland. Of these, forty-five clubs had a Church of Ireland clergyman as either president or secretary. This compared with twenty-two clergymen from other denominations holding the same posts. Predominantly, clubs with Anglican clerical leadership were based in rural areas of Tyrone, Armagh and Cavan.[28] The importance of unionist clubs as a basis for grassroots organisation has been recognised.[29] The relatively high proportion of Church of Ireland clergy holding leadership roles in the clubs, especially when compared with the Presbyterian Church, suggests that such clergy were an important cog in the machinery of running and maintaining unionist enthusiasm, particularly in rural areas where Protestants may have been a minority.

'A MENACE TO LIBERTY': THE CHURCH OF IRELAND REACTION TO *NE TEMERE*

One of the key factors motivating Church of Ireland involvement in Irish unionism was a fear that home rule would allow a powerful Catholic Church to encroach on Protestant liberties. While such a belief was not new, it was given added potency by a papal decree named *Ne Temere*. Issued in 1907 by Pope Pius X, *Ne Temere* declared marriage between a Catholic and non-Catholic to be valid only if the ceremony was carried out by a Catholic priest. In addition, the children of such a 'mixed marriage' were to be raised as Catholics – a factor which, if the decree was enforced, raised the spectre of demographic decline for Irish Protestants. The decree was condemned in 1908 by the Protestant Churches, but it was not until the McCann case of November 1910 that *Ne Temere* became a prominent issue in Irish politics. Agnes McCann, who attended Townsend Street Presbyterian church in Belfast, and her husband, a Catholic, had been told by the local priest that their marriage was invalid in light of the *Ne Temere* decree. Mrs McCann refused to remarry in a Catholic ceremony, and eventually her husband left her, taking their two children with him. William Corkey, the minister of Townsend Street Presbyterian church, publicised the incident, claiming it illustrated the Catholic Church's desire to 'inflict cruel punishment on any members of the Protestant church over whom she gets any power'.[30]

In January 1911 mass meetings were held in Belfast and Dublin to protest against *Ne Temere*. It is likely that the Belfast meeting (held in the Assembly Hall) was organised by the Presbyterian Church.[31] However, it was an ecumenical occasion with John Baptist Crozier, bishop of Down, making the second speech, following the Presbyterian moderator, J.H. Murphy. Crozier claimed *Ne Temere* placed the 'sanctity of home life' under attack from a 'foreign Pontiff'.[32] The demographic implications of *Ne Temere* alarmed Irish Protestants. In addition, for its Irish opponents, *Ne Temere* meant the Pope, as head of both a church and a sovereign state, was advancing the interests of a foreign power to the detriment of the population of Ireland, who were subjects of the British Crown. This assumption allowed opponents of the decree, such as Crozier, to appeal to a strand of xenophobia and 'empire loyalism'.[33] The archbishop of Dublin, Joseph

Peacocke, expressed sentiments similar to Crozier's at the Dublin meeting: *Ne Temere* posed a threat to Protestant 'peace and happiness' from a 'foreign and self-constituted despot'.[34]

Despite the lack of explicit references to home rule in the speeches against *Ne Temere* at the Belfast and Dublin meetings, the press connected the need to oppose home rule with the danger *Ne Temere* posed to Irish Protestants. The *Newsletter* made clear its belief in the impeccable anti-home rule credentials of the opposition to *Ne Temere* in an editorial that claimed the enthusiasm of the Assembly Hall meeting 'forcibly reminded one of the spirit which prevailed at the great Ulster Unionist Convention of 1892'.[35] An *Irish Times* editorial on the Dublin *Ne Temere* meeting asked, if the Catholic Church could set aside British law 'under the Act of Union, what have not Irish Protestants to fear under Home Rule?'[36] The bishop of Kilmore (Alfred Elliot) linked *Ne Temere* with home rule. His letter of apology (for non-attendance) to the Dublin protest stated that the repudiation of the decree may 'fairly be made a test of the toleration which Mr Redmond promises to Protestants' under home rule.[37] In a letter to the *Belfast Telegraph*, Elliot criticised Redmond for not 'giving hope' to Irish Protestants by failing to criticise *Ne Temere*.[38]

The decree attracted opposition from all levels within the Church. In November 1910 (stimulated by the McCann case) the House of Bishops appointed a committee composed of Charles Frederick D'Arcy (then bishop of Ossory), Crozier and the bishop of Derry to prepare a statement on *Ne Temere*.[39] The statement, read to the House of Bishops in February 1911, criticised *Ne Temere* as 'injurious in a moral sense' and a signal that the Catholic Church was able to 'enforce her laws without deference to the authority of the state'. Church of Ireland clergy were asked to 'warn all over whom we have any influence of the terrible dangers attending mixed marriages'.[40] The bishops decided to present the statement as a resolution at the forthcoming General Synod.[41] At the synod, the resolution was seconded by James Campbell, a prominent layman and MP for South Armagh. Campbell claimed Redmond's failure to criticise *Ne Temere* called into doubt the trustworthiness of the 'many verbal assurances and promises of toleration and freedom' Protestants would enjoy under home rule.[42]

Crozier, elected primate by the House of Bishops in February 1911, criticised *Ne Temere* in his speech to the General Synod. In relation to mixed marriages, Crozier asked, 'what right has the Church of Rome to issue laws intolerant, despotic, and hopelessly at variance with the mind of Christ?' He lamented the division caused by *Ne Temere* between Protestants and Catholics, who before the McCann case had been working together for the good of Ireland. Under the union, every grievance 'sentimental or real' had been redressed, and Crozier feared that under a system of 'Irish isolation' religious differences would be accentuated, as was already being demonstrated by *Ne Temere*. *The Irish Times* supported Crozier's speech and the bishops' resolution, again making explicit the belief that *Ne Temere* was a portent of Protestant subjugation under home rule. An editorial asserted that 'the Church had no choice but to denounce this unjust decree. Naturally and inevitably it confirms the fears of many Irish Protestants about their fate under Home Rule.'[43] Following the General Synod, a number of diocesan synods lodged complaints against *Ne Temere*.[44]

Opposition to *Ne Temere* was also expressed in local churches, through sermons or resolutions passed by general vestries. In a sermon preached in Christ Church, Derry, Rev. J. Cox took as his text 1 Corinthians 16:3 ('Quit you like men; be strong'). In words surely intended to evoke the memory of the Apprentice Boys' stand against King James, Cox called for Derry to 'show to the Vatican' that the 'spirit of Protestantism is still strong and still alive as of old within her walls'.[45] The dean of Dromore urged his congregation to 'keep the agitation going till the encyclical is withdrawn'. There was also a need to warn 'our people' of the 'risks they run in marrying one of the Roman Catholic faith'.[46] Preaching in St Mark's, Portadown, Rev. C.K. Irwin criticised Cardinal Logue for issuing a pastoral concerning *Ne Temere* that quoted Deuteronomy 7 (which forbade marriage between the Israelites and Canaanites) in support of an argument against Catholics marrying Protestants. Irwin claimed the Canaanites' promised destruction in Deuteronomy 7 was a 'prophetic forecast as to what they [Protestants] might expect had the Church of Rome the power to put it into execution'.[47]

While sermons offered clergymen the opportunity to express their opinion on *Ne Temere*, the laity could communicate opposition through vestry resolutions. The resolution passed by Killinchy parish church stated *Ne Temere* was a

> direct incentive to Romanist (scamps) to inflict a grievous wrong on Protestant girls, and, like many other Romanist tenets, is utterly opposed to scripture teachings, aside over-riding the law of this realm.[48]

At All Saints in south Belfast a resolution was passed calling for the government to 'take immediate steps to render its operation in this Kingdom void, being contrary to our civil laws and at variance with the principles of civil and religious liberty, of which we are justly proud', while the general vestry of Willowfield parish called upon the Down diocesan synod to take 'such action as it may deem desirable' concerning *Ne Temere*, which had inflicted 'grievous wrongs' on 'unsuspecting Protestants'.[49] In Holywood, County Down the decree was labelled an 'outrage upon morality, a menace to liberty, an insult to the Protestant churches, and as calculated to stir up social and domestic discord in this country'.[50] Resolutions against *Ne Temere* were also passed by a number of churches in Dublin. The general vestries of St Mary's and Clontarf believed *Ne Temere* interfered with Protestant rights and the law of the land.[51] St Matthias' general vestry believed the decree was 'insulting to Protestants' and sent copies of their resolution to the lord-lieutenant, prime minister, chief secretary and A.J. Balfour, leader of the opposition.[52] The bishops' resolution against *Ne Temere* was read in Donnybrook parish church on 5 March, and was printed in the church magazine, where it was 'earnestly hoped' the statement would be 'thoughtfully read'.[53]

The reaction of the Church of Ireland to *Ne Temere* provided a model for its later involvement in the third home rule dispute. Once linked to the political threat of home rule, *Ne Temere* mobilised all sections of the Church of Ireland. Bishops and clergy took part in mass meetings. The House of Bishops passed a resolution attacking the decree; speeches were made at the Church's 'parliament', the General Synod, and diocesan synods also expressed their opposition. At a parish level, clergymen preached sermons and vestries passed resolutions calling for action against *Ne Temere*. In addition, clergymen wrote letters to the press and published pamphlets to publicise the alleged iniquities of the decree – the Church of Ireland Printing and Publishing Company published a pamphlet by Dudley Fletcher, rector of Coolbanagher, Queen's County, examining *Ne Temere*.[54] Therefore, *Ne Temere* provided a trial run for the Church of Ireland's opposition to the third Home Rule Bill in 1912, when a similar pattern (mass meetings, resolutions, synod speeches, sermons) was followed. Additionally, the dispute over *Ne Temere* also allowed the Church of Ireland, at an official 'episcopal' and synod level, to get involved in the political arena under the guise of dealing with an ostensibly religious issue.

'THE GLORY OF TRUE LIBERTY': CROWN AND EMPIRE

Imperialism also motivated opposition to home rule. Some caution should be applied in assigning too much importance to imperialist concerns among Irish unionists. When self-interest was involved, as in 1911–14 (with the threat of home rule), 'popular imperialism' became a factor of 'renewed if still secondary importance as an adjunct to Unionism'.[55] However, imperialism was important for the Church of Ireland; it was in the 'vanguard' of support for the empire and the union among Irish unionists, unsurprising from a 'caste' brought up to believe in the empire's 'civilising mission'.[56] It was feared, in the words of the rector of Warrenpoint, County Down, that home rule was 'injurious to Ireland and the great empire of which it was a part'.[57] The empire was viewed in terms of the British national myth, securing civil and religious liberty. The archdeacon of Connor believed the 'blessings' won by the glorious revolution were under threat, as 'Rome was busy'. However, if Irish Protestants trusted in God, 'he would maintain the liberties of this great empire and preserve to them … the blessings of religious and civil liberty'.[58]

Empire Day religious services provided a means for the Church of Ireland to demonstrate the importance it attached to imperial ideals. Empire Day (held on 24 May, Queen Victoria's birthday) was the creation of Reginald Brabazon, seventh earl of Meath, who hoped to 'nurture a sense of collective identity and imperial responsibility among young empire citizens'.[59] The Church of Ireland's celebration of Empire Day placed it within a wider British and imperial context. In 1909, 1,000 Church of England clergymen preached Empire Day sermons regarding 'our imperial obligation',[60] while similar services were held in Anglican churches throughout the empire.[61] Preaching at a service in Kilmore, County Armagh, Rev. William Jones reminded his congregation of their 'duty' to defend what God 'has given to us, and to use the gift for His glory and the good of the human race. In this matter we are God's trustees.'[62] Such sentiments hint at the importance of Church of Ireland members' sense of imperial identity. If they were indeed 'trustees' of God's gift of the empire, home rule, as a supposed threat to the integrity of this gift, must be resisted.

The outpouring of grief at Edward VII's death and the enthusiastic celebration of George V's coronation provide another examples of how the Church of Ireland viewed the crown and empire. The select vestry of Kilbroney in south Down passed a resolution recording 'loyal and heartfelt sorrow' at the death of Edward VII. They agreed to pray that the future King, George V, would govern in 'righteousness and peace'.[63] Memorial services were held to mark the death of Edward VII, a feature common with Anglican churches throughout the empire. Such services were often well attended – 1,000 were present in Willowfield, over double the normal congregation.[64]

The coronation of George V was marked throughout the Church of Ireland. The General Synod passed a resolution declaring a hope that God would bless the new sovereign so that 'he may see his empire strong, loyal and united, prosperous and happy'. Archbishop Crozier offered George V the Church of Ireland's 'loyal expression of our humble and dutiful attachment to the throne and constitution'.[65]

At a parish level in the Church, the coronation was marked by street parties and church services. While explicit references to the political situation were usually absent from these services, unionism was celebrated in general terms through the elevation of the British empire's worth. In Enniskillen parish church, the dean of Clogher claimed the coronation represented all that the British empire stood for: 'belief in God; the glory of true liberty; the freedom of every man to worship according to the dictates of his conscience'. The coronation allowed them to 'rejoice' that they were 'loyal citizens' of this empire.[66]

The idea that the coronation offered an opportunity to demonstrate loyalty to the crown and empire was a theme of the celebrations. Church of Ireland clergy were often involved in the various local committees set up to organise coronation day festivities – a role they would also play in organising Ulster Day in 1912. Four local clergymen were appointed to the planning committee in Lisburn, with Canon Pounden joining the committee tasked with preparing an address of welcome to the King.[67] The address informed George V of Lisburn's 'deep sense of loyalty to your throne and person'.[68] The select vestry of Muckno in Monaghan passed a resolution affirming 'loyal devotion' to George V.[69] Special services were held in Portrush and Portstewart, and St Patrick's church hall in Coleraine held a coronation party for the children of the town.[70] An inventive means of celebrating the coronation was seen in Bangor, as the St Comgall's select vestry resolved to plant a 'coronation tree' on the morning of the coronation.[71] After planting the tree, the rector of St Comgall's alluded to the imperial aspect of the day by claiming loyalty to the Crown in north-east Ulster was the strongest anywhere in George V's 'wide dominions'. He hoped the tree would keep alive in the young 'the same loyal spirit that now possesses us'.[72] R.B. Cooke, rector of All Saints in Belfast, wrote in the parish magazine that he hoped the coronation would convince the disloyal proportion of the country to be 'brought into closer touch with truth and liberty'. Cooke believed if Irish nationalists realised the new king was on the side of truth and liberty, 'it would be a great means of promoting their loyal allegiance to our King and empire'.[73] The *Irish Churchman* presented the coronation celebrations as a demonstration of Ireland's imperial identity and determination to 'preserve the traditions of the empire and to maintain unimpaired the nation's power and influence in the world'.[74]

If the coronation confirmed, for the Church of Ireland, Ireland's imperial identity, it also served to reinforce the church's own self-perception as forming part of the British empire. For John Henry Bernard, the coronation united the Irish Church with other churches in the Anglican communion. Reflecting his high-church leanings, Bernard urged Archbishop Crozier not to sanction a coronation service that did not use the word 'altar', as this would differentiate the Irish coronation service from those in other Anglican Churches. Bernard consciously used political language to enforce his point: 'I hope that you will not insist upon Home Rule in such a matter, for we all want to be Unionists in things ecclesiastical as in things civil.'[75] If the empire provided an ecclesiastical unity for Bernard, the dean of Clogher believed the empire provided a spiritual unity. The religious ceremony of the coronation demonstrated an 'empire wide belief in God Almighty, the King of Kings'.[76] B.J. Plunkett, rector of St Ann's in Dublin, reflected a widespread belief that the empire was a providential gift from God for the spread of Christianity and civilisation.[77] In a coronation sermon reproduced in St Ann's church magazine, Plunkett claimed God had given the 'British nation' supremacy, as through the empire George V was king of 300 million non-Christian people. God had given the greater part of the 'heathen and Mohammedan' world into England's possession for the 'loving purpose' that 'England's strength should be the moral destruction of the Eastern and African races.' Therefore, Plunkett urged his congregation to support evangelism; failure to do so was 'distinctly anti-Christian, distinctly anti-British'.[78]

In a study of Australian Anglican imperial identity, Robert Withycombe suggests Empire Day celebrations in Australia united the Australian Churches and society with the empire in 'moral and imperial idealism, and economic and defence self-interest'.[79] It is possible that Empire Day and the coronation provided a similar role for the Church of Ireland. In reinforcing the 'common bond of an "imagined community" inhabiting a vast and far flung empire',[80] Empire Day (and the coronation, which was also celebrated throughout the empire) may have provided the Church of Ireland with a sense of status borne from a belief that it – and Ireland – formed an integral part of the moral, spiritual and civilising force of the empire. A fear that this imperial identity would be lost in a home rule Ireland partly motivated the Church's enthusiastic participation in Irish unionism.

LOVING IRELAND MORE: ALL-IRELAND UNIONISM

An all-Ireland unionism was espoused by the majority of politically active clergy. This reflected the mood in the Church at a wider level, as financial ties strengthened the institutional unity of the Church of Ireland. Membership of the Church in Belfast had grown from 75,000 in 1891 to 115,000 in 1910, but, as Crozier pointed out at the 1910 Church of Ireland Conference, it was 'painfully undermanned as regards [its] clerical staff'.[81] In 1911 the diocese of Down and Connor and Dromore could only afford to pay sixty-six clergy in Belfast. To allow provision for more, a number of southern dioceses offered financial aid to the Church in Belfast. Meath, Kilmore and Cork (along with Armagh and Derry and Raphoe) had contributed to the fund.[82] In his 1910 speech to the Down diocesan synod, Crozier acknowledged the help the Church of Ireland in Belfast received from dioceses in the rest of Ireland in rectifying the paucity of clergy. He emphasised that the financial aid from the south strengthened opposition to home rule from the Church in Belfast, which would continue to abhor separate treatment for Ulster under home rule. He asserted that, as in 1886, Ulster would refuse to accept the 'bribe' of a separate parliament: 'God forbid we should sell the inheritance of our fathers by cutting ourselves adrift from our fellow countrymen of every class and creed in the land with which our fondest hopes are for ever bound.' The reason for devotion to the union and loyalty to their fellow churchmen in the south 'was not because they loved England only … but because they loved Ireland more'.[83] In his first speech at the General Synod as primate, Crozier also emphasised the importance of Church unity. He saw signs of hope in the practical sympathy displayed by the south in helping with congested areas of the north, such as Belfast, while from the north there was a 'strong determination not to desert them [the Church of Ireland in the south] in the political crisis with which the country is threatened'.[84]

Dublin diocese issued an appeal to its churches in February 1911, asking each congregation to send in contributions to help fund the shortfall of clergy in Belfast. They needed to help the Church in Belfast as they were members of one body, 'and if one member suffers all the members suffer'. Political justification for aiding the Church in Belfast was also offered:

Not many years ago Ulstermen were tempted to desert their brethren in the South, and to leave them to their fate by the offer of a Home Rule Bill which would allow them to manage their own affairs; they indignantly rejected the offer; they declared that they would stand or fall with their brethren in the South. We cannot forget that. In the time of need of this Heart of Ulster we are bound to come to their help.[85]

Parishes in Dublin responded generously to the appeal. A report in the church magazine of Donnybrook parish called for a contribution of £18 per annum (£90 in total over five years) to the Belfast appeal.[86] By November, a total of £100 had been raised.[87] By 1913, the parish of Howth has raised £83, an increase of £33 on the target set by the select vestry.[88] St Ann's, a parish close to the centre of Dublin, hoped to raise £100 over five years for the Belfast appeal.[89] St Fin Barre's Cathedral in Cork also contributed to the Belfast appeal, despite 1910 having been a 'difficult' year financially for the parish.[90]

The undesirability of separate treatment for any part of Ireland under home rule was emphasised by Bishop Alfred Elliot at the 1910 Kilmore diocesan synod. Elliot lamented the financial and religious consequences of home rule, yet prayed that should home rule 'ever come, it may come with complete separation between the two countries'.[91] Similarly striking sentiments were expressed by Canon Dudley of St Patrick's, Coleraine at an election meeting for H.T. Barrie. In the case of England 'in a moment of madness' granting home rule to Ireland, Dudley asked that England 'leave them alone … withdraw her troops, and tell the police to stand aside, and leave the rebels to the loyalists of Ulster and elsewhere. Then they … would make Ireland great and free for Protestant and Roman Catholic alike'.[92] R. Dixon Patterson, rector of Ardmore, County Armagh, addressing an Orange service in 1911, also called for 'total separation' if the government pursued home rule, as a response to the 'place-hunting, power-loving politicians'. If home rule was forced upon Ireland, 'proudly though sadly they would take the moulding of their country's future into their own hands. Britain might not have intended it, they did not like it, but the final doom of Ireland would then be – total separation.'[93] It was probably not surprising that Elliot, bishop of a diocese including parts of Fermanagh, Cavan and Monaghan as well as Leitrim, called for separation instead of some form of preferential treatment for Ulster. However, Dudley and Patterson, both based in north-east Ulster, did not advance separate treatment for Ulster as a course of action. Their rhetoric served to illustrate the lack of any pronounced sympathy for Ulster exclusion among the clergy at this early stage in the third home rule 'crisis'.

Church of Ireland clergy involved in unionist clubs were keen to stress an all-Ireland conception of the clubs' role. In proposing the formation of Strandtown Unionist Club in Belfast, Rev. Mr Peacocke, rector of St Mark's, Dundela emphasised the clubs should join Irish unionists into 'one solid phalanx in North, South, East and West' and link them with organisations in England and Scotland to educate the electorate regarding the danger of home rule.[94] C.E. Quin, rector of Derriaghy, told Dunmurry Unionist Club that Ulster unionists should not 'accept special terms in Ulster and desert their friends in the South'.[95] At a meeting of Bangor Unionist Club, held in St Comgall's parish hall, Rev. J.I. Peacocke pointed out that members of the Church of Ireland in the south and west of Ireland 'would feel most the power of a home rule parliament', as nationalists already 'had their eyes on the Cathedrals of the Church of Ireland in the south and west'.[96]

In 1910 and 1911 there was little indication that members of the Church of Ireland viewed Ulster as entitled to separate treatment or some form of exclusion from home rule. It is unlikely that they did *not* see Ulster as distinct, but rather the clergy believed the force of unionist arguments against home rule for all of Ireland would ultimately prevail. Admittedly, a number of Ulster-based clergy articulated Ulster-focused militaristic sympathies, particularly during the 1910 election campaigns.[97] However, calls for physical resistance demonstrated an Ulster bias that was out of step with the mood in the Church, and militaristic rhetoric, although a tantalising precursor to events in 1913–14, represented a minority opinion during 1910. Even when pro-Ulster sympathy was expressed, it appeared to come with a lack of enthusiasm. Shortly after the Craigavon demonstration, when Edward Carson had pledged to set up a government for Ulster in the case of home rule, the Literary and Debating Society of St Thomas' in south Belfast held a debate on the motion: 'Ulster is justified in the present crisis in forming a Constitution of her own'. The motion was carried, although by an underwhelming majority, 18 voting for and 11 against.[98]

The all-Ireland unionism of the Church of Ireland was challenged by the small minority of clergy who held home rule views. The Liberal *Ulster Guardian* printed statements by a number of Protestants, including three Church of Ireland clergymen (in the south), proclaiming the toleration of Protestantism by Catholics. In stark contrast to reports emanating from the *Irish Churchman*, these clergymen commented on the 'kindness' and 'courtesy' of their 'obliging' Roman Catholic neighbours.[99] The most articulate home rule supporter in the Church of Ireland was James Owen Hannay, rector of Westport in County Mayo and a prolific author who wrote under the pseudonym George Birmingham. In a statement that originally appeared in the *Morning Leader*, Hannay claimed the 'northern working man' 'speaks occasionally as if the kicking of royal crowns into the Boyne would be a pleasing pastime'.[100] Archbishop Crozier publicly termed Hannay's statement a 'libel' on the Belfast and northern working man,[101] an allegation that elicited a lively personal correspondence between the two men.

Hannay rejected Crozier's allegation of libel. The phrase 'to kick the King's crown into the Boyne' was 'picturesque and rhetorical'. However, the Ulster unionist 'appeal to arms' in effect kicked the King's crown into the Boyne as armed resistance would 'destroy constitutional authority'.[102] The disagreement boiled down to differing conceptions of the legitimacy of Ulster unionist resistance to home rule and the sincerity of the Ulster unionist claim to loyalty. Crozier believed the 'northern working man' desired to live under the King and the British constitution and 'would resist any attempt to place Ireland under Papal domination'. In addition, the northern working man was 'desperately in earnest and passionately loyal to our King'.[103] Hannay agreed that if there was a risk of Ireland being placed under papal domination, rebellion was justified. However, while rebelling, he would not call himself loyal to the King, whose authority he was 'defying', or to the empire, whose constitution he was 'threatening'.[104] This private correspondence, already ill-tempered, grew more divisive after Crozier claimed that, as chief pastor of the Church of Ireland, he had treated Hannay mildly.[105] Hannay termed Crozier's means of rebuking a 'brother clergyman' unbiblical, as instead of speaking to him in private, Crozier began with a public denunciation which went against Christ's instructions in Matthew 18:15.[106] Crozier believed Christ's words referred to injuries done to an individual, whereas Hannay's statement was an 'unjust accusation' against the members of a church of which he was a priest. The northern working men had a right to be defended by their arch-bishop when 'unjustly attacked'.[107] Hannay's reply was returned to him by Crozier endorsed with the statement 'returned unopened by direction of the Lord Primate'.[108]

The Hannay–Crozier quarrel confirmed the impression created by the pro-Ulster minority within the Church of Ireland – namely, that the issue likely to cause division within the Church on political matters was the position of Ulster. While criticism of Ulster came at this time only from maverick figures such as Hannay it was able to be dismissed with the kind of righteous indignation prac-tised by Crozier. Later in the third Home Rule Bill period, after Ulster Day and the appearance of the UVF, more mainstream unionist figures in the Church of Ireland in the south began attacking Ulster unionism in terms similar to those of Hannay in 1911. However, such tension was avoided in 1910 and 1911 as the small percentage of clergy who endorsed separate action by Ulster was eclipsed by those who desired a united front against home rule.

CONCLUSION

The events of 1910–11 pointed, to a greater or lesser extent, to elements that would characterise the Church of Ireland's involvement in the third home rule crisis. There was an element of continuity in the Church's active involvement in support of Irish unionism and its espousal of anti-Catholic and imperial rhetoric to define its strong advocacy of the union. Such long-established elements con-tinued throughout the third home rule period, as did clerical involvement in unionist clubs and the Orange Order. The issue of *Ne Temere* galvanised Irish Protestant opinion and demonstrated that the Church of Ireland and the Presbyterian Church could, and would, work together on issues of common interest. While the Church of Ireland's reaction to the McCann case provided a template for its involvement in Irish unionism, the pan-denominational nature of the Belfast *Ne Temere* protest foreshadowed the ecumenism that would be seen at a parish level during 1912–14, with the holding of 'united' services for union-ist clubs and the Ulster Volunteer Force.

The Church of Ireland also emerged, in 1910 and 1911, as a Church largely united on the issue of home rule. Unity between different theological factions was evident, as demonstrated by the position on home rule of the high-churchman John Henry Bernard, bishop of Ossory, and the broad-church Charles Frederick D'Arcy, now bishop of Down and Connor and Dromore. For Bernard, addressing the Ossory diocesan synod, the chief danger of home rule was an 'act of spoliation', transferring Church of Ireland land and property to the Catholic Church. Bernard argued that Westminster had confirmed the Church of Ireland's rightful claim to its property when the Church was disestablished. It would be a 'monstrous injustice' for this promise to be reversed by 'any local Parliament sitting in Dublin'. Concluding, Bernard pointed out it was the 'duty' of synod members to protect the Church's interests, 'not because we desire "ascendancy" but because we earnestly desire that the Church which we love may be maintained in the future as in the past'.[109]

D'Arcy informed his diocesan synod that home rule would result in Ireland being placed 'under the heel' of the unprogressive, tyrannous ecclesiastical system of the Catholic Church, which would therefore gain absolute supremacy. The consequence for Protestants would be the intolerance towards their beliefs and practices already being demonstrated through the operation of *Ne Temere*. In an echo of Bernard's argument, D'Arcy added that the papal-directed intolerance he envisaged under home rule would see the Church of Ireland's 'prized posses-sions and financial resources' being placed in 'imminent danger', coming under threat from a government 'dominated by Roman influence'.[110] D'Arcy was not viewed as an extremist. The *Church of Ireland Gazette*, commenting on the speech, claimed 'The Bishop is known not to be a politician. His reputation as a scholar and an observer of calm and wise judgement gives his warning a pro-found significance.'[111] Privately, D'Arcy repeated his fear of the Catholic Church. Writing to James Hannay, he claimed home rule would bring 'a tighten-ing of the chain of Roman authority, an effort to thrust Protestants out of every possible position ... Roman tyranny will more and more drive all energy out of the country.'[112]

Significantly, neither D'Arcy nor Bernard were evangelicals. In 1911, D'Arcy was described by the *Newsletter* as a theologian who held 'aloof from either extreme'; upon his death in 1938, *The Times* described D'Arcy as having 'belonged to the school of Broad Churchmen, to whom the *via media* seemed the way of truth and wisdom'.[113] Bernard was distrusted by conservative laymen due to his advocacy of 'certain up-to-date text books' for the Divinity school; in 1911 his elevation to the episcopacy was opposed by an anti-Ritualist grouping within the Church of Ireland.[114] However, D'Arcy and Bernard believed, with the evangel-icals, that the Catholic Church was 'all pervasive in influence, monolithic in scope, imperialist in intention, persecuting in its essential nature, and impoverishing in its social effects'.[115] Therefore, it is overly reductive to ascribe evangelicalism as the progenitor of the anti-Catholic shibboleth so prevalent in the Church of Ireland during the third home rule period.[116] The fact that opposition to home rule within the Church of Ireland was shared by (perceived) ritualists, evangelicals and liberals meant the issue was largely shorn of theological significance.

The unity of differing theological standpoints in opposition to home rule was paralleled politically by the all-Ireland unionism exhibited in 1910–11 by the Church of Ireland. This unity was stimulated from within the Church through the financial aid flowing from the southern dioceses to Belfast. The all-Ireland union-ism was also a reflection of the public position articulated by the leaders of Irish unionism.[117] Certain aspects of the Church's political involvement remained large-ly unchanged throughout the third Home Rule Bill period, such as co-operation with the Presbyterian Church, integration into grassroots unionist organisations and the articulation of anti-Catholic and imperialist arguments. The change – and controversy – within the Church of Ireland on the issue of home rule after 1911 was mainly the result of Ulster unionism's movement from seeing 'Ulster' as a wrecking tactic to an acceptance of some form of Ulster exclusion (in 1912–14). If the Church of Ireland's response to events in 1910–11 tied the Church to Irish unionism, from 1912 the Church was forced to choose between an idealistic all-Irish unionism or a more realistic, Ulster articulation of the unionist creed.

NOTES

1. *The Warden*, 1 October 1909.
2. See p.19–22 for a discussion of the 'McCann case'.
3. *The Warden*, 31 December 1909.
4. *Irish Churchman*, 18 November 1910.
5. Ibid., 25 November 1910.

6. Ibid., 2 December 1910.
7. William Pounden: born County Monaghan, 7 September 1830. Educated at TCD, ordained 1855. Rector of Lisburn 1884–1917. Died 27 August 1917.
8. *Lisburn Standard*, 29 January 1910.
9. Ibid., 5 February 1910.
10. See *Belfast Weekly Telegraph*, 1 January 1910; *Belfast Newsletter*, 28 January 1910; *Lisburn Standard*, 8, 29 January, 26 November, 2, 3 December, 1910.
11. Lisburn Cathedral select vestry minute book, 8 March 1893 (Public Record Office of Northern Ireland (PRONI), CR/1/35D/4).
12. *Belfast Newsletter*, 15 January 1910.
13. Ibid., 6 January 1910; *Belfast Weekly Telegraph*, 8 January 1910.
14. Ibid., 15 January 1910.
15. *BelfastNewsletter*, 30 November 1910.
16. *Irish Times*, 6, 7, 14 January 1910.
17. *Irish Ecclesiastical Gazette*, 3 April 1886; A. Acheson, *A History of the Church of Ireland, 1691–1996* (Dublin, 1997), p.225.
18. *Belfast Newsletter*, 10 January 1906. H.T. Barrie was supported by Canon Dudley, rector of Coleraine (ibid., 2 January 1906). As in 1910, James Craig received the public support of prominent Anglican clergy, such as Canon Pounden (ibid., 11 January 1906).
19. *Irish Churchman*, 21 July 1911.
20. *Lisburn Standard*, 15 July 1911.
21. *Northern Constitution*, 15 July 1911.
22. Down parish, preacher book, 7, 9 July 1911 (PRONI, MIC/1/3a).
23. Armoy parish, preacher book, 7 July 1912, 6 July 1913 (PRONI, MIC/1/334/E/2–3).
24. Willowfield parish, preacher book, 10 July 1910, 9 July 1911, 7 July 1912 (private possession).
25. J.F. Harbinson, *The Ulster Unionist Party 1882–1973: Its Development and Organisation* (Belfast, 1973), p.21.
26. Ibid.
27. *Irish Churchman*, 7 April 1911.
28. Printed list of Unionist clubs of Ireland (PRONI, Ulster Unionist Council papers, D/1327/1/12).
29. P. Buckland, *Irish Unionism II: Ulster Unionism and the Origins of Northern Ireland, 1886–1922* (Dublin, 1973), p.49.
30. A. Megahey, 'God will defend the right', in D.G. Boyce and Alan O'Day (eds), *Defenders of the Union* (London, 2001), p.166.
31. See R.M. Lee, 'Intermarriage, conflict and social control in Ireland: the decree "Ne Temere"', *Economic and Social Review*, 17, 1 (October 1985), p.19.
32. *Belfast Weekly Telegraph*, 14 January 1911.
33. Lee, 'The decree "Ne Temere"', p.19.
34. *Irish Times*, 31 January 1911.
35. *Belfast Newsletter*, 6 January 1911.
36. *Irish Times,* 31 January 1911.
37. Ibid., 31 January 1911.
38. *Belfast Telegraph*, 27 February 1911.
39. Minutes of the House of Bishops, 17 November 1910 (Representative Church Body (RCB) Library).
40. Ibid., 15 February 1911.
41. Ibid., 24 April 1911.
42. *Irish Times*, 26 April 1911.
43. Ibid., 26 April 1911.
44. For example, at Clogher (see *Fermanagh Times*, 12 October 1911) and Dublin (see *Irish Times*, 21 October 1911).
45. *Belfast Weekly Telegraph*, 11 February 1911.
46. *Lurgan Mail*, 18 March 1911.
47. *Ulster Gazette*, 18 March 1911.
48. Killinchy parish vestry minute book, 25 March 1911 (PRONI, CR/1/10D/5A).
49. *Belfast Weekly Telegraph*, 24 April 1911, 6 May 1911.
50. *County Down Spectator and Ulster Standard*, 28 April 1911.
51. *Irish Times*, 24 April 1911.
52. St Matthias' vestry minute book, 21 April 1911 (RCB Library, p.44. 5. 4).
53. Donnybrook church magazine, April 1911 (RCB Library, p.246. 25).
54. *Irish Times*, 9 February 1911; Dudley Fletcher, 'Rome and Marriage: an examination of the recent papal decree, "Ne Temere"' (TCD, Donoughmore papers, Don/K/40/37).

55. A. Jackson, 'Irish Unionists and the Empire, 1880–1920: classes and masses', in Keith Jeffery (ed.), *'An Irish Empire'? Aspects of Ireland and the British Empire* (Manchester, 1996), pp.128, 137–8.
56. D.H. Hume, 'Empire Day in Ireland, 1896–1962', in Jeffery (ed.), *'An Irish Empire'?*, pp.153–4.
57. *Belfast Weekly Telegraph*, 8 January 1910.
58. Ibid., 8 July 1911.
59. J. English, 'Empire Day in Britain, 1904–1958', *Historical Journal*, 49, 1 (2006), p.248.
60. Ibid., p.255.
61. R. Withycombe, 'Australian Anglicans and imperial identity, 1900–1914', *Journal of Religious History*, 25, 3 (October 2001), pp.294–301.
62. *Ulster Gazette*, 3 June 1911.
63. Kilbroney vestry minute book, 16 May 1910 (PRONI, MIC/1/88).
64. Willowfield preacher book, 20 May 1910.
65. *Irish Times*, 26 April 1911.
66. *Fermanagh Times*, 29 June 1911.
67. *Lisburn Standard*, 27 May 1911.
68. Ibid., 24 June 1911.
69. Muckno vestry minute book, 30 May 1911 (PRONI, MIC/151/D/2).
70. *Northern Constitution*, 24 June 1911.
71. St Comgall's select vestry minute book, 5 June 1911 (PRONI, CR/1/87/D/3).
72. *County Down Spectator*, 30 June 1911. However, it appeared this loyal spirit did not extend to upkeep of the church grounds – in 1914 the select vestry noted that the coronation tree 'was not in a healthy state' and was to receive 'temporary nourishment'. The vestry resolved to ensure the tree was 'properly looked after in the autumn'. St Comgall's select vestry minute book, 8 June 1914 (PRONI, CR/1/87/D/3).
73. All Saints' parish magazine, July 1911.
74. *Irish Churchman*, 30 June 1911.
75. Bernard to Crozier, 9 April 1911 (PRONI, Peacocke papers, MIC/87).
76. *Fermanagh Times*, 29 June 1911.
77. See John Wolffe, *God and Greater Britain: Religion and National Life in Britain and Ireland, 1843–1945* (London, 1994), p.224.
78. St Ann's church magazine, July 1911 (RCB Library, p.344. 25).
79. Withycombe, 'Australian Anglicans and imperial identity', p.301.
80. English, 'Empire Day in Britain', p.249.
81. *Belfast Newsletter*, 12 October 1910.
82. *Irish Times*, 5 November 1910.
83. *Belfast Newsletter*, 4 November 1910.
84. *Irish Churchman*, 12 May 1911. Crozier was sincere in his early expressions of all–Ireland Unionism – as Primate, he agonised over the possibility of partition (see Chapters 6 and 7 of this volume).
85. Ibid., 10 February 1911.
86. Donnybrook church magazine, January 1911 (RCB Library, P.246. 25).
87. Ibid., November 1911.
88. Howth church magazine, September 1913 (RCB Library, P.373. 25).
89. St Ann's church magazine, February 1911 (RCB Library, P.344. 25).
90. St Fin Barre's general vestry minute book, 9 April 1911 (ibid., p.497. 5. 5).
91. *Belfast Weekly Telegraph*, 8 October 1910.
92. *Northern Constitution*, 17 December 1910.
93. *Belfast Weekly Telegraph*, 15 July 1911.
94. Ibid., 8 April 1911.
95. Ibid., 1 July 1911.
96. *County Down Spectator*, 20 October 1911.
97. See *Belfast Newsletter*, 28 November 1910, 3, 6, 10 December 1910.
98. St Thomas' Literary and Debating Society minutes, 23 November 1911 (PRONI, CR/1/36/H/2).
99. *Ulster Guardian*, 28 January 1911.
100. *Belfast Evening Telegraph*, 26 June 1911.
101. Ibid.
102. Hannay to Crozier, 24 August 1911 (TCD, Hannay papers, Mss/3455/432).
103. Crozier to Hannay, 25 August 1911 (ibid., Mss/3455/433); Crozier to Hannay, 30 August 1911 (ibid., Mss/3455/437).
104. Hannay to Crozier, 26 August 1911 (ibid., Mss/3455/434).

105. Crozier to Hannay, 30 August 1911 (ibid., Mss/3455/437).
106. Hannay to Crozier, 31 August 1911 (ibid., Mss/3455/438); Matthew 18:15 urged differences of opinion between believers to be settled privately, as far as possible.
107. Crozier to Hannay, 1 September 1911 (ibid., Mss/3455/441).
108. Hannay to Crozier, 2 September 1911 (ibid., Mss/3455/442).
109. *Irish Times*, 22 September 1911.
110. *Belfast Weekly Telegraph*, 4 November 1911.
111. *Church of Ireland Gazette*, 10 November 1911.
112. D'Arcy to James Owen Hannay, 10 November 1911 (National Library Ireland, Hannay papers, Ms/8271/71).
113. *Belfast Newsletter*, 29 March 1911; *The Times*, 2 February 1938.
114. N.J.D. White, *John Henry Bernard, Archbishop of Dublin: Provost of Trinity College, Dublin. A Short Memoir* (Dublin, 1928), p.11; *Irish Times*, 29 July 1911.
115. D. Hempton, *Religion and Political Culture in Britain and Ireland: from the Glorious Revolution to the Decline of the Empire* (Cambridge, 1996), p.111.
116. As Hempton claims, ibid., p.113.
117. A. Jackson, *Home Rule: An Irish History, 1800–2000* (London, 2003), pp.120, 122–3; C. O'Leary and P. Maume, *Controversial Issues in Anglo-Irish Relations, 1910–21* (Dublin, 2004), p.15.

2

'The citadel of Protestantism and liberty'?
The Church of Ireland Episcopate and Ulster Day

The 1912 General Synod and Ulster Day were, apart from the First World War, the most important events in defining the Church of Ireland's position towards home rule. Corporately, the General Synod pledged the Church's opposition to home rule, although this display of political partisanship provoked criticism. At an episcopal level, the Balmoral and Ulster Day demonstrations, showpiece Ulster unionist occasions, were supported by northern Church of Ireland bishops. However, their involvement was opposed privately by bishops of southern dioceses. Ulster Day provided the first significant instance during the third Home Rule Bill period of the potential division home rule could cause between the Church in Ulster and the rest of Ireland. Therefore, the tensions and contradictions inherent in the Church of Ireland's stand on home rule were revealed by the events of 1912 and personified by Charles Frederick D'Arcy, John Henry Bernard and John Baptist Crozier, the most important members of the episcopal bench. The different positions they held concerning Ulster, largely revealed in 1912, coloured the political discourse of the Church of Ireland for the remainder of the third home rule period.

THE 1912 GENERAL SYNOD

On 16 April 1912 the Church of Ireland held a specially convened General Synod to consider the possible effects of home rule. The synod was held on the initiative of Crozier, and unanimously endorsed by the House of Bishops.[1] The special General Synods held to oppose the first and second Home Rule Bills, in 1886 and 1893, provided precedents for the Church of Ireland's action in 1912. A more immediate influence may have been the decision of the Presbyterian and Methodist Churches to hold conventions to discuss the threat of home rule. Walker interprets the Presbyterian convention, held in February, as an attempt to dispel nationalist propaganda that the only opposition to home rule came from the Church of Ireland.[2] However, a letter from Crozier to the convention provided evidence of the increasingly 'pan-Protestant' nature of Irish opposition to home rule. Crozier's letter, read aloud at the convention, stated that the opposition of the Presbyterian Church to home rule would be echoed by the Church of Ireland. In Crozier's opinion, the threat of home rule had 'welded together' the whole Protestant community in Ireland, with the result that an 'overwhelming majority' of Church of Ireland members 'stand shoulder to shoulder with the great mass of our Presbyterian brethren'.[3]

As primate, Crozier delivered the opening address to the General Synod, and tackled home rule from the standpoint of a self-confessed 'patriotic Irishman'.

From this patriotic position, in which Ireland was 'as dear to the members of the Church of Ireland as to the so-called Nationalists', Crozier outlined three objections to home rule. Firstly, he prophesised the erosion of Protestant rights and liberties. The 'popular, clap-trap cry' of 'Ireland a nation once again' was 'utterly absurd' without agreement on the necessary safeguards to prevent the majority from 'tyrannising … the loyal minority'. Secondly, Crozier believed home rule would lessen Ireland's privileged position in the empire. Irishmen were 'freemen of the greatest empire on which the sun has ever shone', but home rule would surrender this 'national greatness' and turn Ireland into a 'petty province of England … a paid tributary … an appendage or a colony of the imperial crown'. Thirdly, Crozier feared home rule would inevitably produce 'anarchy and civil strife'. Fear of 'civil strife' had already 'roused the fighting spirit of the toilers in the province where industry and self-reliance and peacefulness must prevail'. Despite this reference to Ulster, Crozier declared it was not his duty to pass on Ulster unionists a 'sentence of approval or disapproval'. However, he imbued Ulster unionism with a spiritual devotion that arguably carried a degree of moral sanction:

> When men of the old Puritan stock and creed open their meetings day after day with prayer, and by singing 'O God, our Help in ages past', they have the stage of self-sacrifice, unto death. They have resolved to resist extra-constitutional measures by extra-constitutional means; and this they will do for faith and fatherland.

In the face of the dangers posed by home rule, Crozier urged the synod to depend on God and pray that Ireland would be saved from bigotry, intolerance and strife.[4]

Following Crozier's speech, a number of resolutions against home rule were proposed by key speakers. These resolutions were composed by six bishops, aided by a sub-committee of the Standing Committee of the General Synod. The six bishops included the two archbishops (Crozier and Joseph Peacocke), two bishops from Ulster dioceses (D'Arcy and Maurice Day, bishop of Clogher) and two from southern dioceses (Bernard and James Bennett Keene, bishop of Meath).[5] The first resolution, moved by Joseph Peacocke, archbishop of Dublin, affirmed the Church of Ireland's allegiance to the throne and 'unswerving attachment to the legislative union', and stressed the non-party political nature of the Church of Ireland's stand. The bishop of Kilmore agreed, pointing out that 'the tidal wave or the forest fire or the volcanic eruption did not mean politics to those who were endangered by it'. Any grievance that did exist was on the 'side of the loyalists, both secular and clerical'.

The second resolution was moved by the provost of Trinity College Dublin, Anthony Traill. It suggested that Ireland's prosperity and industry was dependent upon the union, and that home rule would 'unrest [*sic*] our advance' by placing the progressive element in society under the unprogressive element. The resolution also stated that the property of the Church of Ireland and Protestant civil and religious liberty would not be safe under a parliament 'in which we should be outnumbered by men who are dominated by traditions and aspirations wholly different from our own'.

The third resolution, proposed by D'Arcy, affirmed a desire to maintain Ireland's union with the imperial 'mother-country', and a hope that Protestants in England would support Irish Protestants in opposing home rule. D'Arcy's 'patriotic' argument was similar to Crozier's. The best interests of Ireland would be served, not by having her own parliament, but by retaining the link with the imperial parliament that indirectly controlled so much of Britain's empire. D'Arcy chose to highlight the political, rather than religious, consequences of home rule, pointing out that total separation was the end goal of nationalist aspirations, and in the third Home Rule Bill was the 'machinery ... by which the Unionists of Ireland, and especially the Unionists of Ulster, might be tied hand and feet, while the Nationalist vulture picked their bones'. Here it was a carnivorous political party that was to be feared, not a rapacious Catholic Church.

However, while D'Arcy's speech showed signs of a sense of Irish patriotism, there were also subtle hints at his growing connection with Ulster, as opposed to Irish, unionism. Significantly, D'Arcy was sympathetic towards possible Ulster unionist resistance to home rule, postulating the scenario of the 'men of Ulster' being mown down by the 'rifles and maxim guns' of Britain at the 'instigation of a Nationalist Parliament' for the 'crime of loving welfare, the glory, the citizenship of Great Britain better than life itself'.[6]

Press reaction to the General Synod was generally positive, especially in Ulster. The *Belfast Newsletter* believed the synod had performed a dual function. Irish Protestant unity had been strengthened by aligning the Church of Ireland with the Presbyterian and Methodist anti-home rule conventions. The synod was also held to have influenced an English Protestant audience. While a 'large majority' of English Anglicans were opposed to home rule, 'those of them who are moderate Radicals will not refuse to listen to the earnest appeal of their brethren in Ireland'.[7] The *Belfast Weekly Telegraph* supported the synod's entrance into the home rule debate; the Church of Ireland had more to lose from home rule than any other Protestant Church, because, as the former established church, 'it might be argued that it would be no harm to despoil her of some of the property she obtained through connection with the state'. In addition, unlike the Presbyterian and Methodist Churches, the Church of Ireland was 'more vulnerable and more open to attack ... as its members are scattered throughout the rural districts of the South and West'.[8] The *Irish Times* acknowledged the 'dangers and disadvantages' for a Church in entering the political arena. As a spiritual institution, a Church 'has no concern with secular politics', while the differing political views of the Church's members should be 'meticulously' respected. However, the Church of Ireland General Synod was justified in opposing home rule, as the views expressed represented 'the opinions of probably 99 per cent of the members of the Church', while the 'minute minority' had 'ample opportunity' to communicate their position. The synod also acted patriotically to defend Ireland's interests from a Home Rule Bill that would (echoing Traill) 'arrest national progress and subordinate the progressive to the unprogressive elements of the community'.[9]

Clearly, the anti-home rule tenor of the specially convened General Synod met with approval from the majority of synod members and the unionist press in Ireland. However, a vocal challenge to the dominant position was mounted both at the synod and in the letters page of the *Irish Times*. Opposition centred around James Owen Hannay and a coterie of southern laymen, including Hutchinson Poe and Walter Kavanagh, who were in regular contact before the synod. Poe feared the synod would turn into an attack on the Catholic Church. In what could be described as a 'Burkean' argument, Poe argued that such an attack would be detrimental as under home rule the Catholic Church would prove to be the

Church of Ireland's 'staunchest ally' in resisting the spread of socialism. Poe claimed a 'considerable' number of clergy and laymen shared his and Hannay's views.[10] Walter Kavanagh informed Hannay of his intention to make a protest against the introduction of political questions in the synod.[11]

Hannay and Kavanagh opposed the first resolution (affirming allegiance to the union) moved at the General Synod. If, he claimed, Hannay had been asked to oppose the current Home Rule Bill, he might have supported the resolution, as he disliked Asquith's bill. However, he believed the resolution was asking them to oppose *any* Home Rule Bill, a position from which he 'absolutely and totally dissented'. Hannay declared he spoke for a minority 'not insignificant in the matter of numbers ... intelligence and capacity'. Kavanagh resented turning the synod hall into a 'political debating chamber'. To illustrate his argument, Kavanagh pointed to the widely held claim, endorsed by John Henry Bernard, that a home rule parliament would 'rob' the Church of Ireland of its property. Such a statement, if made on a political platform, would be dismissed. However, when made with 'all the authority and solemnity of a bishop of our Church' at a synod, the argument was taken seriously. Kavanagh believed Bernard's argument was unfounded, and held that under home rule the Church of Ireland would have the 'same liberty as of old'. Hutchinson Poe opposed the second resolution (which raised the possibility of religious discrimination under home rule) as it represented only the views of Protestants in Ulster. In the south and west of Ireland, many Protestants had no fears of any 'possible encroachments' on religious liberties from 'their Roman Catholic neighbours'.[12] Despite the vocal opposition of Hannay, Kavanagh and Poe, only five members of the synod voted against the resolutions (out of an attendance of 402).[13]

Hannay's intention to speak at the synod was privately supported by John Healy, editor of the *Irish Times*. Healy believed 'J.B.C.' (presumably a reference to John Baptist Crozier) would try to prevent Hannay from intervening. Healy advised Hannay to write to Crozier stating his intention to move an amendment to the first resolution. If Crozier appeared intent on blocking him, Hannay should threaten to inform the press: 'I don't think he [Crozier] would dare to face a scandal.'[14] However, Healy misjudged Crozier's attitude. Following the synod, Crozier informed Hannay how 'truly anxious' he had been that 'your father's son – and an author who has brought credit to Ireland' had the opportunity of 'stating in the synod of his Church his honest convictions'.[15] Crozier sought reconciliation with Hannay following their ill-tempered 1911 dispute concerning the 'Belfast working man'. He invited Hannay to join the University Club, offering to second his membership. Crozier hoped the past was behind them and that once again they could be 'old and valued friends. I *know* you love Ireland as I too do.'[16] D'Arcy also appeared eager for Hannay to be allowed to speak at the synod. Writing shortly after the synod was announced, D'Arcy assured Hannay he would not be shouted down and promised to 'do anything in my power which may help towards fair play'.[17] The apparent eagerness of Crozier and D'Arcy to sanction Hannay's wish to state pro-home rule views at the synod seems incongruous in the light of their own staunch unionist position. It is possible they supported a free expression of views at the synod out of a genuine desire to accommodate differing political positions. In addition, Crozier and D'Arcy may have reasoned that as Hannay was supported by such an insignificant number, it would be churlish and counter-productive to prevent him from speaking. Paradoxically, the articulation of minority views may have benefited the unionist case and played well in England. By willingly allowing minority views to be expressed, the leadership of the Church of Ireland demonstrated confidence in their own political position as well as displaying a degree of moderation.

While the opposition expressed at the synod came from members largely supportive of home rule, the *Irish Times* published a number of letters critical of the General Synod's political nature from churchmen anxious that the Church adhere to strict neutrality. This correspondence tended to cast doubt on the Jeremiads concerning the future of the Church of Ireland under home rule, or questioned the wisdom of discussing politics at the synod.[18] The only allegation of a perceived Ulster bias at the synod came in a letter signed 'Churchman and Unionist'. The Church of Ireland had 'hoisted the flag of Belfast's provisional government committee', this writer complained; '"Pro Belfast", not "Pro Patria" is now her motto.'[19] The correspondence published in the *Irish Times* implied a higher degree of opposition to the Church of Ireland's increasing involvement in politics than evidenced by the voting and speeches made at the synod, although caution should be applied before drawing more general conclusions from the correspondence. The claim made in a number of the letters that opposition to the synod was widespread is difficult to substantiate. The overwhelming majorities recorded in support of the various resolutions suggest that substantial support for the opposing view was wishful thinking. The General Synod remained the main representative body for articulating the views of the Church of Ireland at a corporate level and would be expected to reflect divergences of opinion on participation in politics, if they existed. However, the dissentient voices should not be ignored. While the argument that the Church should not be involved in politics was probably held by very few, its advocates were vocal and articulate and kept the issue alive throughout 1912.[20] Also, the arguments raised against the General Synod were heard again when the Church in Ulster threw its weight behind Ulster Day. The controversy over the General Synod was in many ways a trial run for the much more controversial and significant question of whether the Church of Ireland should endorse the covenant and Ulster Day.

'TRUE NATIONALISTS': D'ARCY AND CROZIER'S INVOLVEMENT IN IRISH UNIONISM

D'Arcy's General Synod speech confirmed the position he had been developing towards home rule since becoming bishop of Down in 1911. In 1912 he emerged as the most vocal episcopal opponent of home rule and defender of Ulster's interests. In an interview with the *Daily Telegraph* in January, D'Arcy aimed to convey to an English audience that Ulster unionism was in 'earnest' and that opposition to home rule was not a bluff. Ulster unionists opposed home rule as they were 'devoted to liberty' and 'essentially a free people' who believed home rule 'would really threaten their civil and religious liberties'. What Ulster Protestants feared most of all was 'religious tyranny'. While English Roman Catholics may have been 'mild and cultivated', D'Arcy asserted that in Ireland Catholicism had a history of 'political antagonism'. Under home rule the Catholic Church would be free to act as it pleased, as a home rule parliament 'would be completely under the domination of the Roman Church in Ireland'.[21]

D'Arcy elaborated on his *Daily Telegraph* interview in a contribution to *Against Home Rule*, a collection of essays written by prominent unionists – Andrew Bonar Law provided the preface, Edward Carson the introduction and there were contributions by, among others, A.J. Balfour, Leo Amery and the marquis of Londonderry. Published in April 1912, *Against Home Rule* was wished a 'popular readership' by the *Belfast Newsletter*, which also hoped the book's cheap price of one shilling would encourage wide circulation. The *Newsletter* particularly commended D'Arcy's contribution to *Against Home Rule* as a 'masterly exposition of Unionist policy'.[22]

D'Arcy's essay in *Against Home Rule* dealt with the 'Religious Difficulty under Home Rule'. He stated at the outset that the deepest conviction of all against giving Ireland a separate legislature and executive was that 'the religious difficulty, which is ever with us here, would be increased enormously'. Irish Protestants feared 'Roman aggression' more than in 1886 and 1893, and if home rule was 'forced upon them' Protestants would be 'face to face with a struggle for liberty and conscience such as this land has not witnessed since the year 1690'. D'Arcy rehearsed a number of arguments familiar from his rhetoric in 1911. The supposedly intolerant nature of Catholicism, illustrated by *Ne Temere*, was reinforced by a further papal intervention, the motu propiro *Quantavis Diligentia*, which he stated meant that any Catholic who 'without permission from any ecclesiastical authority, summons any ecclesiastical person to a lay tribunal and compels them to attend publicly such a court, incurs instant excommunication'. D'Arcy feared that in a home rule Ireland the Catholic Church would have the power to enforce this edict, which had previously been rendered impossible by the 'custom of the country'. The threat to Church of Ireland property under home rule was also emphasised. For D'Arcy, the endowments of the Church of Ireland had been established by the generosity of Church of Ireland clergy in the aftermath of disestablishment, and the church buildings of the Church of Ireland were held by 'exactly the same title as that by which the English Church holds Westminster Abbey'.[23]

D'Arcy's essay seemed addressed to a primarily English readership, with references throughout to the apparent lack of comprehension of Irish affairs in England. For example, *Ne Temere* 'has been enforced in Ireland in a manner which must seem impossible to Englishmen'. The 'mild and cultivated form of Romanism' in England had coloured the opinion of the 'average Englishman' to the extent that the Catholic Church could not possibly be seen as a threat.[24] English Liberals who argued home rule would destroy the power of the Catholic Church in Ireland were mistaken, as from the outset 'clerical domination … would be the ruling principle of an Irish Parliament' due to the strength of the 'Roman Ecclesiastical System'.[25] D'Arcy wanted to convey to English Protestants the sense of impending doom facing their Irish counterparts if a separate parliament was granted to Ireland. In *Against Home Rule*, as with his *Daily Telegraph* interview, D'Arcy acted as an apologist for Ulster unionism, defending and justifying the fears of Ulster Protestants to their English counterparts. It was a mark of D'Arcy's standing in England that he was chosen to contribute to the book along with such an influential cast of politicians – clearly he was seen as the Irish churchman most likely to be a persuasive voice in England.

The impression that D'Arcy was attempting to influence English opinion is strengthened by his correspondence in the first half of 1912 with the archbishop of Canterbury, Randall Davidson. D'Arcy had heard, via the dean of Westminster, that Davidson was interested in Ireland and so sent the archbishop a number of articles stating the unionist case. These papers included an outline of the percentage of Roman Catholics employed in county councils and as poor law union officials in Ireland.[26] D'Arcy also sent Davidson an article from the *Newsletter* entitled 'Home Rule controversy: some relevant facts', which dealt with the issue of fair employment in Ireland, explaining:

> The enclosed from today's *Belfast Newsletter* puts facts very clearly. You will see that in Munster and Connaught there are only 3 Protestant county councillors out of a total of 374, although most of the enterprise, even in those parts of this country, is to be found amongst the Protestant minority. Yet the English public are gulled with the phrase 'Protestant Ascendancy', and even Cabinet Ministers repeat it. Trusting you will pardon me for troubling you with these things – my excuse is that it is a matter of life and death for us.[27]

The following day D'Arcy sent Davidson another letter, enclosing more information, including an Ulster Unionist Council-published pamphlet entitled 'Tolerance in Ireland: what are the facts?' D'Arcy pointed out how 'it is a simple truth that the only real toleration in Ireland is on the part of the Protestant and Unionist section of the population'.[28]

Crozier's General Synod speech was also indicative of his pronouncements on home rule in the first half of 1912. Like D'Arcy, he gave an interview to the *Daily Telegraph* in January. While Crozier praised Ulster unionists as men 'convinced that their religion and liberty of conscience were absolutely at stake', the views expressed in his interview were subtly different from D'Arcy's interview in the same paper a week earlier. Crozier appeared more concerned than D'Arcy about the effect home rule would have on the whole island of Ireland, which explained his focus on the sectarian division home rule would cause and the related effect on the prosperity of the country. Crozier wanted Irishmen to be 'left alone' to put their 'theoretical politics' aside for a few years, so that those who 'really love their country' would come forward to improve it agriculturally, industrially and educationally: 'By such means as these we can best prove ourselves to be true Christian patriots.'[29] Crozier's view, repeated in his synod speech, was that home rule would harm all the people of Ireland, and because the Church of Ireland loved Ireland, her 'native land', home rule must be opposed.

Crucial to such a 'patriotic' opposition to home rule was a belief that Ireland formed an integral part of the empire. This imperial sentiment, expressed in Crozier's General Synod speech, echoed views he had expressed earlier in the year. In February, Crozier spoke at a meeting held in Armagh to inaugurate the foundation of a 'union of Little Empire Builders and Daughters of the Empire'. For Crozier, because they 'loved Ireland so much, they must love the great Empire of which they formed part'. The supreme example of patriotism was Jesus, who was 'the greatest patriot the world ever saw' on account of his concern for his country and Jerusalem. They should oppose home rule because they loved Ireland, and for Ireland home rule would mean 'people fighting, and the people with money, people who owned mills, people who were able to work' leaving the country. Fortunately for Ireland and the empire, the 'Daughters of Empire' were on hand to teach the 'little Empire Builders' patriotic songs which would help make Ireland 'healthy, happy, and prosperous'.[30]

Crozier, like D'Arcy, was highly involved in Ulster unionism. One week before the General Synod, massed ranks of Ulster unionists had paraded at Balmoral, in south Belfast. A sequel to the Craigavon meeting in 1911, Balmoral was attended by Andrew Bonar Law, the leader of the Conservative party, and over seventy MPs. Employing imagery from the 1689 Siege of Derry, Bonar Law reminded Ulster unionists that they were members of a 'besieged city' that held the pass for the empire:

> The timid have left you; your Lundys have betrayed you; but you have closed your gates. The Government have erected by their Parliament Act a boom against you to shut you off from the help of the British people. You will burst that boom.

A religious service, officiated at by Crozier and the Presbyterian moderator, opened proceedings. Crozier prayed that the king would be saved from 'evil counsellors' and pleaded for Ireland: 'Deliver us, we pray thee, from those great and imminent dangers by which we are encompassed. And continue to protect thy true religion against the designs of those who seek to overthrow it.'[31] This prayer indelibly linked the two great requests made to God by unionist clergy: deliverance from home rule and protection from those who sought home rule in order to promote their sectarian agenda.

The Balmoral meeting provoked a number of differing interpretations within the Church of Ireland. Crozier's participation aroused opprobrium in the *Irish Times* from 'a curate' who believed 'our ecclesiastical superiors are blind to the splendour of the vision which we young men are straining after. Will their eyes be ever opened – or will they see when it is too late?'[32] A more vitriolic response came from Pierce O'Mahoney, a southern layman, who believed Crozier's opening prayer was 'absolutely and wickedly false'. O'Mahoney had informed the 'insolent Prelate who uttered it that he had lowered the dignity of his office by his presence at the Belfast meeting, which was pregnant with bigotry and intolerance'.[33] However, unsurprisingly the unionist-supporting Church of Ireland press praised Balmoral. The *Church of Ireland Gazette* viewed it in an all-Ireland context as evidence of the 'great and bitter cry of indignation' coming 'from the four provinces of Ireland, on behalf of the rights and liberties of Protestants, who desire to remain members of that Empire which has been built up by their blood'.[34] The *Irish Churchman* lent a more provincial spin to the demonstration, claiming it represented Ulster's 'unalterable attitude of opposition to Home Rule'. The *Churchman* believed 'the strongest argument against Home Rule is Ulster, with her teeming thousands of successful business men and industrious farmers', a view illustrating the paper's narrower Ulster-focused opposition to home rule.[35]

The journalist Marcus Tanner believes such pro-Ulster sentiments explained Crozier's involvement at Balmoral, where Crozier 'threw himself into the cause of the "Protestant province" and the arming of the Unionist population without a backward glance'.[36] However, it is doubtful whether Crozier interpreted his participation at Balmoral in such terms. Writing to Lady Londonderry, Crozier described the Balmoral demonstration as being 'wonderfully glorious ... and the grim determination of those masses of men I shall never forget. It was the making of History.' Crozier had been a guest of Lady Londonderry at Mount Stewart, with, among others, Carson and Bonar Law, before the demonstration. Crozier thanked Lady Londonderry 'for having me as one of the select circle of true Nationalists'.[37] The assertion that Crozier and his fellow Balmoral speakers were 'true Nationalists' suggests Crozier believed defending Ireland (and not just Ulster) from home rule represented true (British) nationalism, and that Balmoral was a stage in this battle.

For the Church of Ireland, Balmoral was a fitting prelude to the General Synod, as it raised questions concerning the legitimacy of the Church's involvement in politics. Balmoral also foreshadowed Ulster Day, the largest Ulster unionist demonstration of the period. Ulster Day proved controversial within the Church of Ireland for a number of reasons. The northern bishops' support of Ulster Day was opposed publicly by the same elements that had criticised the General Synod – pro-home rule members and those opposed to any ecclesiastical participation in politics.[38] However, the northern bishops, by supporting an obviously pro-Ulster policy, rendered irrelevant the argument used at the General Synod that opposition to home rule was justified as it represented a non-partisan political position. Southern bishops, largely united on the legitimacy of participation in politics and opposition to home rule, privately opposed Ulster Day and the role played by the Church of Ireland in Ulster because of the demonstration's emphasis on Ulster particularism.

CROSSING THE RUBICON: THE CHURCH OF IRELAND AND ULSTER DAY

Ulster Day was the largest and most ambitious Ulster unionist demonstration of the entire home rule period. Belfast was smothered with conspicuous representations of Britishness. The *Church of Ireland Gazette* described the scene as 'unforgettable': 'the city was a mass of bunting. Belfast people are accustomed to flying the flag, but never before was anything like this seen';[39] the *Newsletter* claimed the great mass of union flags symbolised a spirit of 'attachment to the Union, loyalty to the King and to the Constitution'.[40] The purpose of Ulster Day was to demonstrate this sense of attachment, as well as providing a potent exhibition of the strength and apparent unity of Ulster unionist opposition to home rule. The day was to culminate in the signing of a document, the 'Solemn League and Covenant', which unionists around Ulster would put their name to. The Covenant pledged those who signed it to

> Stand by one another in defending for ourselves and our children our position of equal citizenship in the United Kingdom, and in using all means which may be found necessary to defeat the present conspiracy to set up a Home Rule Parliament in Ireland.

Home rule was declared as 'disastrous to the material well-being of Ulster as well as of the whole of Ireland, subversive of our civil and religious freedom, destructive of our citizenship'.[41] The Covenant appealed to its target audience, with ultimately 471,414 Ulster men and women signing the covenant or the declaration.[42] Ulster Day was a marked unionist propaganda triumph, brilliantly planned by James Craig, who ensured that the tools of a nascent mass media were on hand to record the centrepiece event of the day – Carson's signing of the covenant. This event, so important in Ulster unionist image-making and symbolism, was filmed for a wider British and country audience.[43] However, its planners hoped Ulster Day would be seen as more than a well-executed propaganda triumph. With its implicit threat of violence, the covenant suggested Ulster unionists could not be persuaded or coerced into a home rule Ireland. The announcement, in August 1912, of Ulster Day signalled the beginning of a flurry of Ulster unionist activity, with Carson scheduled to speak at mass meetings in provincial centres around Ulster in the week leading up to Ulster Day (28 September) when the 'Solemn League and Covenant' would be signed.

Thomas Sinclair, the leading Presbyterian layman largely responsible for drafting the Covenant, was tasked with approaching Crozier and the heads of the other Protestant denominations to ascertain their opinion on the advisability of holding Ulster Day church services.[44] His overtures were successful – the Ulster Unionist Council (UUC) later announced that Ulster Day should be marked by 'solemn religious' services in each 'convenient locality'. The arrangement of these services was to reside in the hands of local committees.[45] Further evidence of the religious nature of Ulster Day was provided by the establishment of a clerical sub-committee to help with the planning, composed of a number of laymen and the (Dublin-born) dean of Belfast, the Presbyterian moderator and the Methodist president.[46] Ulster Day illuminated the two-way relationship between the Protestant Churches and the Ulster unionist hierarchy. It became clear that the Church of Ireland in Ulster was generally eager to lend support to Ulster Day. Equally, the decision to seek the imprimatur of the leading Protestant clergymen, and the setting up of the clerical planning committee, suggested the UUC was conscious of the value of gaining the support of the Churches if the demonstration was to prove a success.

In public, D'Arcy was the first bishop to support Ulster Day. In a letter to the local press he welcomed the holding of Ulster Day services, as Ulster unionists had a 'great need to humble ourselves before God, to confess our many shortcomings, and to seek for Divine assistance'. They also needed to pray for 'self-control' so that their 'determination to resist intolerable injury may not hurry them into acts of retaliation which would weaken their moral influence, and degrade a noble cause'. D'Arcy emphasised the overtly political nature of the Ulster Day services by stating they should include a prayer 'for the final overthrow of a policy which can bring nothing but strife and misery to our country'.[47]

D'Arcy's call for prayer on Ulster Day was followed by a 'pastoral' issued by the northern bishops (including D'Arcy). With a (presumably) Crozier-influenced turn-of-phrase, the pastoral referred to the ongoing 'great crisis' in the religious and political history of 'our beloved native land'. Therefore, constancy and earnestness in prayer were required so that God, in his 'bounteous goodness', may 'overrule all things to the glory of His name and the greater good of His church and people'. To facilitate such prayer, special services of 'humiliation', confession of sin, and intercession for Ireland's political leaders were announced for 22 September. The pastoral expressed the hope that if they waited 'upon God in humility and faith, He will bring us and our country in safety through the present crisis'.[48]

D'Arcy sent a public letter to the clergy in his diocese interpreting the 22 September services of intercession as an opportunity to prepare for Ulster Day, thereby connecting the 22 September services and Ulster Day in a manner the pastoral had avoided. According to D'Arcy, 'there can surely be no better preparation for the great decision of the 28th than that the first day of that historic week should be thus set apart'.[49] D'Arcy's letter also outlined the structure that the Ulster Day church services should follow, providing another link between the 22 September and Ulster Day services. By issuing guidelines for Ulster Day services in his interpretation of the 'pastoral', D'Arcy gave a fairly clear indication that the 'preparation' he had in mind for his clergy was that they get ready to sign the Covenant and support Ulster Day. The *Newsletter* agreed with D'Arcy's interpretation of the intercessory services as 'no better preparation could have been made for Ulster Day, and nothing could have appealed more to the inner consciousness of the men and women of the North of Ireland to whom the claims of religion occupy the most sacred place in their lives'.[50]

D'Arcy preached at the Ulster Day service in Belfast Cathedral, the largest service seen in Belfast: 'Every available inch of space was occupied, and hundreds were unable to obtain admission.'[51] Lessons were read from Isaiah and Ephesians and Psalm 46 was sung, along with the by now ubiquitous hymn, sung to signify unionist defiance, 'O God our help in ages past'. Pointing out that only matters of the 'most surpassing importance' could justify signing the covenant, D'Arcy based his sermon around the following assertion:

> We maintain that no one has the right to deprive us of our heritage of British citizenship and to subject us to a Government which stands for all that we and our forefathers have striven against. We hold that no power has the right to sell us into slavery.

D'Arcy attempted to grant the Covenant strong moral justification by claiming it signified the desire of Ulster unionists to continue serving God by passing on 'unimpaired to our children that heirloom of religious liberty which our forefathers bequeathed to us'. Ulster Day was also intended, he alleged, to benefit Protestants in the south and west of Ireland and was not a 'selfish endeavour to keep privilege, or even security for ourselves'. D'Arcy aimed to salve any consciences troubled with the prospect of violence and armed resistance implied by the Covenant. In what amounted to a form of just war theorising (that he would more rigorously define at the outbreak of the Great War), D'Arcy cautioned:

> We must face the fact that there are things worse than war ... and we must realise that the conditions of life in this world are such that war becomes possible whenever the foundations are shaken.[52]

D'Arcy recognised the step he, and by implication the Church of Ireland in his diocese, would be taking if he endorsed the Covenant. In effect, he would be validating resistance to the lawfully constituted government of the United Kingdom, by force if necessary, in defending the right of Ulstermen to remain part of that same United Kingdom. D'Arcy later claimed the decision facing him as to whether or not to sign the Covenant 'involved the risking of everything. It was clear that the Covenant meant a real crossing of the Rubicon.' D'Arcy believed that very many of the clergy in his diocese would be guided by the position he took regarding the Covenant. His decision to cross the Rubicon, and lend wholehearted support to Ulster Day, was most profoundly influenced by the advice of Lord MacNaghten, a law lord and D'Arcy's old parishioner and friend from his time as rector of Billy. MacNaghten believed that to 'deprive a community, against its will, of the citizenship and liberties into which its members were born would be a political outrage'. This political outrage was only made possible by suspending the Constitution.[53] MacNaghten's blessing, D'Arcy later recalled, was of 'decisive importance' in encouraging the leading clergy in Down and Connor and Dromore to sign the Covenant.[54] A letter from Crozier to Archbishop Davidson, written in 1914, confirmed D'Arcy's interpretation of events in *Adventures*. Davidson had asked Crozier how D'Arcy had justified signing the covenant. Crozier's reply was a summary of a statement made to him by D'Arcy:

> Lord MacNaghten: 'From the legal point of view Ulster men are perfectly justified in signing the Covenant because the Constitution is suspended.'

He further stated that loyalists should be bound together by the Covenant and could not be defeated.

The Bishop of Down has just given me the above statement.[55]

D'Arcy's support of Ulster Day revealed a pro-Ulster sympathy possibly surprising from a Dublin-born bishop of the Church of Ireland. A number of factors influenced his decision to support a policy that seemed to imply the abandonment of the Protestants of the south and west of Ireland to a home rule parliament. D'Arcy's leadership of the most populous (and Ulster unionist) diocese in Ireland, allied to his long-standing professional connection with Ulster, perhaps inevitably led him to sympathise with an Ulster-focused political strategy. It is also likely that D'Arcy's belief in eugenics reinforced his partitionist instincts. In November 1911, D'Arcy had been appointed as an office bearer of the newly formed 'Eugenics Education Society'.[56] This was an offshoot of the 'Belfast Eugenics Society', of which D'Arcy was chairman. This society, founded in 1911, became in effect a pressure group, campaigning for the extension of the Mental Deficiency Act to Ireland.[57] D'Arcy believed 'rigorous scientific proof' demonstrated 'civilisation will be in danger from extinction' if the increase continued of individuals 'well below the average human standard'. In the prevailing poor social conditions, the 'feeble minded and inefficient members of society' were marrying more and 'multiplying more rapidly than the rest of the population'.[58] However, luckily for D'Arcy, he observed that he was fortunate enough to be bishop of a diocese that had the lowest percentage of insane people in Ireland; indeed, Ulster was the sanest province in Ireland, with a mere 4.2 per 1,000 of its population certified as 'lunatics'.[59] In his 1912 diocesan synod speech, held after Ulster Day, D'Arcy quoted the 1911 census returns for Ulster to illustrate how the province was more prosperous and better educated than the rest of Ireland. For example, 'in Cork city the illiterates are 6.5 per cent, in Dublin city 5.3 per cent, in Belfast only 3.6 per cent'. D'Arcy also pointed out that the 'proportion of the insane in this part of Ulster is not only far below the rest of Ireland, but far below the rest of the United Kingdom'. D'Arcy admitted he would rather not have to make such 'odious' comparisons, but the 'false statements' of Ulster's slanderers had to be exposed.[60] The *Belfast Telegraph* described D'Arcy's speech as 'vigorous and stirring' and deserving of the attention of all who 'love their country'.[61] The *Newsletter* reported admiringly that D'Arcy's speech had been reproduced in the *Church Times* (a Church of England High-Church newspaper), which had 'many radicals' among its readership. The *Newsletter* believed the figures quoted by D'Arcy were 'stubborn facts which should silence for ever Radical and Nationalist slanderers of Ulster's fair name and province'.[62] Eugenics provided an intellectual rationale to D'Arcy's growing identification with Ulster – his diocesan synod speech was not merely anti-home rule, but partitionist in feeling.

While D'Arcy enthusiastically endorsed Ulster Day, southern bishops were rather more circumspect. Led by Joseph Peacocke (archbishop of Dublin) and John Henry Bernard (bishop of Ossory), southern bishops decided against holding 22 September intercessory services or issuing a statement endorsing Ulster Day. Bernard had received a series of letters in August from Lord Bessborough, a southern layman. To mark Ulster Day, Bessborough suggested a special religious service should be held in 'every Protestant place of worship in Ireland on the same day and hour'. This would be 'very striking'. However, Bernard opposed this idea – he marked the letter 'I demurred from this.'[63] It is likely Bernard was not willing to hold a special service that risked identifying the Church of Ireland with the particular Ulster-focused policy entailed by Ulster Day. When Bessborough next wrote to Bernard, he agreed with Bernard that it would be a mistake for the Church to 'take any definite political step [or] unite itself in any way with any political party'.[64]

Correspondence between Bernard and Peacocke made clear that the southern bishops were concerned that support for Ulster Day would suggest the Church of Ireland identified with Ulster, as opposed to Irish, unionism. On 1 September Peacocke wrote to Bernard to explain that D'Arcy's decision to hold Ulster Day services was taken unilaterally, 'very unwisely and without consultation with the Primate and the other Bishops in Ulster'. D'Arcy would, in Peacocke's opinion, commit the Church of Ireland in Down and Connor and Dromore 'in the eyes of the general public in Ireland and Great Britain to the acceptance of whatever action may be taken by the meeting'. Peacocke claimed the other northern bishops were 'much put aback by Down's action' but had agreed that special prayers and intercession should be offered in the northern dioceses on 22 September, 'and thus, as far as possible, avoid identifying the church generally with the proceedings of the meeting of the 28th'. Peacocke believed if similar intercessory services were to be held in the south, they must not be identified with the 'Belfast meeting' or the Covenant. The southern bishops also had to consider the position of 'our clergy and people outside Ulster', who may face hostility 'throughout the three other provinces' in revenge for the 'Belfast movement'.[65]

Peacocke's rejection of the Covenant was shared by Bernard and the bishop of Cork (William Meade), making clear the tensions between the stand advanced by D'Arcy and what southern bishops were prepared to countenance. Meade agreed that Ulster Day should not be observed by the Church of Ireland in the south as he was 'sure that the great majority of the laity in the south would strongly object to being in any way identified with the Ulster Movement'.[66] Later in September, Peacocke confirmed that '*All* the bishops are glad we are not taking action that would bring us into line with the Ulster movement and meeting on the 28th.'[67]

However, Peacocke resolved to issue a prayer of intercession for Ireland for use in public worship, although the precise form and date of use were initially a matter of debate. Meade believed the prayer should be used on 15 September, although Peacocke disagreed with this date as it was obviously 'disconnecting ourselves' from our 'Ulster brothers'. Instead, Peacocke believed Bernard's idea – of using the prayer (which Bernard would write) on the Sunday before parliament opened in October – was the best policy to pursue.[68]

Bernard's opposition to Ulster Day did not appear, from his Leighlin diocesan synod speech, to be the result of any personal dislike of D'Arcy or Ulster. Bernard appealed for money to aid D'Arcy's diocese in appointing clergy to service the growing Church population in Belfast. In 1911 appeals for Belfast were encouraged by pointing to Ulster's solidarity with Protestants in the rest of Ireland in opposing home rule. However, for Bernard, speaking on the eve of Ulster Day, helping the Church of Ireland in Belfast carried no semblance of gratitude for their Ulster brethren's supposed political selflessness. Helping Belfast 'was a matter that had nothing to do with politics, whether civil or ecclesiastical. It had only to do with the elementary Christian duty of helping their neighbours, their brethren in Christ.'[69] Bernard may have made this statement for a number of reasons. Although the Church of Ireland in Belfast, led by D'Arcy, had apparently decided to act in the interests of defending Ulster from home rule, a spiritual obligation remained for Anglicans in the rest of Ireland to help their northern counterparts. Bernard may also have been attempting to justify to his own synod members the financial aid required for Belfast, which many may have opposed due to Ulster Day. Whatever the reason, Bernard endorsed help for Belfast during the lead up to Ulster Day, an early suggestion that whatever the political differences within the Church, perceived spiritual unity could ensure institutional unity.

Peacocke's speech to the Dublin diocesan synod, made after Ulster Day, demonstrated his continued opposition to home rule and belief that the Church should be involved in politics. After the General Synod no one could 'mistake the opinion of the great mass of the members of our Church on this question [home rule] as expressed by its chosen representatives or the position it has now taken up'. Peacocke also claimed Ulster Day 'has shown plainly the feelings of the great mass of the Protestants of this country in regard to the bill now before Parliament', surprising sentiments from a man who had privately ensured the Church of Ireland outside Ulster did not officially endorse Ulster Day or the Covenant. However, it could be argued that Peacocke had *not* endorsed Ulster Day in his diocesan synod speech, but merely stated a fact. His assertion that only 'lawful means' should accompany 'our prayers' to avert the 'coming revolution' suggested he may still have had objections to the Covenant.[70] Judging from the diocesan synod speeches of a number of other southern bishops throughout 1912, it is unlikely their reasons for not endorsing the Covenant were an unwillingness to oppose home rule or an objection to involving the Church in politics.[71] The bishop of Meath, John Bennett Keene, speaking at his diocesan synod (held after Ulster Day), opposed home rule and called for Ireland to be 'let alone'. As with Ossory and a number of other southern dioceses, Keene pointed out that Meath was contributing money to Belfast to help pay for church workers (in Meath's case, £2 per parish).[72]

While the southern bishops did not agree with identifying the Church of Ireland in the south with Ulster Day, Peacocke's 1 September letter to Bernard suggested that the northern bishops, apart from D'Arcy, were also reluctant to lend official endorsement to Ulster Day. However, only one bishop came close to criticising Ulster Day in public. Speaking at the Ardagh diocesan synod before Ulster Day, Alfred Elliot, bishop of Kilmore, Elphin and Ardagh, claimed 'all moderate men regretted the aspect of things caused by the determination of Ulster to resist the imposition of Home Rule'.[73] Elliot also referred to the 'awful response' being prepared by Ulster. Elliot's critique of Ulster Day probably resulted from a realisation that the possibility of separate action implied by the Covenant meant the diocese of Ardagh, which was outside Ulster, would be isolated in a home rule Ireland. Elliot may also have borne in mind the lukewarm reception accorded to ecclesiastical moves against home rule at the previous year's Ardagh Synod. A resolution describing home rule as 'disastrous' was proposed by a layman in his capacity as a 'representative of the Church of Ireland in Ardagh'. The resolution, when put to a vote, received fourteen votes in support and fourteen votes against, and was withdrawn.[74] However, at the Kilmore diocesan synod, held in Cavan after Ulster Day, Elliot praised Ulster, which, although the 'least inviting part of Ireland', was in 'general prosperity ... far in advance of the other provinces'. Elliot did not think it fair or likely that the 'brain and muscle, to which Ulster's condition is due' would accept 'without coercion' home rule.[75] The change in tone from Elliot's Ardagh speech may have been because Ulster Day passed off peacefully – it was easier to endorse a 'risky' event once it had occurred and the 'awful response' had turned out to be not so awful after all. In addition, Elliot probably tailored his rhetoric to suit an audience composed largely of Ulstermen who were likely to have welcomed Ulster Day.

If Elliot's Ardagh speech offered a modicum of support to Peacocke's claim that the northern bishops were not enthusiastic supporters of Ulster Day, his argument was weakened by the statements and actions of the remaining northern bishops, who all signed the Covenant. However, beneath the surface unity, ambiguities existed in the northern bishops' support of Ulster Day. The bishop of Clogher, Maurice Day, preached at the united Ulster Day service in Enniskillen. After the service, Day was the second signatory of the Covenant (behind the earl of Erne). In his sermon, Day emphasised it was not his duty to urge people to sign the Covenant: 'This is a matter each of us must decide in his own conscience and in the sight of God'. Day desired, as a 'bishop of the Church of Ireland', to identify himself with the 'spiritual side' of Ulster Day as 'no efforts of ours can be successful without the help and blessing of God'. At the conclusion of his sermon, after outlining the perilous state faced by Protestants under home rule, Day called for unionists to 'use, as we are asked to-day, all lawful means for the preservation of our liberties – civil and religious', as well as asking God to 'help and deliver us'.[76] In referring to the Covenant as a 'lawful means' of resisting home rule, it seems that Day either seriously misunderstood the covenant or was engaged in a degree of wishful thinking. The less than legal aspect of the Covenant was alluded to by the *Fermanagh Times* in its Ulster Day article, which included Day's sermon. It pointed out that leading up to Ulster Day 'no attempt was made to minimise or gloss over the rigid meaning of the [Covenant's] clauses or the fateful import of its logical consequence'.[77] Day may have wanted to see the Covenant as 'lawful' to justify his own signing of it – or he may have been very subtly suggesting that the unlawful action promised by the covenant was not the right course for Ulster unionists to follow. A comparison can be drawn between Bishop Day's Ulster Day sermon and a speech he made to the Clones and Monaghan unionist clubs on Empire Day. Both events were archetypal unionist occasions and at both Day demonstrated an affinity with unionist rhetoric. On Empire Day he announced his love for the union flag and hoped it would 'always be unfurled and never taken down'. However, as at Ulster Day, he emphasised the need for a lawful stand against home rule. Day 'was not one of those who would advocate anything that was not in accordance with the law of the land', but anything that was lawful should be done to oppose home rule.[78] Day's views on the extent to which home rule could be resisted illustrate the very difficult position in which the Covenant placed him. Perhaps as a result of the widespread support accorded Ulster Day from the mass of Ulster unionists, Day felt the need to endorse the Covenant; however, at the same time he appeared opposed to its implied threat. This tension probably explained his rather confusing behaviour on Ulster Day, where on the one hand he advocated only lawful means of opposition to home rule, yet signed the Covenant.

Peacocke had claimed the 22 September services were an attempt by the northern bishops to avoid identifying the Church with Ulster Day. If true, they were undermined by D'Arcy's interpretation of the intercessory services as a means of preparing for Ulster Day. However, George Chadwick's interpretation of the intercessory service seemed to support Peacocke's claim. Chadwick, the bishop of Derry, sent his clergy a letter outlining the form the 22 September intercessory services should follow. He emphasised the intention of the service was not to 'pervert the pulpit to the purposes – even the legitimate purposes – of a party platform'. He hoped the services would ensure 'political passion may be softened and regulated by grace'.[79] However, despite this avowedly apolitical interpretation, Chadwick's intercessory service sermon at Derry Cathedral implicitly supported the Covenant. While admitting the decision to sign the Covenant was a matter of individual conscience and that the 'whole Church of Ireland in General Synod assembled should not decide that question', Chadwick implied that not to sign the Covenant was spiritually deficient: 'To shift one's responsibility, one's political responsibility upon another man was utterly alien from the spirit and the generous and unselfish teaching of Christ and his apostles.' Chadwick justified resistance to the state, implicit in the Covenant, by arguing there was a limit to obedience: '"Bond servant, obey your master in all things" would be an utterly demoralising mandate unless checked and controlled by the influence of much higher laws.' With a restricted House of Lords imperilling parliamentary government and a promised Irish parliament likely to be led by the representatives of 'cattle drivers', obedience to the state was limited – instead, unionists should 'appeal to a greater person than Caesar'. Drawing a parallel with the Siege of Derry ('worshippers harder pressed and sorer tried than we, yet by the mercy of God victorious'), Chadwick invoked 'the protection, the deliverance, the vindication of the King of Kings'.[80] Chadwick's desire for a non-political intercessory service may have been sincere, but his sermon demonstrated the difficulty in achieving this aim. The intercessory service was essentially a form of worship necessitated (in the bishops' opinion) by political circumstances – it was naïve for Peacocke (and Chadwick) to assume these services would abstain from rallying the faithful and challenging the doubtful ahead of Ulster Day.

Like D'Arcy, Crozier's statements prior to 22 September linked the intercessory service with Ulster Day. In a letter to the clergy of Armagh diocese, Crozier pointed out that 22 September *and* 28 September were set aside as special days of intercession and prayer 'on behalf of our beloved native land'. The letter outlined the form such services should follow, and Crozier expressed his hope that 'nothing may keep any of our people away from the House of Prayer on Sunday 22nd, and on Saturday 28th'. A special collect was printed, to be used in the services, confessing sin and calling on God to 'look in mercy upon us thy servants at this time of anxiety and distress. Deliver us we pray thee, from these great and imminent dangers which threaten the welfare of our Church and country.'[81] Crozier made a spectacular intervention at the Ulster Day proceedings in Belfast. During the Covenant-signing ceremony in the City Hall, 'a despatch rider burst into the hall' bearing a heliogram from Crozier to Carson: 'May God give you strength and wisdom to guide aright Ireland's faithful sons in trying to save our beloved native land from degradation, disaster, religious strife, and civil war.'[82] Crozier's sermon at the private chapel of Castle Saunderson in Fermanagh continued in the vein of his previous statements on home rule by emphasising Irish patriotism. Conveniently, in Crozier's text (2 Samuel 12:10) 'we notice that Joab speaks as a devoted patriot ready to do or die for the safety of his native land.' Crozier called for God to save Ireland from a 'patriotism' that allowed cattle houghing and murder – such behaviour 'prostituted' real patriotism. True, God-given patriotism was a readiness to 'suffer the loss of all things for their native land'. It was in this spirit that Ulster unionists had acted, calling on God to help them prevent the 'degradation of their native land and the dismemberment of the great Empire'. Those who signed the Covenant were 'brave men struggling for civil and religious liberty'.[83] Thus, Crozier represented Ulster Day as a patriotic protest on behalf of all the people of Ireland against home rule. Nevertheless, Crozier faced, at a national level, the same difficulty that confronted the bishop of Kilmore: how to reconcile support for Ulster unionism while representing Church of Ireland members worshipping outside Ulster. Crozier's patriotic inter-pretation of Ulster Day was unsurprising in light of his other statements on home rule, and also explained why he felt able to endorse the Covenant. The only way Crozier, as primate of Ireland, could support Ulster Day was to see it as having an 'all Ireland' patriotic dimension instead of being a myopic Ulster-focused initiative.

The fact that the Covenant was drawn up by a Presbyterian, Thomas Sinclair, and inspired by a centuries-old Presbyterian document (the 1643 Scottish Parliamentary Covenant) has led to claims that it represented the Presbyterian nature of Ulster unionism.[84] In addition, it has been claimed Irish Anglican cler-ical support for the covenant represented the 'Presbyterianisation' of the Church of Ireland.[85] Akenson interprets support for the 'distinctly Presbyterian' Ulster Covenant as evidence of the 'cultural hegemony that the Ulster-Scots held over the entire Protestant population of the north of Ireland'.[86] However, these claims are challenged by a number of pieces of evidence. D'Arcy, the staunchest sup-porter of the Covenant, was a Dublin-born Anglican; and although D'Arcy had a great affinity with Ulster, there is little evidence he had 'gone native'. Crozier's support for the Covenant was not that of an 'Ulster-Scot', but of a self-confessed patriotic Irishman motivated by a desire to defeat home rule for all of Ireland. In addition, there is no evidence that D'Arcy or any other northern bishop viewed the Covenant as a Presbyterian document. Perhaps more significantly, southern bishops never mentioned the Covenant's Presbyterian antecedents as justifica-tion for their opposition to it. It is likely that the Covenant's Anglican opponents would have seized on its supposed Presbyterian nature to argue against the north-ern bishops' participation in Ulster Day, if such a perception was widespread. Anglican support for the Covenant is most adequately explained when placed in the context of growing Irish Protestant co-operation in response to the threat of home rule. When opposing home rule, competing denominational identities were subsumed under the unity provided by being 'Protestant' and unionist. Such unity was perhaps most potently demonstrated at a parochial level in Ulster, in joint unionist club and Ulster Day religious services.[87] At a high-political level within the Church, denominational co-operation was illustrated by Crozier's let-ter to the Presbyterian Convention and practically demonstrated by the ecumeni-cal composition of the Ulster Day clerical sub-committee.

CONCLUSION

One implication of the events of 1912 was that the Church of Ireland *mattered* in the increasingly tense battle over home rule. D'Arcy and Crozier's interviews with the *Daily Telegraph* and D'Arcy's contribution to *Against Home Rule* highlighted these bishops' desire to play a role on the political stage. The wide reporting and attendant praise of the General Synod suggested the position taken by the Church of Ireland was worthy of attention. Diocesan synods were seen as representative of Protestant opinion outside the confines of the Church of Ireland. The anti-home rule resolutions of laymen at the Clogher, and Down and Connor and Dromore synods were praised by the *Newsletter*.[88] The Clogher synod demonstrated how Protestants in rural areas, as in Belfast, were 'practically unanimous in their determination to resist a measure which they know would bring disaster to the country'.[89] The *Newsletter* praised the Down and Connor and Dromore synod's resolution, as it was necessary that 'Radicals and Nationalists should have no excuse for asserting that [Protestant] hostility to Home Rule is weakening.' The unanimous support of the resolution made it 'impossible for any man who wishes to tell the truth to say that those who are represented in the synod are prepared to acquiesce in Home Rule if the Bill should become an Act'.[90] Like the Presbyterian anti-home rule convention, which had a Scottish and English non-conformist audience in mind,[91] the Church of Ireland general and diocesan synods were intended to speak to an audience not solely confined to their own members. The unionist press, particularly in Ulster, repeatedly stressed the representative nature of the synods and hoped that 'English radicals' and nationalist 'slanderers' would be silenced by the arguments put forward.

Another significant feature of 1912 was the apparently easy and widespread acceptance of the Church's involvement in politics. It is possible that the bishops who spoke at the General Synod genuinely believed their opposition to home rule was non-party political, or in some way above the sordid nature of party politics. However, it was harder to make such an argument in support of Ulster Day, which clearly identified the Church with an Ulster-focused anti-home rule policy, despite D'Arcy and Crozier's protestations to the contrary. Ulster Day involvement also differed from the General Synod's resolutions in another crucial way – it held out the possibility of resisting the state, by armed force if necessary. This may have been expected to pose significant theological problems for bishops of a Church pledged to support the 'lawfully instituted authorities'. MacNaghten's statement circumvented this problem for D'Arcy, as, if the constitution was suspended, it followed that the 'authorities' were not lawfully instituted.

D'Arcy also defended political involvement with some conveniently chosen biblical texts. He presented Christ as the supreme example of the legitimacy of involvement in politics during a sermon in Down parish church shortly after Ulster Day. He turned to Matthew 22:15–22, where Christ's answer to the Pharisees – that they should 'Render unto Caesar what is Caesar's' – was seen as an answer to the major political issue of early first-century Israel: how far Israelites should obey Rome. Christ recognised that Israel was already incorporated into the imperial system of Rome and 'taught quite plainly that, not in a narrow, exclusive nationalism but in a frank acceptance of the imperial authority was to be found the way of safety for His people'.[92] D'Arcy indulged in a hermeneutical 'leap' when applying this passage in order to justify not merely the right of ministers to comment on politics, but the right of ministers to take the 'imperial' side in such comments. First-century Israel, in D'Arcy's interpretation, equated with twentieth-century Ireland; first-century Rome paralleled twentieth-century Britain. The implication appeared to be that ministers should 'Render unto Britain what is Britain's'. It was ironic, in light of the fact that D'Arcy was defending ministers' political involvement in the aftermath of Ulster Day, that he affirmed a 'frank acceptance' of imperial authority – as Ulster Day had pledged the majority of Protestants in Ulster to resist imperial authority if home rule was passed. However, such comments were easier to understand in light of another supreme irony – that D'Arcy and his fellow unionists were only prepared to resist the imperial authority in order to remain subject to that same authority, in an Ireland free from home rule.

Any controversy that existed over the political nature of the General Synod hinged on differences over whether or not a church should be involved in politics. Ulster Day raised similar concerns, but further (private) controversy was created by a belief among southern bishops that to endorse Ulster Day moved the Church of Ireland away from an all-Ireland form of unionism. As already seen, a number of northern bishops sought to answer such criticism by claiming the Covenant was fighting home rule for all of Ireland (a point made by D'Arcy and Crozier in their Ulster Day sermons). This was not accepted by their southern counterparts. It could be argued that the Church's decision in the north to endorse Ulster Day was the pivotal event in this period. Publicly, the Ulster bishops, led by D'Arcy, were committed to whatever policy the Ulster unionist leadership decided to follow in opposing home rule. Arguably, by supporting the covenant the Ulster bishops were bound to support the soon to be formed Ulster Volunteer Force – it would have been illogical, and even immoral, to sign a covenant that pledged its signatories to use 'any means' to resist home rule and then baulk when those means involved the establishment of an Ulster unionist paramilitary wing.

The private dispute over the Covenant also established the main lines of division within the episcopate. D'Arcy was the most articulate and forceful 'Ulster' unionist bishop. Bernard seemed to be the most significant 'southern' unionist bishop (it was Bernard that Peacocke turned to for advice on the Covenant, and Bernard who drafted the opening-of-Parliament prayer for the Church in the south). Crozier's repeated references to his 'beloved native land' and his espousal of a 'patriotic' opposition to home rule suggested that as early as 1912 he recognised the need to plot a torturous middle route between the nascent partitionist instincts of D'Arcy and the increasingly unrealistic all-Irish unionism espoused by Bernard and his fellow southern bishops. This pattern, crudely put, of D'Arcy against Bernard, with Crozier playing a mediating role, was followed for the rest of the third home rule period.

Church of Ireland involvement in Ulster Day demonstrated the almost inexorable drift of the most populous part of the Church to a predominantly Ulster-focused opposition to home rule. As with the political representatives of Ulster unionism, it is difficult to discern whether D'Arcy and the other Ulster bishops saw Ulster Day and the increase in militancy as a 'bluff' intended to defeat home rule for all of Ireland, or as a sign that preserving Ulster's place in the union was already the best unionists could hope for. At a welcoming reception after his first diocesan synod in 1911, D'Arcy was greeted on behalf of the clergy by Canon Pooler, who stated that what they had to offer their new bishop was the 'knowledge that he is called to preside over a diocese which will be increasingly the citadel of Protestantism and liberty in Ireland'.[93] By Ulster Day, it appeared the Church of Ireland in parts of Ulster was poised to exclude their Anglican brethren in the rest of Ireland from the protection of the citadel.

NOTES

1. Minutes of the House of Bishops, 16 January 1912 (Representative Church Body (RCB) Library, Dublin); also Minutes of the Standing Committee of the General Synod, 18 January 1912 (RCB Library).
2. G. Walker, 'The Irish Presbyterian anti-Home Rule convention of 1912', *Studies: An Irish Quarterly Review*, 86, 341 (Spring 1997), p.71.
3. *Ulster Gazette and Armagh Standard*, 3 February 1912.
4. *Belfast Newsletter*, 17 April 1912; *Belfast Weekly Telegraph*, 20 April 1912.
5. Minutes of the House of Bishops, 16 January 1912 (RCB Library).
6. *Belfast Newsletter*, 17 April 1912; *Belfast Weekly Telegraph*, 20 April 1912. A fourth resolution was moved by the bishop of Derry, asserting that Home Rule would not 'tend to the pacification of Ireland' (ibid).
7. *Belfast Newsletter*, 17 April 1912.
8. *Belfast Weekly Telegraph*, 4 May 1912.
9. *Irish Times*, 17 April 1912.
10. Hutchinson Poe to James Owen Hannay, 19 March 1912 (National Library of Ireland, Hannay papers, Ms 8271/93).
11. Walter Kavanagh to Hannay, 26 March 1912 (ibid., Ms 8271/95).
12. *Freeman's Journal*, 17 April 1912.
13. *Belfast Newsletter*, 18 April 1912.
14. John Healy to Hannay, 12 April 1912 (National Library of Ireland, Hannay papers, Ms 8271/98).
15. John Baptist Crozier to Hannay, 17 April 1912 (ibid., Ms 8271/102).
16. Crozier to Hannay, 18 April 1912 (ibid., Ms 8271/103).
17. Charles Frederick D'Arcy to Hannay, 25 January 1912 (ibid., Ms 8271/88).
18. *Irish Times*, 18, 19 April 1912.
19. Ibid., 23 April 1912.
20. For example, J.O. Hannay's article in *Church of Ireland Gazette*, 12 July 1912.
21. *Daily Telegraph*, 10 January 1912.
22. *Belfast Newsletter*, 17 April 1912.
23. C.F. D'Arcy, 'The religious difficulty under Home Rule', in S. Rosenbaum (ed.), *Against Home Rule: The Case for the Union* (London, 1912), pp.204–11.
24. Ibid., p.206.
25. Ibid., p.211.
26. D'Arcy to Davidson, 8 March 1912 (Lambeth Palace Library, Davidson papers, vol. 389/1).
27. D'Arcy to Davidson, 12 March 1912 (ibid., vol. 389/8).
28. D'Arcy to Davidson, 13 March 1912 (ibid., vol. 389/10). Davidson's responses to D'Arcy's entreaties are not extant. However, it is unlikely he shared D'Arcy's staunch Ulster Unionist sympathies: in 1914, in the midst of the Curragh Crisis and Larne gun-running, he acted as a mediator between Asquith and Bonar Law (see Chapter 4 of this volume).
29. *Daily Telegraph*, 18 January 1912.
30. *Lurgan Mail*, 10 February 1912.
31. *Belfast Newsletter*, 10 April 1912.
32. *Irish Times*, 12 April 1912.
33. *Ulster Guardian*, 27 April 1912.
34. *Church of Ireland Gazette*, 12 April 1912.
35. *Irish Churchman*, 12 April 1912.
36. Marcus Tanner, *Ireland's Holy Wars: The Struggle for a Nation's Soul, 1500–2000* (New Haven, 2001), p.273.
37. Crozier to Lady Londonderry, 10 April 1912 (Public Record Office of Northern Ireland (PRONI), Lady Londonderry papers, D/2847/1/7/5).
38. This is explored in the following chapter.
39. *Church of Ireland Gazette*, 4 October 1912.
40. *Belfast Newsletter*, 28 September 1912.
41. R. McNeill, *Ulster's Stand for Union* (London, 1922), p.105–6.
42. J. Bardon, *A History of Ulster* (Belfast, 2001), p.438.
43. A. Jackson, 'Unionist myths, 1912–1985', *Past and Present*, no. 136 (1992), pp.164–85.
44. Ulster Day committee minute book, 14 August 1912 (PRONI, Ulster Unionist Council papers, D/1327/2/7).
45. *Belfast Weekly Telegraph*, 24 August 1912; see Chapter 3 for a discussion of clerical involvement in these organising committees.

46. Ulster Day clergy committee minute book (PRONI, Ulster Unionist Council papers, D/1327/2/7). The minutes note that arrangements for the Ulster Hall Ulster Day service were left in the hands of the clergy committee: 5 September 1912.
47. *Belfast Newsletter*, 26 August 1912.
48. *Church of Ireland Gazette*, 6 September 1912.
49. Ibid., 13 September 1912.
50. *Belfast Newsletter*, 23 September 1912.
51. *Northern Whig*, 30 September 1912.
52. Ibid., 30 September 1912.
53. C.F. D'Arcy, *Adventures of a Bishop* (London, 1934), pp.189–90.
54. Ibid.
55. Crozier to Davidson, 17 March 1914 (Lambeth Palace Library, Davidson papers, vol. 389/241–4).
56. *Ulster Echo*, 16 November 1911.
57. G. Jones 'Eugenics in Ireland: the Belfast Eugenics Society, 1911–1915', *Irish Historical Studies*, vol. 28 (1992), p.85.
58. *Church of Ireland Gazette*, 21 June 1912.
59. Ibid., 27 September 1912.
60. *Belfast Newsletter*, 6 November 1912.
61. *Belfast Telegraph*, 6 November 1912.
62. *Belfast Newsletter*, 30 November 1912.
63. Lord Bessborough to Bernard [n.d. August 1912] (British Library, J.H. Bernard papers, Add. Ms 52782/4–5).
64. Lord Bessborough to Bernard, 31 August 1912 (ibid., Add. Ms 52782/8–9).
65. Peacocke to Bernard, 1 September 1912 (ibid., Add. Ms 52782/10–12).
66. Peacocke to Bernard, 5 September 1912 (ibid., Add. Ms 52782/13–14).
67. Peacocke to Bernard, 13 September 1912 (ibid., Add. Ms 52782/15–16).
68. Peacocke to Bernard, 5 September 1912 (ibid., Add. Ms 52782/13–14).
69. *Irish Times*, 19 September 1912.
70. Ibid., 15 October 1912.
71. For example, at the Cashel and Killaloe diocesan synods: ibid., 26 June 1912; *Church of Ireland Gazette*, 26 July 1912.
72. *Irish Times*, 25 October 1912.
73. Ibid., 11 September 1912.
74. Ibid., 15 September 1911.
75. Ibid., 10 October 1912.
76. *Fermanagh Times*, 3 October 1912.
77. Ibid., 3 October 1912.
78. Ibid., 30 May 1912.
79. Bishop of Derry's circular to clergy, 11 September 1912 (TCD, J.H. Bernard papers, Mss 2388/49).
80. *Weekly Telegraph*, 28 September 1912.
81. *Irish Times*, 21 September 1912.
82. *Lurgan Mail*, 5 October 1912.
83. *Fermanagh Times*, 3 October 1912.
84. G. Walker, *A History of the Ulster Unionist Party: Protest, Pragmatism, and Pessimism* (Manchester, 2004), pp.33–4.
85. D. McConnell, 'The Protestant Churches and the origin of the Northern Ireland state' (Queen's University Belfast, unpublished Ph.D. thesis, 1998), p.221.
86. D.H. Akenson, *God's Peoples: Covenant and Land in South Africa, Israel and Ulster* (Ithaca, 1992), p.186.
87. See Chapter 3, this volume.
88. See *Fermanagh Times*, 10 October 1912; *Belfast Newsletter*, 6 November 1912.
89. *Belfast Newsletter*, 5 October 1912.
90. Ibid., 6 November 1912.
91. Walker, 'Irish Presbyterian anti-Home Rule convention of 1912', pp.71, 73–4.
92. *Church of Ireland Gazette*, 18 October 1912.
93. Ibid., 10 November 1911.

3

'A force to be reckoned with'?
Church of Ireland Clergy, the Covenant,
and Ulster Day

Canon Pounden, writing in the Lisburn Cathedral magazine, reviewed the position of unionists at the start of 1912. While they were 'unmoved' in their strong claim to membership of the empire, he anticipated a struggle in the forthcoming year to maintain their position in the union. Demonstrating a providential understanding of God's role in unionism, Pounden asserted that 'God is on our side and will make all things turn out for our good and His glory.'[1] As Pounden predicted, the third Home Rule Bill increasingly impacted on Church life in Ulster in 1912. Like their synodical counterparts, vestry meetings passed strongly worded resolutions against home rule. Most strikingly, the majority of clergy in Ulster mirrored the action of their bishops by endorsing Ulster Day. Support was practical – clergy were often key members of committees involved in organising Ulster Day activities – and spiritual, as sermons were preached lending moral justification to the Ulster Covenant. In addition, clergy continued throughout 1912 to make Protestantism, and appeals to God, central in the definition of their political stance. According to F.W. Austin, rector of St Columba's in east Belfast, the 'driving force' of unionist opposition to home rule was religious. The engine of this religiously motivated opposition was Protestantism, which was 'formative of individual and national character and its value they often only began to realise when they had neglected its principles and departed from them'. Protestants faced a Catholic Church that was 'reactionary and intolerant', and so they must make 'Irish Protestantism a force to be reckoned with'.[2] The majority of Church of Ireland clergy in Ulster strove throughout 1912 to make their church such a force.

SUPPORT FOR UNIONISM AT A PAROCHIAL LEVEL

A case study indicating the extent of clerical support for Ulster unionism was provided by the visit of Winston Churchill to Belfast in February 1912. Along with John Redmond and Joe Devlin, the nationalist MP for West Belfast, Churchill was scheduled to speak in support of home rule at a Liberal meeting in the Ulster Hall. The Ulster Unionist Council resolved to prevent such a 'desecration' of the Ulster Hall, a unionist shrine since Churchill's father's famous anti-home rule speech in 1886. Unionists intended to pack the Ulster Hall the evening before the Liberal meeting and refuse to leave the following day. In the face of such resistance, the Liberal meeting was moved to Celtic Park, in a nationalist area of Belfast. The UUC reaction provoked accusations in the Liberal press that free speech was being suppressed, and even sympathetic papers such as *The Times* doubted the wisdom of the unionist tactics.[3] However, the *Belfast Newsletter* was supportive, and saw Churchill's intention to speak in the Ulster Hall as a 'challenge, and a truculent one'; Churchill was being deliberately provocative, and his intention was to 'impress us and the rest of the United Kingdom with the full menace of Home Rule'.[4]

The Ulster unionist response to Churchill's visit was supported by all sections of the Church of Ireland in Ulster. Archbishop Crozier believed the decision to prevent the Liberals from using the Ulster Hall was the 'only alternative to cruel and irresponsible rioting and street murder'.[5] Crozier was not alone in fearing violence if Churchill spoke in the Ulster Hall. Dublin Castle ordered extra troops and police to Belfast, and Ulster unionist leaders also feared rioting.[6] Crozier believed Churchill should be allowed to speak somewhere in Belfast, but hoped he would be convinced that Ulster was in 'deadly earnest'. He wrote to Lady Londonderry: 'I would provide 50,000 men to line the streets and let him pass in solemn silence with the intimation that these were the loyal outposts that bid him defiance but not to touch him!!'[7] A similar concern for order was demonstrated in F.W. Austin's endorsement of the UUC response to the Churchill visit. Austin, rector of St Columba's, told Ballynafeigh Unionist Club that they needed to remember the policy of 'no surrender' – especially of 'no surrender' to 'Romish demands' – and must continue to follow their leaders faithfully, as 'to run beyond their leaders was as bad as to lag behind'.[8] At an Orange meeting in Lisbellaw, County Fermanagh, Rev. E.W. McFarland and Rev. Mr McTighe supported the UUC decision to prevent Churchill from speaking in the Ulster Hall. McTighe claimed to support free speech, but argued that the Churchill visit was an 'exceptional case', intended to give substance to the lie that Ulster was weakening against home rule. It followed that the UUC 'were right in taking advantage of the only means in their power to nail that lie'.[9] Chairing a meeting to mark the formation of Armaghbrague Unionist Club, Rev. Charles Berwick referred to Churchill's visit as that of a 'gentleman from London' who was protected by the military 'or perhaps they accompanied him as a guard of honour'. Unionists did not want any of Churchill's safeguards, as their safeguards 'would be the same as in the past: their loyal hearts and strong right arms'.[10]

The Churchill visit acted as an encouragement for Ulster unionism. They could claim to have scored a perceived victory over a government minister and their nationalist opponents, as Churchill was forced to change the venue for his speech from the Ulster Hall to a football ground in a nationalist part of Belfast. Clerical rhetoric on the meeting reflected this optimism and illustrated their willingness to be involved in events that bound the Ulster unionist community together and gave a sense of common purpose. Arguably, clerical involvement in the Churchill furore mirrored their role in the *Ne Temere* controversy one year earlier, which had also acted to bring the various elements of Ulster (and Irish) unionism together. However, the Churchill visit can also be viewed as a prelude to unionist defiance later in 1912. By endorsing the rather rambunctious tactics of the UUC, clergy suggested they would not be averse to supporting action against home rule that fell outside the norm of conventional political opposition. This would be seen to a greater degree in their participation in Ulster Day.

Clerical involvement in the Balmoral demonstration of Easter 1912 also foreshadowed their later role in Ulster Day. Services of 'preparation' were held ahead of the demonstration that tended to stress the importance of God's providence as a weapon in the unionist armoury. For Canon Davis, preaching at a united service for Belfast's unionist clubs, God was their leader in the 'great moral warfare they were waging for civil and religious liberty'.[11] Willowfield Unionist Club (in east Belfast) was reminded of God's blessing at a service in the local parish church, attended by 500 people.[12] The rector of Willowfield, Canon Harding, attempted to maximise what he perceived as the spiritual lesson of the threat of home rule. While reassuring the congregation that God would bring Irish unionism 'safely through the struggle', Harding suggested the 'chastise-ment' of the 'present position' was a result of their lack of loyalty to Christ and failure to attend their 'respective places of worship'.[13] At the following month's select vestry meeting, a letter was read from the honorary secretary of Willowfield Unionist Club thanking the vestry and Canon Harding for the use of the church for their service.[14] Christ Church in Lisburn held a 'Balmoral' service for Lisburn Unionist Club, with the Craig brothers present among the 1,000-strong congregation. The rector, R.H.S. Cooper (who was also a member of the unionist club), reminded the congregation of God's guiding hand in their history, which encouraged them to 'take courage, and declare to their enemies that they had a King who reigned, even Christ the Lord'.[15]

The Balmoral services indicated the pulpit's potential as a medium through which clergy could attempt to exert some degree of political influence. Sermons lamenting the future of Ireland and Protestantism under home rule, backed up with supposedly apposite biblical texts, could be a powerful rhetorical device. The preacher book of Holywood parish church recorded that 800 people attended an afternoon service for the local unionist club and Orange lodge, a considerable increase on the average attendance of around 330 for a morning service.[16] The rector, Canon Moore, preached on Samuel 10:12 ('Be of good courage and let us play the men for our people'), a text which 'conveyed a most suitable and appro-priate message'. Moore expressed his reluctance to preach politics from the pulpit, but believed he would fail in his duty as a Christian minister if he did not advise 'his flock' of the impending danger and their responsibility in opposing home rule. The congregation's duty was to ask for God's guidance and blessing, as doing so meant they could count 'upon his [God's] approval in offering all lawful opposition to legislation which they believed would be disastrous to the prosperity, liberty and peace of the land they loved'.[17] For Archdeacon Pooler, as with Canon Moore, God's providential blessing bolstered belief in the apparent inevitability of the defeat of home rule. Preaching in November to a congrega-tion including members of the Hollymount Unionist Club and Orange lodge, Pooler pointed to the siege of Derry as proof that God was not always on the side of the 'big battalions'. Pooler welcomed support from England and Scotland but 'in the extremity we have two sources of strength on which to depend – God and ourselves; and thank God we can depend on both'.[18]

Unionist club services were not vehicles for one particular denomination to flex their political muscle. Rather, it appears the clubs were seen by Church of Ireland clergy as a means of instigating closer relationships between the Protestant Churches. Such co-operation was understandable and pragmatic con-sidering the precarious demographic make-up of Protestantism in Ireland. Unionist clubs were composed of men from every denomination, so the increased attendance at unionist club services was not surprising. However, the fact that members of other denominations were prepared to attend services in Church of Ireland churches was a practical demonstration of the Protestant ecu-menism strengthened by the threat of home rule. The rhetoric of clergy at union-ist club meetings and services emphasised the neutral denominational aspect of such occasions. The rector of Mary Magdalene (in south Belfast) told the Balmoral and Upper Malone Unionist Club that they were brought together on a 'sensible platform' of a 'common Protestantism and a common Unionism'.[19] Rev. R.H.S. Cooper believed 'all denominations had been drawn together to give them strength in the battle'.[20] Archdeacon Pooler claimed the threat of home rule had brought unity and strength and 'welded' Protestants 'into a line of defence against which [their] opponents will break in impotence'.[21] It is not apparent that unionist clubs were more likely collectively to attend Church of Ireland services than those of any other Protestant denomination. However, unionist club services demonstrated that Church of Ireland clergy were eager to incorporate unionism into the life of their parishes. Such services, especially when accompanied by providential rhetoric, provided a powerful seal of approval for the unionist clubs and by extension their opposition to home rule, and, arguably, for Ulster unionist militancy.

When seen in the context of the Churchill visit, the Balmoral demonstration and continuing support for unionist clubs, the anti-home rule tenor of many 1912 general vestries is understandable. Resolutions against home rule passed at these meetings demonstrated that the General Synod – held after the majority of general vestries – reflected the mood of the Church of Ireland at a parish level in Ulster. General vestry meetings, held annually, were a fairly accurate indicator of the issues animating the Church of Ireland locally. The general vestry acted like a mini-parliament by allowing those (men) who had registered as vestrymen to elect select vestry members to run the life of the parish in the year ahead. It was also customary for the parochial clergy to give a speech at the general vestry that surveyed the life of the parish in the previous year and looked forward to the coming year. A number of clergymen made home rule a theme in their speeches; for example, Canon Davis, rector of St Jude's in south Belfast, hoped they would not allow the perceived threat of home rule to 'interfere with the growth and development of Christ's work in this parish'.[22]

Clerical speeches against home rule made at general vestry meetings echoed similarly expressed opposition to the first and second Home Rule Bills, as did the resolutions passed against home rule in 1912. The majority of resolutions stressed the representative nature of general vestries. The attendance at the meeting in Limavady was apparently the largest for 'many years'. A resolution recounting the main unionist arguments against home rule was proposed, stating that the parish, 'representing over 1,000 persons', believed home rule would destroy 'civil and religious liberty, imperil the property of the Church, bring about civil strife, and lead to the disruption of the empire'.[23] The representative function of the general vestry – affirmed in the Limavady resolution – mirrored how some Anglicans viewed the General Synod.[24]

The impression that general vestries were perceived as vehicles for articulating Protestant opposition to home rule was strengthened by the forwarding of resolutions to prominent politicians. Willowfield general vestry received letters of thanks from Edward Carson and Andrew Bonar Law for sending them its unanimously passed resolution against home rule.[25] The resolution against home rule passed by St Thomas' (on the Lisburn Road in south Belfast) was sent to Carson, as well as to the prime minister, Herbert Asquith. The resolution declared the 'strong and emphatic protest' of the 'registered vestrymen of the parish of St Thomas' Belfast' against the Home Rule Bill,[26] and drew a letter of acknowledgement from Asquith's secretary (preserved in the vestry minute book). Carson showed he valued the support offered by such resolutions by sending a handwritten letter of thanks to the vestry's secretary. Carson thanked St Thomas' for the 'emphatic protest against the Home Rule policy of the government'.[27]

Looking at the clerical (and lay) involvement in the Churchill visit, Balmoral demonstration, unionist club sermons and general vestry meetings, a picture emerges of the Church of Ireland in Ulster largely united in opposition to home rule. While this was a continuation of the political positioning of clergy and laity in 1910–11, events in Ulster in 1912 tended to stress the increasing importance of the province, rhetorically and strategically, to the unionist cause. Ulster Day was a suitable culmination to events in 'secular' Ulster unionism in 1912, building on the apparent success of the Craigavon meeting one year earlier and the Balmoral demonstration. Ulster Day also provided Church of Ireland clergy based in Ulster with a highly prominent position in Ulster unionist politics.

ULSTER DAY

Ulster Day received an enthusiastic reception from the majority of Church of Ireland clergy in Ulster, who demonstrated their support in a number of ways and through a number of forums. Clergy were members of committees that organised Ulster Day demonstrations in towns around Ulster, sermons were preached and speeches made endorsing the Ulster Covenant, and Ulster Day services were held in Church of Ireland churches.

The membership of Ulster Day organising committees reflected the various elements of Ulster unionism. Organising committees were largely concerned with deciding where the Covenant should be signed in each locality, and the arrangements for Ulster Day church services. The presence of clergy (from both the Church of Ireland and Presbyterian Churches) on the committees, alongside representatives from the Orange Order and unionist clubs, provided evidence of the importance of the Protestant Churches in providing leadership and a degree of organisational impetus to Ulster unionism. Clergy were particularly important in rural areas – in parts of Armagh, north Antrim, Tyrone and Fermanagh they often played leading roles on the organising committees.[28]

As well as organisational assistance, clergy used the opportunity provided by unionist meetings to encourage active support for Ulster Day. The rector of Maguiresbridge, Thomas Troughton, did not want to be governed by a 'class of men like the Nationalist Party' and urged the Maguiresbridge Unionist Club to support Ulster Day.[29] At a meeting of Whiteabbey and Greenisland Unionist Clubs, J.A. Carey, rector of Whitehouse, claimed unionists should sign the covenant to 'make it plain that they were not prepared to betray the trust which had been bequeathed to them by their forefathers'.[30] Canon Pounden, who led Lisburn's Ulster Day organising committee, gave a vote of thanks to Edward Carson for speaking at a huge pre-Ulster Day demonstration in the town. Pounden hoped 'many thousands' would 'register their names on the coming Ulster Day'.[31]

The clerical support for Ulster Day demonstrated in organising committees and unionist meetings was also expressed from the pulpit. Like the bishops of Down, Derry and Armagh (D'Arcy, Chadwick and Crozier), clergy used the services of intercession on 22 September explicitly to support Ulster Day. The dean of Dromore pointed out that the day of humiliation was called due to the 'momentous action about to be taken [in] Ulster on Saturday next when we sign a Solemn League and Covenant'. Ulster Day was not merely a 'theatrical' gesture or 'bluff', but a sign that the Protestants of Ulster would 'shrink from no sacrifices' in defending their 'civil and religious liberty'.[32] The archdeacon of Armagh (speaking in St Mark's, Armagh) defended his, and his Church's, close connection with Ulster Day. If home rule was 'merely a political question and not also a religious one, he did not think he would bring it into the pulpit'. However, he claimed home rule *was* a religious question, as their 'Church and Protestantism, their lives and liberties were in danger'. The archdeacon invited the congregation to sign the covenant in St Marks, and admitted that some had objected to having the signing ceremony in a church. However:

> They had made the question a matter of prayer to God in that house; if that was right how could it be wrong to finish the job there, and so to stamp with the seal of religion their endeavour under God's help to avert the terrible calamity which confronted them.[33]

The curate of St Mark's, Newtownards, L.V. Uprichard, used his intercessory service sermon to explain the importance of Ulster Day being a success. With the possibility of a home rule Ireland dominated by an allegedly intolerant Catholic Church threatening Protestant freedom of worship, Uprichard hoped he would see 'every loyal son' come to the church before signing the covenant. Doing so would allow them to draw near to God and pray that 'He will deliver us from the terrible calamity which now threatens the Church of Ireland and Protestantism in this country.'[34]

Judging from a number of preacher books, the intercessory services in Belfast were well attended and more popular than regular Sunday services. The intercessory service held at St Columba's, east Belfast, had an attendance of 225, whereas the average attendance was around 200.[35] This increase appeared to be a response to the particular circumstances surrounding Ulster Day: St Columba's was not a typical 'Orange' church – a remark in the preacher's book on 12 July 1914 (for a service that attracted only 145 people) noted that it was a 'Holiday – many away!'[36] Attendance at Knockbreda was also higher than average;[37] at Willowfield in east Belfast 520 attended – an increase of around 100 above the average, while St Jude's in south Belfast also recorded an increase (356, as against an average of 300).[38]

Similarly, Ulster Day church services held in Church of Ireland churches around Ulster were generally well attended. Alongside the main united religious service in Lisburn, held in the Grain Market (attended by 10,000 people, 'easily the largest congregation ever seen in Lisburn'[39]), individual churches in the town also held their own services on the morning of Ulster Day. Four hundred attended the service in Lisburn Cathedral, a large increase on the average attendance of 250.[40] The service was held at 1.30 p.m. to allow those engaged in mill work the opportunity to attend.[41] In Downpatrick, 1,000 attended the Ulster Day service in Down Cathedral, while in Dundrum the parish church was 'filled to overflowing'.[42] Killinchy parish church held two Ulster Day services; in the morning 19 came, while in the evening 53 attended (the average attendance was around 45).[43] Over 2,000 attended the service in Lurgan parish church.[44] Large congregations attended both St Columba's and Willowfield on Ulster Day: 300 in St Columba's and 600 in Willowfield.[45]

The increased attendances at intercessory and Ulster Day services is harder to account for than those at unionist club services. In the case of a 'united' Ulster Day service being held in a Church of Ireland church (as with a unionist club service), the congregation would have been swollen by members from other denominations. Such united services may have been held in Church of Ireland churches due to the predominance of Anglicans in a certain area,[46] or simply as a result of the larger size of a particular church – although such factors could equally result in a united service being held in a Presbyterian church in areas of Presbyterian majorities. However, in many provincial towns in Ulster, such as Lisburn, Lurgan and Coleraine, each denomination held its own Ulster Day service. The increased attendance at such services, along with the intercessory services (a distinctively Church of Ireland occasion), suggested the presence of a number of 'floating Anglicans', who may have been drawn to church for a number of reasons. The services may have been viewed as an opportunity to feel part of an occasion binding together the unionist community; nominal members of parishes may have attended simply for a sense of security in a time of crisis. Certainly, the services of intercession, also intended by the bishops to mark a day of 'humiliation', were part of a long tradition of response to times of national crisis (including the Irish Famine[47]), suggesting the service may have been viewed as the conventional way to respond to the 'national crisis' of an impending home rule settlement.

The sermons preached at Ulster Day services were largely consistent with the providential rhetoric of unionist club services earlier in 1912. The dean of Dromore called for the Covenant to be signed in God's name, as God had blessed the work of Ulster Protestants by turning the 'most barren' province in Ireland into 'the garden of the Lord'. However, under home rule Ulster would be the 'milch cow' of Ireland and the Catholic Church would 'stamp out' freedom of thought and liberty. As a result, it was their 'religious duty' to oppose home rule: 'For the sake of our country, ourselves, our children, and our God we will not have it.'[48] Similar obligations were impressed on the congregation at the Killylea Ulster Day service by the preacher, Canon Tichborne. Failure to sign the covenant 'would be a serious dereliction of duty on the part of a free people'. However, those who did decide to sign the Covenant pledged themselves to resist oppression, 'animated by Christian courage … and assured that God will defend the right and crown all our efforts with success'. The rector of Tandragee (John McEndoo) drew on his influence with his congregation by stating 'if it would be any guide for those present he and his household would, after the service, affix their signatures.'[49] Rev. W. Giles of Killowen encouraged his congregation to put their faith in God, reminding them of how their forefathers had been sustained by such faith until they too overcame the dangers that had confronted them.[50] Appeals to the past were also made by Canon Davis of St Jude's. 'No matter what the consequences might be to them', Davis hoped his congregation would do as much as their ancestors had done in defending their religious and civil liberty: 'They would refuse to obey the behests of a Parliament in Dublin, nor would they ever put themselves under a yoke which their forefathers broke from.'[51] A report on Ulster Day in the parish magazine of St Mark's, Dundela (in east Belfast) summed up what seemed to be the attitude of the majority of Church of Ireland clergy and laity in Ulster. Ulster Day was 'one of the most momentous points in the history of our nation'. It was 'no light thing' for 'almost half a country' to 'rise up like one man and solemnly before God pledge themselves to resist to the uttermost a change proposed by the governing body of the country'. The 'grim determination' of the signatories should have left no one in doubt that 'this is a big thing' and a 'landmark in the history of Ireland'. A firm belief in God's particular favour towards Irish unionism was held to motivate attendance at the Ulster Day service in St Mark's:

> Our own parish church was well filled, and many of our parishioners we trust went home from the solemn service with faith strengthened and confidence more surely established that He who rules over all will see that His church and people shall not be dismayed.

The Covenant and declaration were signed by 600 men and women at St Mark's on Ulster Day.[52]

There were few instances of opposition to Ulster Day from the ranks of Church of Ireland clergy in Ulster. Rev. T. Harvey of Holy Trinity in Portrush appeared keen to make the intercessory service the non-partisan event the northern bishops' pastoral letter perhaps rather optimistically suggested it should be. In his intercessory service sermon, Harvey recognised that home rule was a question on which more than one opinion might be held, and 'trusted that nothing would be done which might lead to an unconstitutional course of action of which the Church could not approve'.[53] There was certainly no recommendation of Ulster Day in his sermon. If anything, the pointed reference to the undesirability of unconstitutional action could be seen as an indirect criticism of the Ulster Covenant. It is likely that Harvey's decision not to endorse Ulster Day resulted in criticism. Writing to Harvey privately, the clerical critic of unionism James Owen Hannay praised him for refusing 'to prostitute the church to the service of a political party'. With characteristic vigour, Hannay charged the northern bishops of making the Church of Ireland an 'adulteress' by their support of Ulster Day, which pushed her 'into the obscene rites of deities more debased than Baal or Ashtorath'.[54] In direct contrast to D'Arcy's later publicly stated claim that Christ was a first-century imperialist,[55] Hannay asserted that 'no man – were he fifty times a bishop – has a right to identify the cause of Christ with that of loyalist Herodians or nationalist Pharisees'. It was a 'horrible kind of blasphemy' to claim Christ would support one political party over another. Hannay hoped it would encourage Harvey to know that if he was made to suffer, he was 'at least true to the spirit of the Master'.[56]

John Frederick MacNeice, rector of St Nicholas' in Carrickfergus, also refused to endorse the Covenant. Although an Ulster Day service was held in St Nicholas', MacNeice's sermon opposed the Covenant. The thrust of his argument was religious, not political. Recognising the militancy implicit in the Covenant's terms, MacNeice held that the Church must fight under 'Christ's banner, and in Christ's way, and need not borrow the weapons of the kingdoms of the world'. He shrunk from a policy that, in the last resort, entailed civil war. Realising he held a minority position, MacNeice did not ask anyone to adopt his view.[57] Carrickfergus was unusual in that all Protestant clergymen refused to sign the Covenant, a stand in which MacNeice may have been instrumental.[58] The 'conscientious scruples' of the Carrickfergus clergy 'exposed them at the time to some adverse criticism', although MacNeice was praised by the Liberal *Ulster Guardian* for his display of 'moral courage' in refusing to endorse the Covenant.[59] His criticisms of it were not those of a home rule clergyman such as Hannay. Despite the claims of a recent biographer, MacNeice was a unionist, a fact attested to by the *Ulster Gazette*: 'Mr MacNeice's Unionism is of too staunch a character and has been too often manifested … for him to risk being dubbed a Home Ruler because he is commended in a Home Rule organ.'[60] In 1914 MacNeice informed the archbishop of Canterbury that 'I am a Unionist. I am not a Volunteer. I am not a Covenantor.'[61] MacNeice was certainly a fairly unusual figure in the Church of Ireland in this period, remaining consistently opposed to participation in politics, whether Ulster unionist, southern unionist or home rule. His position on the Covenant should be viewed as the practical out-working of an almost quietist belief that the Church of Ireland's loyalty was above all to God and Christ, and consequently that it should have no great involvement in politics.[62]

The most vocal opposition to Ulster Day came from southern Anglican opin-ion. Canon Sterling Berry, a County Dublin rector who became bishop of Killaloe in 1913, also criticised participation in Ulster Day. Preaching in Booterstown parish church, Berry condemned the bishops ('our leaders') for the political tenor of the 1912 General Synod and their involvement in 'political demonstrations'. Berry did not believe the Church should be involved in political participation of the type suggested by Ulster Day in case it 'recoil[ed] upon the Church'.[63] It is likely that Berry's opposition to the Covenant was borne of ideological rather than political concerns, as he remained largely consistent in his rejection of ecclesiastical involvement in what could be perceived as militaristic politics – he later opposed the ethical defence of participation in the First World War constructed by preachers and theologians.[64] However, unlike MacNeice, Berry became highly involved in politics, and was one of three bishops to support the anti-partition of Ireland manifesto in 1917.[65]

In addition to its rejection by the southern bishops, the wisdom of supporting the Covenant was also questioned by a number of correspondents to the *Irish Times* and the *Church of Ireland Gazette*. The Covenant was rejected for pledg-ing its signatories to unquestioning obedience to unionist leaders, resistance to any future Irish parliament, and support of any proposed Ulster parliament. Such policies entailed the 'end of constitutionalism in politics' and would lead to 'anarchy and civil war'.[66] A number of letters expressed a reluctance to associate the Church with 'political agitation'.[67] A letter in the *Gazette* expressed discom-fort at too closely following the lead of the 'Irish Unionist Party', as 'we cannot feel sufficient confidence in any party to justify such a general welcome as we are expected to extend to the "Solemn League and Covenant"'.[68] The fact that such objections were aired in the pages of predominantly southern-based union-ist journals suggested Ulster Day was perceived in the south as a symbolic renunciation of all-Ireland unionism.

CONCLUSION

A number of times during 1912 Charles Frederick D'Arcy had claimed to be act-ing as the representative of his diocese when making anti-home rule speeches. His letter of apology to the Balmoral meeting stated: 'Let me say that my whole heart is with you, and that I know I speak for the clergy and laity of the Church of Ireland in this diocese of whom I am officially representative.'[69] Shortly after the General Synod, D'Arcy replied to a resolution of sympathy sent from the select vestry of Lisburn Cathedral, which had offered him good wishes and a speedy recovery from the flu that had kept him from attending Balmoral. D'Arcy explained:

> By permission of my doctor I came to Dublin for the synod, as I was most anxious to take part in our great demonstration against Home Rule. I considered it most important to represent the diocese of Down and Connor on that platform.[70]

The reaction of the Church of Ireland at a local level in Ulster to events in 1912 appeared to justify D'Arcy's claim that he represented his diocese at a political level. The majority would have agreed with D'Arcy's endorsement of Ulster Day – as proved by the alacrity with which Ulster Day services were arranged, their large attendance and partisan nature of the intercessory services. Events at a parish level in 1912 in Ulster demonstrated that the General Synod and Ulster bishops' support of Ulster Day were in tune with the mood of their dioceses. The integration of unionism into the life of Church of Ireland parishes in Ulster was expressed before Ulster Day (and the General Synod) in unionist club attendance at church services and vestry resolutions passed against home rule. Such overt identification with Ulster unionism at different levels within the parish churches made it almost inevitable that the covenant would be supported.

There was a degree of rhetorical support for Ulster unionist resistance – or at least unconstitutional tactics – from clergy in 1912. Clerical endorsement of the UUC response to Churchill's visit at the start of the year suggested they would contemplate and accept extreme tactics. The rhetoric at a number of general vestries reflected Bonar Law's apparent abandonment of constitutional propriety made in his Balmoral pledge to support to any extent Ulster unionist resistance.[71] The general vestry of Willowfield promised 'to use every means to prevent it [home rule] being placed on the statute book'.[72] The general vestry of Desertmartin articulated their trust in the unionist leadership and expressed their readiness to contemplate extreme measures in defence of the union:

> We object to being deprived of our free and equal rights under the present constitution of the United Kingdom, and we are prepared to adopt any course recommended by our leaders to prevent such a yoke being placed on our necks.[73]

The most obvious manifestation of clerical support for resistance in 1912 was their organisational involvement and spiritual endorsement of Ulster Day.

Clerical involvement in Ulster Day should not necessarily be held to imply wholehearted support for any threatened Ulster unionist militancy. Indeed, according to the archdeacon of Dromore, E.D. Atkinson, there was a feeling of 'uncertainty' among clergy before the Covenant was published. After receiving assurance from James Craig that clergy could 'conscientiously' subscribe to it, Atkinson persuaded 'several of my brethren who appealed to me for guidance in the matter' to sign the Covenant.[74] Charles Grierson, dean of Belfast, sought to encourage the congregation at the Belfast Cathedral intercessory service to sign the Covenant. However, he also called on them to pray that God would restrain 'reprehensible acts'. Such acts brought 'disgrace upon a noble cause' and angered God. It was in the face of provocation that 'the law of love came in'. Grierson assured the congregation that 'if they approached God in this spirit the cause they had at heart, and which they believed to be God's cause, would be won, and that, by the grace of God, by a bloodless victory'.[75] In a similar vein, Canon Pounden believed the holding of church services on Ulster Day was a 'guarantee that a peaceful demonstration is to be held'.[76] The curate of St Mark's,

Newtownards reassured his congregation that they would not have to resort to armed resistance. God, their 'refuge and strength', would avert civil war: 'Many times before in the history of our country the hand of providence has intervened, and it was certain that in our time this hand would not desert us.'[77] Pounden's Ulster Day sermon attempted to provide a degree of moral justification for the Covenant. He did not believe it inevitably entailed armed resistance and violence: it would 'prove efficient by its moral weight; it is no doubt couched in no mistakable terms, yet it proposes to go no further than the exigencies of the time require'. He asked that 'weak minded and unnecessary objections' were put aside, as 'the best men of our day' in 'church and state' had framed the Covenant. For Pounden, the Covenant provided stability, strength and unity, and was not 'treason' – rather, it was the Liberal government that had committed treason by aiming to deprive Irish Protestants of their position in the empire.[78]

While a number of prominent clergymen offered a pacific interpretation of Ulster Day, clergy were left with little room to manœuvre when the implied militancy of the Covenant became a reality in 1913 with the formation of the Ulster Volunteer Force (UVF). However, the desire of clergy to reflect the political culture of Ulster unionism, demonstrated by their support of the Covenant, meant the UVF received a warm welcome from all but the few who had opposed the Church's involvement in Ulster Day. The apparent restraint of prominent clergymen such as Grierson and Pounden actually provided a framework for providing justification for the UVF. The alleged order provided by the Covenant was posited as a justification for the UVF by its clerical apologists, while the calls for reliance upon God expressed at intercessory and Ulster Day services were repeated at UVF services in 1913–14.

Like their bishops, it was clear that clergy who both supported and opposed Ulster Day were not concerned with the Presbyterian antecedents of the Covenant. If anything, the events of 1912 highlighted the co-operation of the Presbyterian Church and Church of Ireland. Arguably, Ulster Day suggested the Church of Ireland was the dominant partner in this denominational relationship. In the weeks before Ulster Day, the *Newsletter* published four lists outlining where Ulster Day services would be held. Of the 368 services advertised, 49 per cent were to be held in Church of Ireland churches, with 35 per cent in Presbyterian churches.[79] It is likely the Church of Ireland probably held more Ulster Day services as a result of its strength *vis-à-vis* the Presbyterian Church in the west of the province. In addition, in large provincial towns in the northeast of Ulster with a Presbyterian majority, Anglican clergy often ensured there was an Ulster Day service in the local Church of Ireland church. For example, in Newtownards, the Anglican rector of St Mark's arranged to hold an Ulster Day service instead of attending a single united act of worship. He did this for a number of reasons: it was the unanimous decision at a meeting of local Anglican clergy that such a service should be held; it would demonstrate the strong opposition of the Church of Ireland in Newtownards towards home rule; and no building in Newtownards was capable of holding the large number of people that would attend a united service. However, it was arranged that a display of Protestant unity would be preserved, with Presbyterian clergy taking part in the Ulster Day service in St Mark's.[80]

As with bishops such as D'Arcy and Crozier, clerical support was an important element of Ulster unionism in 1912. Politically, the involvement of Church of Ireland clergy in Ulster unionism throughout 1912 provided an organisational impetus, seen most clearly in the lead up to Ulster Day. Church of Ireland clerical support may also have lent an air of respectability to Ulster unionism. The value of having the erstwhile established church as a firm patron of Ulster Day was shown in an article in the London *Daily Mail*. The comments of over 300 Ulster-based Protestant clergy were published endorsing Ulster Day. Nearly half (137) came from Church of Ireland ministers, whose comments were given prominence. Intended for an English audience for whom Anglican opinion may have counted more than Presbyterian, the article emphasised the importance of the clerical statements as coming from men of peace for whom 'only the deepest conviction of imminent peril can have constrained ... to pen their vivid lines'.[81]

While clergy acted as *de facto* representatives of a political party in various meetings and committees, their role as ministers of the Church played an equally important part. Through sermons and speeches, a moral framework founded on a belief in God's providential favour towards unionism was girded to the sometimes unconstitutional nature of Ulster unionist opposition to home rule. The importance of confidence in God's providence should not be overlooked. While difficult to quantify the influence of such a belief, it is likely a providential understanding of God's role in unionism encouraged clergy that Ulster Day would succeed in its ultimate aim of defeating home rule.

The all-Ireland unionism espoused by the Church of Ireland in 1910–11 was not explicitly rejected in 1912. For Canon Dudley, rector of Coleraine, Ulster Day had an all-Irish dimension: 'The Ulster people were pleading not for themselves, or through any merely selfish desire for their own prosperity, but for the true welfare of the whole nation.'[82] However, by supporting the perceived sacred bond of the Ulster Covenant, Church of Ireland clergy were tied to the political strategy of the Ulster unionist leadership. That year –1912 – established the lines of division within the Church of Ireland, between clergy who actively promoted the Church's involvement in politics and those who feared it would damage the Church, and between clergy who would come to support Ulster exclusion and those who feared partition.

NOTES

1. Lisburn Cathedral magazine, January 1912 (private possession).
2. *Belfast Newsletter*, 17 January 1912.
3. A.T.Q. Stewart, *The Ulster Crisis: Resistance to Home Rule 1912–1914* (London, 1967), pp.50–1.
4. *Belfast Newsletter*, 17 January 1912.
5. Crozier to Lady Londonderry, 18 January 1912 (Public Record Office of Northern Ireland (PRONI), Lady Londonderry papers, D/2847/1/7/3).
6. Stewart, *Ulster Crisis*, pp.51–2.
7. Crozier to Lady Londonderry, 26 January 1912 (PRONI, Lady Londonderry papers, D/2847/1/7/4).
8. *Belfast Newsletter*, 3 February 1912.
9. *Fermanagh Times*, 1 February 1912.
10. *Ulster Gazette*, 24 February 1912.
11. *Belfast Newsletter*, 8 April 1912.
12. Willowfield parish preacher book, 31 March 1912 (private possession).
13. *Belfast Weekly Telegraph*, 6 April 1912.
14. Willowfield parish vestry minute book, 9 May 1912.
15. *Lisburn Standard*, 13 April 1912.
16. Holywood parish preacher book, 10 March 1912 (private possession).
17. *Belfast Weekly Telegraph*, 16 March 1912.
18. *Down Recorder*, 9 November 1912.
19. *Belfast Weekly Telegraph*, 9 March 1912.
20. *Lisburn Standard*, 13 April 1912.

21. *Down Recorder*, 9 November 1912.
22. St Jude's vestry minute book, 4 April 1912 (private possession).
23. *Belfast Newsletter*, 27 April 1912.
24. The Earl of Desart believed the General Synod offered Protestants (and particularly southern Protestants) a 'voice' on Home Rule: *Church of Ireland Gazette*, 19 April 1912.
25. Willowfield vestry minute book, 9 May 1912 (private possession). Receipt of the letters was recorded in the select vestry minute book, although the letters are not preserved. The resolution was passed on 12 April 1912. See also Trinity Church vestry minute book, 11 April 1912, for a resolution against Home Rule forwarded to Carson (PRONI, CR/1/3/5/2).
26. St Thomas' vestry minute book, 18 April 1912 (PRONI, CR/1/36/D/4).
27. Ibid.
28. *Lurgan Mail*, 7 September 1912; *Northern Constitution*, 14 September 1912; *Ulster Gazette*, 21 September 1912; *Fermanagh Times*, 26 September 1912.
29. *Fermanagh Times*, 5 September 1912.
30. *Belfast Newsletter*, 13 September 1912.
31. *Lisburn Standard*, 21 September 1912.
32. *Lurgan Mail*, 28 September 1912.
33. *Ulster Gazette*, 28 September 1912.
34. *Newtownards Chronicle*, 28 September 1912.
35. St Columba's, Knock preacher book, 22 September 1912 (private possession).
36. Ibid., 12 July 1914.
37. Knockbreda preacher book, 22 September 1912 (PRONI, CR/1/24G/6).
38. Willowfield preacher book, 22 September 1912; St Jude's preacher book, 22 September 1912 (private possession).
39. *Lisburn Standard*, 5 October 1912.
40. Lisburn Cathedral preacher book, 28 September 1912 (PRONI, CR/1/35F/6).
41. Lisburn Cathedral magazine, October 1912.
42. *Down Recorder*, 5 October 1912.
43. Killinchy preacher book, 28 September 1912 (PRONI, CR/1/16F/6).
44. *Lurgan Mail*, 5 October 1912.
45. St Columba's preacher book, 28 September 1912; Willowfield preacher book, 28 September 1912.
46. For example, Fermanagh: *Fermanagh Times*, 5 October 1912.
47. See P. Gray, 'National humiliation and the Great Hunger: fast and famine in 1847', *Irish Historical Studies*, 30, 126 (November 2000), p.199.
48. *Lurgan Mail*, 5 October 1912.
49. *Ulster Gazette*, 5 October 1912.
50. *Northern Constitution*, 5 October 1912.
51. *Belfast Weekly Telegraph*, 5 October 1912.
52. St Mark's Dundela parish magazine, October 1912 (private possession).
53. *Northern Constitution*, 28 September 1912.
54. James Owen Hannay to Rev. T. Harvey, 30 September 1912 (TCD, Hannay papers, Mss/3455/500a).
55. See Chapter 2, of this volume.
56. Hannay to Harvey, 30 September 1912 (TCD, Hannay papers, Mss/3455/500a).
57. John Frederick MacNeice, *Carrickfergus and its Contacts: Some Chapters in the History of Ulster* (Carrickfergus, 1928), pp.72–3.
58. Christopher Fauske, *'Side by Side in a Small Country': Bishop John Frederick MacNeice and Ireland* (Church of Ireland Historical Society, 2004), p.6.
59. MacNeice, *Carrickfergus and its Contacts*, p.72; *Ulster Guardian*, 5 October 1912.
60. *Ulster Guardian*, 5 October 1912. Fauske claims MacNeice had gone to Carrickfergus with a 'reputation as a Home Ruler' and tentatively suggests MacNeice stopped being a Home Ruler 'on the day the Anglo-Irish treaty was signed'. Fauske, *Bishop John Frederick MacNeice and Ireland*, p.15.
61. John Frederick MacNeice to Randall Davidson, 1 April 1914 (Lambeth Palace Library, Davidson papers, vol. 389/309–12).
62. A point he made in a sermon at Carrickfergus, 9 July 1922; see Fauske, *Bishop John Frederick MacNeice and Ireland*, p.11.
63. *Church of Ireland Gazette*, 20 September 1912.
64. See Chapter 5, of this volume.
65. See Chapter 6, of this volume.
66. *Church of Ireland Gazette*, 30 August 1912.
67. Ibid., 6 September 1912; *Irish Times*, 9 September 1912.
68. *Ulster Gazette*, 13 September 1912.

69. *Belfast Newsletter*, 10 April 1912.
70. Lisburn Cathedral select vestry minute book, 19 April 1912 (PRONI, CR/1/35D/4).
71. Stewart, *Ulster Crisis*, pp.56–7.
72. Willowfield vestry minute book, 12 April 1912 (private possession).
73. *Northern Constitution*, 8 June 1912.
74. E.D. Atkinson, 'The Covenant', in S. King and S. McMahon (eds), *Hope and History: Eyewitness Accounts of Life in Twentieth-Century Ulster* (Belfast, 1996), pp.33–4.
75. *Belfast Newsletter*, 23 September 1912.
76. Lisburn Cathedral magazine, September 1912.
77. *Newtownards Chronicle*, 28 September 1912.
78. *Lisburn Standard*, 5 October 1912.
79. *Belfast Newsletter*, 14, 17, 19, 23 September 1912.
80. *Newtownards Chronicle*, 14 September 1912.
81. *Daily Mail*, 28 September 1912.
82. *Northern Constitution*, 5 October 1912.

4

'The Red Hand of Ulster'?
The Church of Ireland and the Ulster
Volunteer Force, 1913–14

In 1912, James Owen Hannay (under the pseudonym George Birmingham) published *The Red Hand of Ulster*, a satirical, fictional look at Ulster unionist resistance to home rule.[1] The novel tells the story of an attempted revolution in Ulster, financed by Joseph Peterson Conroy, a bored American businessman, and led by an array of Irish unionists. Lord Kilmore, the narrator, is an almost bewildered observer of events, sucked into involvement with Conroy by a domineering unionist hostess, Lady Moyne. Gideon McNeice, 'one of the fighting men of the Irish Unionist Party', and Colonel Malcolmson, a retired colonel (and member of the Church of Ireland), drill the rebellious Ulster unionists, who use arms smuggled into Ulster aboard Conroy's boat, the *Finola*.

Through the character of the dean, rector of Kilmore and a leading Orangeman, Birmingham lampooned the involvement in unionist politics of the Church of Ireland hierarchy. The dean explained that the 1912 General Synod appeared to be on the side of unionism only because unionism was always right. The Church of Ireland 'would be quite as much on the side of the Liberals if they would only drop their present programme which happened in every respect to be morally wrong'. The dean argued that political questions involved differences of opinion among 'honest men': 'But all honest men are opposed to Home Rule, which is therefore not a political question.' His flying of the union flag from the church spire signalled the start of the rebellion. Inside the church, the dean held a service for those who would take part, rifles in hand.

The rebellion, when it arrives, is provoked by the government banning a huge anti-home rule demonstration in Belfast's botanic gardens. Although they succeeded in establishing a provisional government, the Ulster unionists were angered by the army's reluctance to engage in combat. McNeice complained that the soldiers 'fired over our heads'; Malcolmson asserted: 'We're not going to stand any more fooling.' The newly established Ulster provisional government ordered the English government to 'conduct the war in a proper business-like way ... or ... clear out of Ireland altogether ... and leave us to manage Ireland ourselves'. The English government's protestation that such terms amounted to 'Home Rule of the most extreme kind' fell on deaf ears. *The Red Hand of Ulster* ends with Ireland under her own government, and the dean and other leaders of the rebellion congratulating each other on how the third Home Rule Bill was defeated by 'the unfaltering attitude of the Ulster loyalists'.

The Red Hand of Ulster was published on 30 July 1912 (Birmingham started writing it at the end of April 1912, shortly after the General Synod).[2] One of Birmingham's biographers has accurately claimed *The Red Hand of Ulster* sounds like a 'bizarre combination of Gilbert and Sullivan comic opera and a work of astute political prophecy'.[3] The events that unfold in Birmingham's novel were in some ways an accurate harbinger of real-life events in Ulster during 1913–14. In January 1913 the Ulster Volunteer Force was formed, apparently to act as the armed wing of Ulster unionism. Arms were smuggled into Ulster in 1914, although the *Fanny*, not the *Finola*, acted as the carrier. Significantly for this chapter, like the dean in *The Red Hand of Ulster*, the actual Church of Ireland clergy often played a leading role in legitimising and encouraging Ulster unionist militancy, supporting the establishment of the UVF and related developments such as the Larne gun-running. However, while the UVF received moral and practical support from the Church of Ireland, the reality of the Church's role in the UVF was more complex than in Hannay's satire. A number of clergy seemed genuinely fearful at the prospect of violence and used their influence to restrain volunteers. Archbishop Crozier's all-Ireland unionism was strained by his support for the UVF, while Charles Frederick D'Arcy emerged as a firm supporter of some form of Ulster exclusion.

'TO RISK THEIR LIVES AND SHED THEIR BLOOD'? CHURCH OF IRELAND CLERGY AND THE ESTABLISHMENT OF THE ULSTER VOLUNTEER FORCE

Military-style drilling in unionist clubs and Orange lodges had begun in 1911 and increased rapidly in 1912 – it was estimated that in December 1912, 216 drill practices took place in Ulster.[4] The rationale behind drilling was explained by Rev. S.R. Anderson, rector of Lack in County Fermanagh. Speaking to Irvinestown Unionist Club, Anderson claimed drilling offered the best method of resistance against the impending 'dictation' of a home rule parliament by enabling unionists to 'join hands and advance with fullness of joy to risk their lives and shed their blood on behalf of the great privileges they now enjoyed'.[5] Anderson's support for drilling extended to allowing Lack Unionist Club the use of his rectory's grounds for regular drill practice during July and August.[6] Rev. W.B. Stack, another Church of Ireland clergyman, often drilled the men who met in Anderson's grounds throughout the second part of 1912. Stack also helped drill eighty-eight unionist club members at Tubrid, and took part, along with Rev. W. Black (of Ardess), in a meeting of Kesh Unionist Club at which a number of men carried dummy rifles.[7]

Such militancy resulted partly from the Craigavon demonstration of 1911, where the appearance of a well-drilled county Tyrone Orange lodge had launched the 'craze' for military drilling.[8] However, drilling also drew on a longer tradition of popular loyalist militancy embodied more generally in the Orange Order.[9] A small number of speeches by Church of Ireland clergy made at Orange meetings before Craigavon demonstrated an instinctive recourse to militaristic rhetoric. Rev. S.M. Watts told Orangemen at Derrygonnelly that as home rule threatened religious liberty, they were justified in bearing arms.[10] Speaking at the opening of an Orange hall in Milford, M.B. Hogg, rector of Keady in County Armagh, claimed the threat posed by home rule to 'the dearest principles of their religion' legitimised armed resistance: 'Ulster would fight, and Ulster would be right'.[11] Perhaps the most explicit expression of clerical support for physical resistance to home rule was delivered by Rev. A.E. Sixsmith at a meeting of Kilrea Unionist Club in the week before the Craigavon meeting. Sixsmith believed the one thing worse than war was slavery, and that if they submitted to home rule they would become 'slaves of masters who would trample on them'.

Instead of submission, Sixsmith advocated facing their enemies, and if they 'shot as many of them as they could, and were shot in return, they would at any rate demonstrate their determination and their devotion to their principles'. Sixsmith wanted the 'Protestants of Ulster' to 'stand to their guns, literally not metaphorically' and 'rise as one man against Home Rule, overthrow their enemies, drive them out, pull down the walls about their ears, and destroy them utterly'.[12]

Long-term factors such as traditions of loyalist militancy and the shorter-term influence of Craigavon and the 'Ulster crisis' contextualise the creation of the volunteer force. A more general explanation for the enthusiastic reception accorded the UVF within certain sections of the Church of Ireland in Ulster was the trend for militaristic hobbies. The Church of Ireland Young Men's Society (CIYMS) had a seemingly thriving rifle club, praised by Archbishop Crozier at the society's annual meeting in 1911: 'Shooting trained the eye and steadied the nerves, and if the members of the club were ever called upon they would be able to play a manly part in defence of their country.'[13] The CIYMS rifle club came third in a competition involving the sixty rifle clubs of Ulster, and also held its own competition at which the Church Lads' Brigade rendered valuable service 'with the targets'.[14] The rifle club movement reflected a wider enthusiasm in British churches for organisations with a militaristic ethos, such as the Boys' Brigade and Church Lads' Brigade.[15] The combination of national pride with Christianity seen in organisations such as the CIYMS rifle club resulted in a 'fervent' nationalism and militarism.[16] The *Irish Churchman* explained that 'Ireland determined not to be left behind the sister island in the matter of patriotism, and the outcome was an enthusiastic desire to form miniature rifle clubs in every part of the country, especially the North.'[17] D'Arcy extolled the virtues of the CIYMS rifle club at the society's annual meeting in 1913. The rifle club members seemed to be 'very proficient marksmen indeed'. He believed that every man should be prepared to defend his country, and that universal military training would be a great advantage to the 'manhood' of the United Kingdom. Military training would encourage patriotism and would be a 'means of giving back to us some of that great spirit of devotion to the fatherland which had to some extent been lost in our time, although it had not been lost in Ulster'.[18] Church of Ireland endorsement of the UVF reflected the 'muscular' or 'imperial Christianity' that Wolffe demonstrates provided fertile ground in the rest of Britain for recruitment at the start of the First World War.[19] Support for the UVF built on a wider culture of Christian militarism, reflected in Church of Ireland clerical patronage of rifle clubs.

The establishment of the UVF at the annual meeting of the Ulster Unionist Council in January 1913 confirmed the intention of the Ulster unionist leadership to utilise unconventional tactics in opposing home rule. Membership was limited to 100,000, and only those men who had signed the Covenant could join the force. In the summer of 1913 the UVF's leadership, Sir George Richardson (commander-in-chief) and Colonel W. Hackett Pain (chief of staff), organised the force on the British army model, introducing county regiments. Again, like the British army, separate nursing, transport and special service corps were created.[20]

The UVF received the support of Church of Ireland clergy throughout Ulster. In March 1913 a report to the chief secretary pointed to the 'constant recurrence of certain names as the principal inciters to contingent rebellion'. These names were 'mostly prominent members of the Orange society or Rectors of the late established church'. In an attempt to downplay the threat of 'contingent rebellion', the report claimed Church of Ireland clergy were 'neither the natural leaders of, nor possess any influence with, a large section of Ulster Protestants'. Indeed, according to the report, it seemed reasonable to infer that 'the Presbyterian community of Ulster is not prepared to follow the hot headed Orange leaders'.[21] This memo to the chief secretary was written by Sir James Brown Dougherty, under-secretary at Dublin Castle. Dougherty was close to Presbyterian home rulers and wanted Augustine Birrell (the chief secretary) to discount alarmist police reports.[22] His report should therefore be treated with a certain degree of scepticism, especially as each county inspector's report received by Dublin Castle claimed the main Protestant denominations were involved in whatever drilling was happening in their respective county. Indeed, it is likely the UVF strengthened the growing sense of mutual interest among the Protestant denominations created by the threat of home rule. The county inspector of Antrim believed the home rule crisis and attendant drilling had 'welded the Protestant churches together by a community of interest and feeling which it would have taken at least a generation under other circumstances to bring about'.[23]

The county inspectors' assessments were more accurate than Dougherty's. The UVF helped forge a sense of common identity by bringing together members of the Protestant denominations. United church services attended by UVF contingents strengthened this sense of common identity – acts of worship in Presbyterian and Church of Ireland UVF services followed a familiar pattern, using similar hymns and Bible readings.[24] It is probable that united services were arranged on an *ad hoc* basis by commanding officers of UVF units, who decided which clergymen would take part. These clergymen would then 'arrange amongst themselves what part each will take in the dedication or service. By this means it is hoped any misunderstanding as to precedence amongst the clergy of the various denominations will be avoided.'[25] While this letter (written by UVF headquarters to leaders of the north Antrim volunteers) suggests there may have been potential for denominational controversy concerning the arrangement of UVF services, a more common feature was the ecumenism practised in Newtownards in January 1914. The son of Lord Dunleath, a local unionist grandee, had met with the Church of Ireland rector (William Twist-Whatham) and the Presbyterian minister (William Wright) to arrange a UVF service:

> Wright will encourage the Volunteers who belong to his Church to attend the service in Mr Whatham's Church ... I expect that at least 200 of the Newtownards men will turn up – more than 400 are enrolled in the Newtownards District.[26]

Dunleath may have under-estimated the numbers that would attend the service; according to the *Chronicle*, between three and four hundred volunteers were present, with 'every available seat' taken. The service demonstrated how 'practically every Protestant ... is heart and soul in the movement which has as its roots the defence of his civil and religious liberties'.[27] A similar example of Anglican–Presbyterian co-operation was exhibited at a UVF service in Clare Presbyterian Church in Armagh. The Presbyterian minister, Robert Whan, conducted the service, while his Anglican counterpart, J. McEndoo, delivered the sermon. In order to preach, McEndoo had cancelled the afternoon service in his own church after receiving permission from his bishop (Crozier). Whan paid tribute to the 'broadmindedness, tolerant spirit, and cultivated mind of his Grace, in permitting the church to be closed'.[28]

Dougherty's report to the chief secretary *was* accurate in relation to the attitude of Church of Ireland clergy towards the UVF and drilling. At a preliminary meeting to organise the force, held in Enniskillen in December 1912, Rev. W.B. Stack was appointed honorary secretary for Fermanagh, and elected as the county's representative at headquarters meetings. His brother, Rev. W.A. Stack, was chosen as a divisional representative (for Tubrid, Kesh) to act on the Fermanagh UVF county committee.[29] In July 1913, W.B. Stack was identified as a prime mover in the importation of arms into Fermanagh;[30] in addition, he acted as camp adjutant at a UVF camp at Crom Castle in November, and accompanied Sir George Richardson as he inspected various battalions in Fermanagh.[31] The *Fermanagh Times* claimed the success of the UVF in Fermanagh was largely due to Stack's 'energy, enthusiasm, and military knowledge'.[32] A number of other Fermanagh clergy were involved in the force. R.C. Lapham, rector of Lisnaskea, commanded the volunteers of Lisnaskea and Tyraffy; in December, General Richardson inspected Lapham's men in Lisnaskea parochial hall.[33] A notebook kept by John Bears, a drill inspector who checked on the organisation and drilling ability of various Fermanagh UVF contingents, further reveals the involvement of certain Church of Ireland rectors in the force. Bears' notebook recorded the number of men and senior officers present at each drill he inspected. Bears complimented W.B. Stack's men in Ardess, who carried out drill in 'good style'.[34] However, in Lack, where Rev. S.R. Anderson was the senior officer present, Bears noted: 'No roll books kept. Ordered to be rectified … Squad very slack, require a lot of training. Rifles (wood) out for first time. Told to practise rifle exercises.'[35] The state of the Tempo volunteers (under the command of the local rector, James Wilson) was little better. Bears reported the 'Company book kept only but not marked up. Told to rectify … Require a lot of practice before efficient in squad drill. Told to practise squad drill and skirmishing. Half of these men would be good men if taken in hand by good Instructor.'[36]

However, Bears' comments were made shortly after the force was established, when a lack of expertise would be expected. Also, it was unlikely many Church of Ireland rectors would have any great ability at drilling squads of men unless, like W.B. Stack, they had been members of the army before ordination. It appears that what the Fermanagh clergy may have lacked in military ability, they made up for in enthusiasm. The membership book of the Fermanagh UVF listed nineteen members as being Church of Ireland clergymen.[37] As a proportion of the Church of Ireland clergy in Fermanagh, nineteen is an impressive figure and suggests that a large section of eligible clergy in Fermanagh supported the UVF enough to join the force. Also, as the Stack brothers were not recorded in the membership book, it is likely the actual number of clergy who were members of the UVF in Fermanagh was higher than nineteen.

Due to a lack of relevant sources, it is difficult to assess the involvement of Church of Ireland clergy in the UVF in the rest of Ulster to the same extent as in Fermanagh. However, it is clear that clerical participation in the UVF mirrored earlier organisational roles taken in unionist clubs or the Orange Order. In Cavan, although drilling was initially on a small scale, the volunteer movement was led by two Church of Ireland clergy (Rev. A.W. McGarvey and Rev. J.W. Askins), as well as Lord Farnham, a local landowner and member of the Church of Ireland.[38] Around Ulster, clergy demonstrated their support for the volunteers in a variety of practical ways – joining auxiliary sections of the UVF,[39] officiating at prize-giving ceremonies,[40] or taking part in fundraising events.[41] In north Antrim, Rev. William Matchette of Ballintoy 'unreservedly' agreed to allow the provisional government the use of his Model T Ford motor car 'in the event of such being required in connection with any of the Forces or Services of the said Provisional Government, subject only to reasonable compensation for loss or damage'. Matchette also signalled his willingness to enrol in the transport section of the UVF, and agreed to drive '*when necessary*', although he would prefer to have a chauffeur assigned.[42] In addition to such practical support for the UVF, clerical patronage was provided by allowing volunteers to use parochial halls for drilling. The select vestry of St Thomas' in Belfast allowed an ambulance section of the local UVF the use of their parochial hall;[43] the Lisburn UVF used the cathedral's school-house for meetings.[44] Perhaps most significantly, massed ranks of volunteers became a familiar sight at Church of Ireland churches throughout 1913 and 1914, providing a potent symbol of the Church's support, in Ulster, for the volunteer movement.

JUSTIFYING MILITANCY

George Chadwick, bishop of Derry, made a concerted effort during 1913 to construct some form of theological defence for armed resistance. In June 1913 he preached at a service held in Derry Cathedral attended by the city's unionist club. It was claimed 400 men were present, of which at least half were drilled. Chadwick based his sermon on the 'render unto Caesar' passage in Matthew's gospel. He believed it absurd to claim the text proved Christ taught 'servile obedience' to the government. A number of supposedly apposite examples were chosen to illustrate that the Bible did not enforce such obedience: Moses opposed the Pharaoh, Samuel dethroned King Saul, and Elisha anointed Jehu king while Ahab still held power. In light of such examples, Chadwick claimed that for Irish unionists to 'shirk from defending' their freedom to worship God, they would be 'rendering to Caesar that which is not Caesar's'.[45] Preaching in Belfast Cathedral to a congregation composed of members of Belfast unionist clubs, Chadwick emphasised armed resistance could be divinely sanctioned. Christ's command to 'resist not evil' was 'a broad general rule, wholly unconcerned with the exceptions in details'. The most 'vital' exception was the one 'which set the ruler free to inspire terror in the hearts of evil doers'. As the source of authority was now 'the people', the intention to deprive Ulster, without her consent, of the 'great heritage of empire' was a rebellion against 'legitimate rule and order'. The great wrong of home rule was to be 'inflicted by fraud and usurpations on a great scale under the eyes of the true ruler, the people whom they [the government] refused to consult'.[46] Chadwick preached on the possibility of 'justifiable violence' at an Ulster Day service in Glendermott parish church, attended by the local UVF contingent. He claimed 'no man could really suppose the Christian religion forbade any violence under any circumstances whatever', and asserted that religious and political liberty were 'causes for which no Christian is to be at liberty to fail to defend'.[47]

Chadwick's defence of militancy was consistent with his earlier statements on home rule. During the *Ne Temere* dispute he had suggested that if the state proposed legislation that meant disobeying the 'voice of God in His scriptures', then the state must be opposed.[48] A more immediate cause of Chadwick's rhetoric may have been the relative paucity in recruitment to the UVF in Derry city.[49] His repeated attempts to cloak the volunteer movement with divine endorsement and a sense of spiritual vitality and Christian duty could have been designed to encourage the faithful to sign up for the UVF, as well as encouraging those who were already volunteers in their belief that the proposed armed resistance was morally righteous.

Chadwick's attack on the government for failing to call an election was repeated by R.G.S. King, rector of Limavady, in his pamphlet: *Ulster's protest: her industrial, political, imperial reasons for refusing to submit to Home Rule. An appeal to Great Britain.* King justified resistance on the basis of the government's 'corrupt bargain' with the Irish party, and the lack of a 'mandate from the people' for home rule. In addition, he saw in the Williamite forces of 1690 a convenient parallel for Ulster unionists in 1913, as both had dared to resist constitutional authority to obtain, or in the case of Ulster unionists, retain, their rights and liberties. An imperial argument was also utilised by King when he claimed many of those drilling and organising the UVF had fought in the Boer War 'for the empire', and that they were certain they would be fighting for the empire in Ulster as well. King concluded his argument by calling for all unionists to 'above all, be true to our glorious and beloved empire'.[50] Such an argument was unsurprising from as ardent an imperialist as King, a prime mover in organising Limavady's Empire Day celebrations in 1913, at which 'a finer pyrotechnical display has never been seen in Limavady'.[51]

The arguments advanced by Chadwick and King were representative of clerical support for militancy. Their defence of the UVF reflected arguments utilised by Ulster unionists to resolve the 'moral dilemma' of resisting the state: the Constitution was suspended by the Parliament Act, the result of a corrupt bargain between Liberals and nationalists, depriving unionists of the opportunity of compelling the government to hold a general election on home rule.[52] In addition, clergy deployed a religious or spiritual defence of militancy. In *Ulster's refusal to submit to a Roman Catholic Parliament*, a second pamphlet by R.G.S. King, the religious argument against home rule was held 'by itself … quite sufficient to justify our determination never to submit to it'.[53] The UVF was bolstered by a belief that 'the God of Hosts would go forth with our armies'.[54] The first anniversary of Ulster Day was marked by religious services at the request of Edward Carson, services endorsed by a northern bishops' pastoral appointing Ulster Day as a 'special day of intercession and prayer on behalf of our beloved native land'.[55] Ulster Day services offered clergy an opportunity of affirming the righteousness of physical resistance. For example, the dean of Dromore trusted that God 'will keep us in the struggle and give us deliverance' if the UVF was 'forced' into a civil war. They would fight because it was their 'religious duty' to resist wrong. The dean urged constant prayer and confession of sin in order to realise their strength came from God.[56] The bishops' desire for prayer and intercession found expression in a series of united prayer meetings held around Ulster throughout 1914.[57] Prayer meetings inevitably implied the legitimacy of Ulster unionism's increasing militancy. Rev. George Stephenson, addressing a huge prayer meeting in Belfast, presented the Old Testament figure of Nehemiah as a 'man of prayer' whose faithfulness and patriotism unionists were encouraged to emulate. They must follow God with 'unquestioning devotion and obedience', whether God led them in the 'ways of pleasantness' or to civil war.[58]

The dean of Belfast, Charles Grierson, confirmed the right of volunteers 'to turn at such a time to your clergy for a clear statement of what they consider to be the moral position of the situation'. Preaching a New Year sermon in St Mary Magdalene to a congregation including members of the South Belfast regiment of the UVF, Grierson defended militancy by resort to the 'God-given principle of love', which demanded the defence of the 'greatest gifts bestowed upon us by God – civil and religious liberties'. He reassured the volunteers that they were 'acting as God would have you act'.[59] In similar terms to Grierson, the archdeacon of Down reassured the South Down regiment of the UVF that they were right to drill and prepare to resist home rule. The 'courage' and 'zeal' displayed by volunteers after prayer meetings demonstrated a belief in God's blessing upon their 'determination'.[60] By cloaking the UVF with a degree of spiritual vitality, clergy reflected their own religiously motivated worldview and belief in a God who answered the politically motivated prayers of the penitent. In addition, to claim God was in full support of militancy may have encouraged support for the UVF among Church members who were not convinced with arguments resting on conditional obedience to the state when faced with the apparent inevitability of armed resistance.

Alongside the moral justification leant to the UVF by clergy was a widely expressed desire for restraint on the part of volunteers. Chancellor Hobson, rector of St Mark's, Portadown, spoke twice in 1913 of the need to restrain violence. At an Orange meeting in March, Hobson called on those present to restrain the 'irresponsible young people, who in times of excitement took up the cudgels when they had no right to do so'.[61] At an Ulster Day service in Lisburn, attended by the Lisburn battalion of the UVF, Rev. R.H.S. Cooper emphasised the 'best way to avoid war and strife was to prepare for battle'. Cooper believed volunteers wanted to live in peace and harmony with their fellow countrymen, and urged the congregation to prevent 'thoughtless parties giving utterances to foolish party expressions'.[62] In his Mary Magdalene New Year sermon, the dean of Belfast also urged the volunteers to 'keep calm' and avoid 'sinful' rioting. Obedience to those in command was emphasised, as the 'issues at stake are too great for hasty and independent action on the part of anyone'.[63] Grierson's appeal for restraint was consistent with sentiments expressed one year earlier at a unionist club service held in the Ulster Hall, when he had thanked God for Ulster unionism's leaders, as 'unerringly had they so far guided the democracy of Ulster'. As a result, unionists should 'move as they [their leaders] bade them move, and never on their own initiative'. In order to emphasise this call to obedience was a call for restraint, Grierson urged those present 'to use all their influence to restrain the irresponsible from excess'.[64] In February 1914, at a service in Belfast Cathedral attended by 1,300 volunteers, Rev. T. Collins acknowledged the threat of civil war and the readiness of every volunteer to sacrifice 'even life itself'. However, in words which may have carried added resonance due to the presence of Sir George Richardson and Lord and Lady Londonderry, Collins maintained the importance of discipline and 'implicit obedience to those in authority'. The Covenant and UVF had, he continued, produced a 'quiet' and 'self-possessed' spirit in Ulster, and instead of 'outbreaks of disorder, you have a calm, deliberate preparation'.[65] In Fermanagh, the rector of Colebrooke urged the volunteers to 'bear and forbear', avoid intemperance, and 'continue to obey as you have obeyed'.[66] The archdeacon of Dromore, E.D. Atkinson, 'earnestly' impressed the Donaghacloney general vestry of their duty in using 'all your influence with others … to maintain that attitude of peaceful self-restraint' and strive for 'peace with honour'.[67] The make-up of Atkinson's select vestry may have explained his call for restraint – the first and second battalions of the West Down volunteers were commanded by Captain Holt Waring, Atkinson's churchwarden, and two other members of Atkinson's select vestry were prominent supporters of the volunteers. However, despite his calls for restraint, Atkinson, along with the Presbyterian moderator, consecrated the colours of the West Down volunteers in May 1914.[68]

Buckland highlights the fact that unionists justified their own militancy by arguing that the UVF served a social purpose by maintaining order in Ulster.[69] Other historians have accepted the view that the UVF attempted to restrain the grassroots of Ulster unionism. Through military rigour, discipline was established and uncontrolled rioting, with its attendant political damage, prevented.[70] In Townshend's opinion, the enrolment of the local paramilitary units into a single force was clearly intended 'to control them as much as to encourage them'.[71] Jackson argues that the UVF was established by the Ulster unionist leadership to bring loyalist militants more directly under control.[72] This 'top-down' view was also held by Cyril Falls, who briefly discussed the origins of the UVF in his history of the 36th Ulster division. Falls believed Carson established the UVF as he realised unorganised resistance would be disastrous and lead to disorder and 'unnecessary bloodshed'.[73] J.J. Lee also viewed the UVF as the creation of the Ulster unionist leadership, intended to 'keep the physical force Unionist element under political control'.[74] Counterintuitively, in this interpretation unionists believed the presence of an armed force prevented violence.

Church of Ireland clerical calls for restraint certainly reflected a top-down view of the UVF, in which the force was only to act at the bidding of the Ulster unionist leadership. The prevalence of clerical calls for restraint may have reflected a fear that disorder was a very real possibility. Support for the UVF and calls for restraint did not represent a false dichotomy – it was possible to support the volunteers (and be a volunteer) while still wishing to avoid violence (as illustrated by Archdeacon Atkinson). Clergy may have recognised the rhetorical value of urging restraint, believing the UVF was intended as a demonstration of the unity of Ulster unionism as well as a means of frightening the government into dropping home rule for all of Ireland, or at the very least all or part of Ulster. The supposed propaganda value of the UVF motivated clergy to both support the force and urge restraint, as outbreaks of disorder would be detrimental to the Ulster unionist case in England.

Clerical calls for restraint also reflected a degree of self-interest. The fear of disorder drove a number of churches to take out insurance policies against damage caused by 'civil commotion'. The impetus to insure churches appeared to come from the diocesan synod of Derry and Raphoe. Captain Ricardo, a prominent layman and leading member of the UVF in Tyrone, urged the synod to move a resolution (passed unanimously) affirming their desire to insure buildings against the risk of damage.[75] In the following months a number of churches in Derry and Raphoe took out insurance.[76] The select vestry of Drumclamph agreed to insure their church against loss or damage 'caused by fire occasioned by riot, civil commotion, insurrection, military or other usurped power'.[77] Insurance in other parts of Ulster was carried out on a more *ad hoc* basis than in the diocese of Derry and Raphoe. Rostrevor select vestry appointed a four-man sub-committee in February 1914 to investigate the advisability of insuring the church 'against malicious injury'.[78] The sub-committee decided to write to an insurance company to discover whether it would accept a policy of £1,000 for the church and £100 for the church school.[79] However, the minutes contain no further evidence as to whether or not the parish was insured. The select vestry of Down parish took out an insurance policy against damage caused by riot or civil commotion, 'in view of possible riots in connection with the forcing of Home Rule upon the loyalists of Ulster'.[80] The outbreak of the First World War appeared to signal the end of the 'civil commotion' insurance policies – in December 1914 the vestry of Lower Moville was informed that the diocesan council would no longer insure their church against civil war.[81] The select vestry of Belleek (in west Fermanagh) viewed the outbreak of war as offering an opportunity to carry out some much-needed repairs to the church building. In May 1914 the repairs were delayed due to the 'disturbed' state of the country,[82] and only proceeded with in September, shortly after the outbreak of war.[83]

Rural parishes seemed more likely than urban churches to take out insurance. Many Church of Ireland populations in rural parts of Ulster, especially in Donegal and Fermanagh, were isolated in predominantly Catholic areas and therefore held to be more at risk from 'civil commotion'. In Belfast, with a larger Protestant population and more firmly established UVF, insurance may have been seen as an unnecessary expense. St Thomas' in Belfast (the parish of William Dowse, dean of Belfast) appeared unwilling to take out insurance. In February a special meeting of the select vestry was held to discuss 'the propriety' of insuring the 'church properties against loss caused by riot and civil commotion, rebellion and insurrection'. The vestry decided to postpone its decision until a more fully attended meeting.[84] The matter was discussed the following week at a vestry meeting, at which Dowse pointed out 'it would cost something like £45 for a period of twelve months'. After 'considerable discussion', it was agreed to post-pone a decision until the vestry's next meeting.[85] In March the question was fur-ther delayed,[86] and there was no further reference to insurance in the minutes, suggesting the issue had been quietly dropped. Two Belfast parishes, Mary Magdalene and St Jude's, declared they had no intention of insuring their church-es against civil commotion (no reason was given for these decisions).[87]

The select vestry of Lisburn Cathedral also declined to take out an insurance policy, a decision it probably came to regret. In March 1914 a special meeting of the select vestry was called to discuss the propriety of insuring the cathedral against 'riot and civil commotion'. The policy would cost £17, 6s, which was considered excessive. In any case, the vestry believed that if damage was done to the cathedral, they would have a claim against the county council.[88] The fol-lowing month's vestry meeting agreed unanimously to take no further action on insuring the cathedral.[89] However, in July, Canon Pounden informed the vestry that the diocesan council had emphasised the need for watchfulness in guarding the cathedral, not from angry home-rulers or riotous loyalists, but from suffra-gists. Pounden believed 'every care was taken and in addition the police were taking active part in this direction'. Unfortunately these precautions were not enough to prevent a group of suffragists from attempting to blow up the cathedral on 1 August 1914. The suffragists' audacious attack failed, succeeding only in destroying the chancel window. The *Lisburn Standard* described the scene soon after the damage was discovered: 'Strewn about the place were pieces of masonry and broken glass; while several handbills danced about between the tombstones in what almost seemed fiendish delight.'[90] The suffragists chose a particularly tense time to set off a huge explosion, in the midst of growing tension between Britain and Germany. Lillian Spender, the wife of Wilfred Spender (a leading member of the UVF), noted in her diary that at about 3 o'clock in the morning, as she was lying awake worrying about what could happen to her husband in the war, she heard what she thought was a 'big gun firing'. This proved to be the explosion at Lisburn Cathedral, caused by 'suffragettes, who blew out the ancient east window in Lisburn Cathedral, the brutes. They were all staying with Mrs Metge, a Lisburn lady and a mad militant, and today I believe nearly all the windows in her house are broken.'[91] In the cathedral magazine, Canon Pounden pointed out that although the noise of the exploding bomb was heard many miles away, 'it was heard also by God in heaven, who suffered not its violence to prosper'.[92] On 11 August 1914 the select vestry of the cathedral held a meeting to consider how to repair the damage. Embarrassingly, considering their earlier refusal to insure the church against civil commotion, the select vestry agreed to pay for the repairs to the cathedral.[93]

While the only physical damage caused to Church of Ireland churches in Ulster in 1913–14 was thus carried out by female suffragists, the threat of civil war was considered real enough for many vestries to take out insurance. In some cases, these insurance policies may have exerted a heavy financial burden on churches. While the Lisburn Cathedral affair was a fairly humorous (and unique) incident, it demonstrated what easy targets churches were. It is possible that the perceived need for many churches to be insured against damage caused by civil war explained calls for restraint, especially in rural areas of Ulster where there was a minority Protestant population. If it was feared churches could be damaged, it was likely clergy would have exerted what influence they had to 'restrain angry passions'.

'DEFENCE, NOT DEFIANCE'? D'ARCY, CROZIER AND THE UVF

The attitude of Charles Frederick D'Arcy and John Baptist Crozier towards the UVF seemed to reflect the balance of justification and restraint displayed by parochial clergy. D'Arcy was a very public supporter of the volunteers, and consecrated the colours of four UVF battalions in his diocese (at Newtownards in February, at Hillsborough in March, Antrim in April, and Ballymena in May).[94] The consecration ceremonies were attended by the UVF leadership and prominent Ulster unionist politicians and landowners (who often presented the colours to the battalion in question). The ceremony was usually an ecumenical occasion, with D'Arcy dedicating the colours and a Presbyterian clergyman offering prayer (or vice versa). In his 1913 Ulster Day sermon, D'Arcy expressed views that would become familiar in his subsequent speeches on the force. He pointed to the 'splendid unity' and 'excellent order' prevailing in Ulster. The lack of rioting was especially important as the 'cause for which they stood was too great and glorious and sacred a thing to be associated with disorder'.[95] D'Arcy's 1913 diocesan synod speech trumpeted the unity and 'spirit of loyalty' in Ulster and the energising moral force of the UVF, which was 'enabling the men of Ulster to set today a glorious example of self-sacrifice for the country's sake – an example which may, we trust, fire the men of England and the men of Scotland to a noble emulation'.[96] At a prayer meeting in February 1914, D'Arcy called for prayer to avert civil war. In his opinion, there was no incongruity in this petition, as the 'volunteer force has so far proved itself a most potent agent for the promotion of peace and order'. Without the UVF, and the resulting 'discipline' and 'self control', there would already have been 'bloodshed'. D'Arcy thanked God for the UVF, as it had 'taught our people the great lesson of order and of the strength and confidence which comes from good order'. Finally, he added the petition 'that the volunteer force may never be called upon to shed their blood in defence of our liberties'.[97]

D'Arcy's calls for order, as with those parochial clergy who urged restraint, were motivated by a belief in the volatility of the rank and file. His initial response to the 'Curragh crisis' (20–25 March 1914) seemed to add to this sense of volatility. The Curragh crisis was caused by a (mistaken) assumption that the government had ordered elements of the army, stationed at the Curragh base, to redeploy preparatory to action against the UVF, orders a number of officers refused to follow. Preaching in St Mary's, Newry on the Sunday after the crisis broke, D'Arcy issued what for him amounted to a rallying cry. Unionists had hope in the midst of such a 'solemn day' as among them were men 'ready to deny themselves and suffer and die, if need be, for their country's cause. Thank God for such men – men who will give themselves for their country and for those things we hold dearest and noblest and best.'[98] D'Arcy's St Mary's sermon appeared a temporary interruption in his pleas for order, a direct result of the heightened tensions created by the Curragh crisis. By the following week he had reverted to his more familiar rhetoric of restraint. Speaking in St Bartholomew's, Stranmillis, he urged continued prayer and watchfulness, and reminded the congregation that 'calm, patient self-control is the supreme need of the present moment'. Ulster unionists needed to avoid any semblance of disorder and maintain the 'grand spirit of self-sacrifice' demonstrated by the UVF in order to restrain 'angry passions' and keep the 'public peace'.[99] The Curragh crisis prompted D'Arcy to send a letter to the clergy of his diocese, calling upon them to exercise influence 'in their own localities' to 'restrain angry passions, to avoid excitement, and to soften resentment'. Clergy should exert all their powers in public and private, to urge parishioners to 'absolute self-restraint in case of provocation'.[100]

D'Arcy summarised his attitude to the UVF in a letter to the London *Times*, written four days before the Larne gun-running (20 April). He presented himself as an eyewitness to the development of the force, who as bishop of a diocese containing Belfast and counties Antrim and Down was 'continually going about through the district which forms the very heart of Ulster'. As a result, he had realised the UVF was of 'inestimable benefit to the whole community'. Volunteers were self-sacrificial, submitted to discipline and exercised self-restraint, all for a 'high patriotic purpose'. The most 'extraordinary result' of the UVF was its influence in 'controlling passions and preventing riot'. In the light of such multifaceted benefits, D'Arcy asked was 'England going to order these men [the volunteers] to be shot, or is she going to take them to her heart and enrol them among those who are willing to give their lives for her welfare?'[101] By writing to a London-based newspaper, D'Arcy intended to present an acceptable face of Ulster unionist militancy to an English audience. As with his interview in the *Daily Telegraph* in 1912 regarding Ulster unionist resistance, D'Arcy's letter to *The Times* revealed a high level of engagement with the Ulster unionist cause and demonstrated the influence he was perceived to carry with English readers.

D'Arcy's endorsement of the UVF, allied to his blessing of colours at Ballymena after the Larne gun-running, was criticised by Colonel Seely, the ex-secretary of state for war. D'Arcy defended his actions in another letter to *The Times*, claiming the UVF had no desire to 'shed blood'. By consecrating UVF colours, D'Arcy was acting no differently from a bishop who consecrated colours for a regiment of the army 'because he believes his country's cause to be a righteous and holy cause, and because he believes the Army's main purpose is the maintenance of peace, and not the shedding of blood'. Nevertheless, the UVF needed rifles, as 'what is the good of an army without weapons?'[102] During a speech in Birmingham, Seely responded to D'Arcy's letter by claiming he found it difficult to understand how a bishop could defend the use of a maxim gun, 'one of the most fiendish inventions that had ever proceeded from the brain of man'. D'Arcy had blessed the UVF 'in the name of the Prince of Peace' and it was his duty to 'either denounce the possession of those engines of wholesale slaughter [the maxim gun] or else forswear his faith'.[103] D'Arcy responded, again in the pages of *The Times*, by claiming the leaders of the Church in Ulster had been doing their best 'to restrain angry passions and to prevent disturbance'. The Curragh crisis was an example, he claimed, of D'Arcy's desire to use 'studiously moderate language' and demonstrated the long-standing 'splendid order and constant watchfulness of the Volunteer Force'.[104]

The image of a bishop blessing maxim guns, promoted by Seely, has proved durable, although D'Arcy maintained he had never seen any guns, 'much less blessed them. What the volunteers possessed in the way of weapons I did not know.'[105] In his biography of James Craig, Hugh Shearman noted that in 1913–14 'we find Dr D'Arcy ... although no firebrand, and indeed an eminently mild man, appearing in his official, ecclesiastical capacity to consecrate Unionist machine guns.'[106] D'Arcy's defence of the UVF in his response to Seely implicitly defended the illegal importation of arms, although in his public statements on the force, D'Arcy clearly viewed the UVF as a top-down force, imposing order upon the Ulster unionist rank and file. His support for the UVF, accompanied by calls for restraint, was consistent with his view that the UVF was never intended to fight – in effect, D'Arcy viewed the UVF as an elaborately constructed propaganda tool intended to persuade the government of the folly of attempting to impose home rule.

Archbishop Crozier displayed, like D'Arcy, a mixture of endorsement and calls for restraint in relation to the volunteers. On Saturday 4 October 1913 Edward Carson inspected the UVF in Armagh. On the Friday night, Carson and F.E. Smith stayed with Crozier in the episcopal palace. Crozier joined Carson the following day on the inspecting platform, providing a visible sign of his endorse-ment of the volunteers.[107] At a UVF service in Newtownards, Crozier presented the Old Testament as a meta-narrative intended to 'let them see from history that God never forgot nor forsook his people, so that no man would ever despair for his native land however dark the outlook might be'. God's benevolence towards Ulster unionism was seen as a spur to further action, not complacency. No man should 'withdraw his hand' from 'building up' the Church and state 'when he had come to realise God's over-ruling providence and their own responsibility for helping to fulfil the divine purpose'. Crozier's desire was for a true confession of individual and national sin so that as a nation they would honour God, allow-ing them to pray 'that the land might be saved from strife and civil war'.[108] In March 1914 a large UVF service was held in Armagh Cathedral. The *Belfast Newsletter* claimed: 'seldom has such a large congregation assembled within the walls of the historic building.' Crozier did not preach, but took part in the service. He urged the congregation, composed of over 700 volunteers, to avoid provoking those who differed from them 'even though those men wished to throw Ireland back into the filth of the Slough of Despond'. They needed to be obedient to their leaders and remember that 'defence and not defiance was their motto'.[109] Crozier also issued a prayer to be used by every Church of Ireland member of the UVF, calling upon God to protect them in 'their time of danger and difficulty'.[110] Wilfred Spender, one of the chief organisers of the UVF, alleged Crozier's support of the UVF made him complicit in the Larne gun-running. Replying (in 1959) to the enquiries of Rev. C. Brett Ingram, Spender described how far from Belfast the imported weapons were distributed: 'I know that Archbishop Crozier at Armagh was brought into consultation. His household used to attend Family Prayers sitting on benches filled temporarily with rifles instead of Bibles.'[111] Spender's reminiscences need to be treated with a fair degree of caution, especially as he was writing forty-five years after the events he described. It also seems unlikely that the only or best place for Crozier to hide rifles in the episcopal palace was in benches. However, it is possible that Crozier, similarly to D'Arcy, supported gun-running as the crowning glory to the 'defence, not defiance' strategy, ensuring the government would drop home rule or be forced into a general election.

D'Arcy's attempts at influencing English opinion through letters to *The Times* were echoed by Crozier, who brought the unionist case to England through sermons and speeches. In March 1914 Crozier attended a Church Missionary Society meeting in Manchester's Free Trade Hall, chaired by the bishop of Manchester (Bishop Welldon), an ardent unionist. The chairman's speech criticised the possibility that those Ulster counties which were predominantly Presbyterian (and therefore 'valuable in connection with the Scottish vote') could vote themselves out of the Home Rule Bill. This left the Church of Ireland, scattered throughout the country, to be 'placed under the dominion of the Parliament in Dublin'. Crozier responded by claiming he would welcome home rule if it would benefit the whole country, but he did not believe it would do so. In a torturous metaphor, he expressed his confidence that home rule would not 'sink' the Church of Ireland:

> If the ship of the Church goes down, please God she will go down as the Titanic went down – with her band playing, and with her engineers at their places beside the engines. But I do not believe it will be so. The Church of Christ has weathered many a storm.[112]

Crozier was similarly optimistic when preaching in Westminster Abbey. He claimed 'they did not despair for their land even in her darkest hour', although he asked for the prayers of the congregation so 'that God might save Ireland from faction, strife and civil war'.[113]

Crozier's platform sharing with the bishop of Manchester and invitation to preach in Westminister Abbey reflected a wider interest among the Church of England episcopate in the 'Irish question'. The archbishop of Canterbury, Randall Davidson, was initially reluctant to engage the Church of England in prayer for the avoidance of 'internecine war' in Ireland, as it would be 'unreal to put out a simple invitation for prayer as though the Constitutional question were beyond the range of human handling'.[114] However, in response to the wide level of support among parochial clergy in England, Davidson came to support calls for prayer. J. Gough McCormick, a rector in London, received 468 favourable replies from other clergy (and only six unfavourable) to his circular calling for a 'solemn Act of Prayer for the one and only object of a peaceful settlement' in Ireland.[115] Davidson hoped bishops in his province would follow the example of the London diocese and appoint the first Sunday of 1914 as a day of intercession for Ireland.[116] He defended the call for special prayers by pointing to the 'troubles and divisions which, with increasing and even clamorous urgency, threaten the people of Ireland'.[117] The bishop of Durham, in a public letter to his diocese, appealed for intercession to avert civil war in Ireland.[118] In March, the dean of Canterbury was a signatory to the 'National Appeal', which demanded dissolution and supported unconstitutional tactics if home rule was passed without being submitted to the country.[119] Hensley Henson, the dean of Durham, stayed with D'Arcy during a visit to Ulster in June 1914. When he returned to Durham, Henson sent a letter to *The Times* in which he claimed home rule would only be effective 'at a cost ruinously great, both to Ireland itself and to the British Empire'.[120]

It was likely the support of English bishops and leading clergymen encouraged their contemporaries in Ireland. The Irish House of Bishops thanked Davidson for the Church of England's prayerful support 'in this time of imminent danger and distress in Ireland'.[121] The archdeacon of Down believed the intervention of the Church of England proved the 'Ulster question' was an 'imperial' issue 'whose roots struck deep into those principles of justice and liberty on which depended the welfare of England and the stability of the empire'.[122] The bishop of Manchester gave a different spin to the archdeacon of Down's belief that the Church of England viewed home rule as an imperial issue. Welldon opposed home rule not least as he was certain the religiously motivated bloodshed threatened in Ulster if home rule was enforced would be replicated in Liverpool.[123]

The apparent interest of Davidson in the home rule dispute may have provoked Crozier to enlist his influence. Shortly after the Curragh crisis, Crozier informed Davidson that 'your grace cannot realise how terribly near we were to it [civil war] in March 19–21'. With tensions running high, Crozier believed a 'ray of hope' in 'this awful crisis' would be provided if Asquith 'were really to offer the exclusion of Ulster till a federal scheme for the whole Kingdom was brought into existence. It would not in the least lessen the *dread* of Home Rule … but I believe it would *prevent* civil war.'[124] Crozier's suggestion that the Curragh crisis risked civil war in Ulster may have exaggerated the true state of affairs, although it revealed his concern at the volatility of the volunteers. On Easter Sunday he wrote a further letter to Davidson, discussing the utility of various solutions to Home Rule and giving his assessment of the 'rank and file'. He informed Davidson that

> you may be sure I am doing and will do all that is possible with the leaders here. But it is *absolutely necessary* that it should be *privately* done, in order that when the time comes to try and lead the men straight (I mean the rank and file) one's influence may be of real value.

Crozier appeared to want to act as a moderating influence, but realised any public tailoring of his position would lessen his ability to influence the volunteers. He believed the role he could play in influencing the rank and file was crucial, as the 'Northern man hates diplomacy' and 'utterly distrusts the word of all official politicians'. However, 'he trusts his own Bishop, clergyman or minister wonderfully and if he gives his word of honour I should never ask him to write it down!' Crozier emphasised the defiant action of Ulster unionists, backing up his point by informing Davidson that Mrs Crozier had recently attended a meeting in Gosford Castle, for instruction in hospital work, as part of the UVF nursing corps. The ladies were taught by 'Red Cross' nurses from England, with some of the 'leading surgeons instructing and directing. And these ladies would have been hunting, or playing golf otherwise!' Back-tracking on his earlier advocacy of federalism, Crozier now believed that if Ulster supported a federal solution, it would be 'terribly difficult … to convince our church folk in the South that we have not betrayed them'. Temporary exclusion was 'impossible', as 'racial and religious prejudice would increase as the end of the exclusion period came nearer'. The best solution was to hear the 'voice of the people' in a general election.[125] Crozier's initial attraction to a federal solution should not be exaggerated, but it did fore-shadow his later support for such a scheme at the Irish Convention, in 1918. His tentative advocacy of federalism also provides a parallel with Edward Carson, who pushed privately, and discreetly, for a federal-devolutionary scheme in 1913 and early 1914.[126] Carson could not publicly back a federal solution, as doing so 'would have destroyed his position among his supporters'.[127] Crozier backed away for similar reasons, fearful that a federal deal would be seen as the aban-donment of southern members of the Church of Ireland.

Crozier's apparent abhorrence of any outbreak of violence and his related intention to point the 'rank and file' in a more pacific direction suggested deep private unease at the increasing strength of the volunteer force. Crozier may have identified Davidson as a point of contact who could convey his assessment of the UVF to high-ranking figures in the government. Such hopes were partially ful-filled when Davidson informed Crozier that after talking with Andrew Bonar Law and Herbert Asquith, he believed the Curragh crisis had furthered and not hindered 'pacificatory possibilities'.[128] In holding out for a general election, Crozier pinned his hopes on a solution that could potentially return an unwelcome result for the unionists, as there was no guarantee the 'voice of the people' would be sympathetic to Ulster unionism. His advocacy of an election suggested he was not in favour of the last-ditch action of military resistance and preferred a con-stitutional way out of the Ulster crisis. He did not even include the permanent exclusion of any part of Ulster in his analysis of the various solutions available to unionists, probably for a similar reason to his rejection of federalism. Permanent exclusion would be a 'betrayal' of the southern Anglicans, leaving them at the mercy of a Dublin parliament.

Like Crozier, D'Arcy also hoped to influence Davidson in his dealings with the government. After Asquith announced his intention to introduce an amending bill to the Home Rule Bill, D'Arcy wrote to Davidson claiming Ulster was close to an outbreak of serious violence:

> If the Home Rule bill becomes law, without very thoroughgoing amend-ment being secured it may become impossible to restrain the forces which are held in check … If very great wisdom is not exercised, there may be a terrible explosion.[129]

D'Arcy wrote to Davidson again shortly after the amending bill had been intro-duced (a bill based on county option and a six-year exclusion period for the affected Ulster counties). He believed that making the Ulster settlement dependent upon a referendum to be held in six years would create 'bitter oppositions'. Nationalists would use 'every influence' to 'introduce more voters of their sort', while Protestant employers would be encouraged to 'get rid of R.C. and Nationalist workers'. D'Arcy thought it 'far better, if exclusion is to be the solution' for a 'clean cut' to be made 'at once by Act of Parliament by means of an agreement between the two great parties'.[130] There are two ways to read this correspondence with Davidson. On the one hand, it could have revealed D'Arcy's private unease at Ulster unionist militancy and fears that his calls for restraint were going unheeded. On the other hand, D'Arcy's courting of Davidson could have been intended as a form of lobbying in favour of Ulster exclusion. Davidson's reply to Crozier concerning the Curragh crisis proved he was in contact with leading figures at Westminster. By emphasising the risk of violence and offering a 'clean cut' as the solution to an impending civil war in Ireland, D'Arcy may have hoped Davidson would convey such views to the prime minister, Herbert Asquith.

D'Arcy did not elucidate whether he viewed exclusion as desirable on a four-county, six-county or nine-county basis. However, his desire for a clean cut, with its implications of permanency, distinguished his position from Crozier, whose desire for an election has been noted. In addition, at the start of August Crozier informed Davidson that exclusion from home rule on a religious basis 'would be the very worst'. Protestant counties would become more and more Protestant, 'the rest of Ireland more Roman – two watertight compartments'. Crozier believed a 'purely geographical separation' (presumably the exclusion of the province of Ulster) would avoid permanent separation. Nine-county exclusion would establish a 'strong Roman Catholic minority', inducing an Irish parliament 'to treat the government of Ireland as a solemn trust for all the people, and avoid the selfish and self destructive policy of such bodies as the Dublin and Sligo corporations'. Crozier's desire for a settlement that would in time produce Irish unity was based on his position as primate of an all-Ireland Church. He pointed out that the Presbyterians, 'whose people are all massed in the North ... do not realise as we do the danger of Ulster exclusion and are the more ready to accept the exclusion of 4 or 5 counties in which something like 300,000 of their co-religionists are living.' However, the Church of Ireland had a 'real stake' in the rest of Ireland.[131] Crozier's preference for a nine-county, temporary solution placed him at odds not just with D'Arcy but also with the Ulster unionist leadership, who one week earlier at the Buckingham Palace conference made clear they would settle for nothing less than permanent six-county exclusion.[132]

CONCLUSION

The original ending of *The Red Hand of Ulster* envisaged Germany offering assistance to the Ulster rebels. This offer of help caused the loyalists to realise the error of their ways and form an alliance with the government in the face of a common enemy. In an interview with the *New York Times*, Hannay claimed the foreign office wanted the ending altered 'in view of the delicate international situation'. However, as the outbreak of the First World War proved, Hannay's original ending was not, as his publisher claimed, 'illogical and fantastic'.[133] War changed entirely the situation in Ireland. Home rule was simultaneously placed on the statute book and suspended; the UVF made good its earlier protestations of loyalty to the Throne and Constitution by offering itself for military service. In hindsight, some tantalising premonitions of the UVF's subsequent role in the British army were provided in the first half of 1914. In March, the Loughgall contingent of the UVF carried out training in a scenario in which they provided assistance to a battalion of British troops under attack from German infantry.[134] Soldiers from the Bedfordshire regiment and the local UVF attended a service in Omagh parish church, 'in some cases actually sharing the same prayer book'.[135] In D'Arcy's April letter to *The Times* defending the UVF, he pointed out that the force was a 'body of troops, 110,000 strong, eagerly fitting themselves for military service, fired with enthusiasm for the flag, ready to die in defence of their British citizenship'. At a time when the regular army had difficulty in keeping up its supply of men, and when the Territorial force was far below strength, D'Arcy found it gratifying that 'there is in Ulster an armed force which would place itself at the disposal of the crown for the defence of the country'.[136]

Hannay's prophetic ability was not entirely obscured by the alteration to his original ending of *The Red Hand of Ulster*. His telling of an imagined Ulster unionist rebellion bore an uncanny resemblance to events in Ulster in 1913–14. Many Church of Ireland clergy evoked comparisons with Hannay's dean, welcoming UVF contingents to church services, providing drilling areas in the form of church grounds, and taking an active part in the force as volunteers. However, the dean was a caricature of clerical opposition to home rule and support for militancy. In reality, many Church of Ireland clergy in Ulster were not prepared to provoke a rebellion and viewed the UVF as an agent of social order, designed to restrain the rank and file. Whether the UVF was an agent of social order is open to question. Tim Bowman has argued the UVF should be viewed as a 'bottom-up' movement, the inevitable outcome of the independent drilling organised by Orange lodges and unionist clubs in 1911–12.[137] The need for repeated requests for order from leading clergymen could be interpreted as recognition that the UVF was not the malleable tool of the Ulster unionist (or indeed clerical) leadership.

Ecclesiastical patronage of the UVF was not so surprising when placed in the wider context of a growing acceptance in church and society for militaristic organisations and hobbies. However, the UVF was a different prospect to a rifle club or a uniformed Church organisation such as the Church Lads' Brigade. By supporting the UVF, clergy were identified with a force that potentially entailed armed resistance to the state. Wolffe argues that organised religion, while reflecting society as a whole, also had a formative influence in strengthening support for war, by producing nationalism of a quasi-religious kind.[138] The Church of Ireland played a similar role in Ulster. Clergy utilised arguments developed to justify the Ulster Covenant to legitimise the UVF – the Constitution was suspended; the government was not the lawful authority; there was no mandate for home rule without a general election – that reflected the politics of unionism. However, the unique contribution of the clergy was their ability to offer the UVF divine endorsement. While difficult to assess the influence of religious arguments, it is likely they convinced devout members of the Church of Ireland (and clergy) to abandon any doubts about their support for the UVF.

The UVF was the practical outworking of the Ulster Covenant's promise to oppose home rule by any means necessary. D'Arcy accepted the 'clean cut' solution, excluding (probably) the six north-eastern Ulster counties from home rule. He viewed the UVF as a 'safety valve' for the rank and file; his correspondence with Archbishop Davidson implied he also viewed the force as a means of convincing the government of the folly of imposing home rule on Ulster. The establishment of the UVF, and the negotiations between the key political players in 1913–14, largely confirmed Ulster unionism's increasing move away from all-Ireland unionism. Some idea of the gulf developing between the Church of Ireland in Ulster and the south and west of Ireland was demonstrated by a dispute between D'Arcy and Sterling Berry, the bishop of Killaloe, at the start of the war.

Speaking at his diocesan synod, Berry (an opponent of clerical support for the Ulster Covenant) declared it a Christian's duty to 'accept and obey' an act of parliament when it became law, pointing in support to Christ's command to 'Render unto Caesar'.[139] Berry's provocative address drew a stinging retort from D'Arcy, who claimed in a letter to the *Church of Ireland Gazette* that only the Quakers held to the same extent his fellow bishop's interpretation of the biblical texts used to justify 'passive obedience'. Ulstermen had armed in defence of their 'birthright', and their struggle was 'against revolution'. Characteristically, alongside such strident rhetoric was D'Arcy's emphasis on the propaganda value of the UVF, which was formed 'not to bring about fighting, but to make Ulster so strong that she could not be coerced'. The outbreak of war provided a retrospective seal of approval to the UVF, which had drilled 100,000 men ready for service.[140]

Crozier shared D'Arcy's conservative, top-down view of the UVF as a propaganda weapon, but significantly differed from D'Arcy as to the area of Ulster to be excluded from home rule. Crozier initially appeared attracted to some form of federal solution to the impasse, but came to favour nine-county exclusion (while preferring a general election as a means of defeating home rule *tout court*) because he believed it held out the possibility of future reconciliation. The combination of Crozier's all-Ireland unionism and overt identification with Ulster unionism was strained by his support for the Ulster Covenant; the events of 1913–14 left him in an increasingly untenable position, supporting a force pledged to protect Ulster in the case of home rule but rejecting the viability of the 'clean cut' solution. Crozier was also influenced by the threat posed to the unity of the Church of Ireland – the dispute between D'Arcy and Berry suggested the potential for public division within the Church leadership over home rule, and specifically the issue of Ulster. The war granted Crozier a temporary reprieve from having to decide one way or the other where his public sympathies lay – with Ulster or all-Ireland unionism – although the Easter Rising and Irish Convention would revive the difficulty.[141]

Alvin Jackson has warned that the 'great moral questions' raised by the third Home Rule Bill crisis are 'incapable of definitive resolution' and are best left to 'priests and philosophers rather than the historian'.[142] However, Church of Ireland involvement in the UVF suggested the 'priests' were culpable in the moral confusion of the period. Some clergy seemed willing to storm the battlements of the Home Rule Bill, while others urged restraint. It is possible many clergy, like their episcopal superiors in Down and Armagh, were divided in their attitude towards the UVF. They recognised the damage that could be done to their standing if they refused to support the force and probably wanted to play a role in the movement. However, at the same time, many clergy probably recognised that if civil war or, less melodramatically, rioting did break out, they would be complicit in a paramilitary force armed with illegal weapons. The ambiguities and complexities in the volunteers' position as 'loyal rebels' were illustrated by the different armies attending church services around Ulster in 1914. In St Mark's, Newtownards, the year began with the UVF being anointed by the leading Anglican churchman in Ireland, and ended with the twelfth battalion of the Royal Irish Rifles, camped near Newtownards, attending morning worship.[143] Fortunately for the Church of Ireland, the 'red hand of Ulster' was not waved in 1914, but this was more through luck – or providence – than judgement, as the potential battlefield of Ulster was replaced by the actual battlefields of France.

NOTES

1. George Birmingham, *The Red Hand of Ulster* (London, 1912).
2. Brian Taylor, *The Life and Writings of James Owen Hannay (George A. Birmingham) 1865–1950* (New York, 1995), p.112.
3. Ibid., p.117.
4. B. Mac Giolla Choille, *Intelligence Notes, 1913–1916* (Dublin, 1966), p.20.
5. *Fermanagh Times*, 16 May 1912.
6. District inspector reports, 24, 27, 30 July 1912, 10 August 1912, 14 September 1912 (National Archives, Kew, confidential reports to Dublin Castle, CO/904/27/227; ibid., CO/904/27/222; ibid., CO/904/27/218; ibid., CO/904/27/214–16; ibid., CO/904/27/185–6).
7. District inspector reports, 11 July 1912, 6 September 1912 (ibid., CO/904/27/250; CO/904/27/208–9).
8. C. Townshend, *Easter 1916* (London, 2005), p.33; R. McNeill, *Ulster's Stand for Union* (London, 1922), p.57.
9. See Townshend, *Easter 1916*, p.33.
10. *Fermanagh Times*, 6 April 1911.
11. *Ulster Gazette and Armagh Standard*, 2 September 1911.
12. *Northern Constitution*, 23 September 1911.
13. *Irish Churchman*, 3 February 1911.
14. Ibid., 14, 28 July 1911.
15. John Wolffe, *God and Greater Britain: Religion and National Life in Britain and Ireland, 1843–1945* (London, 1994), pp.229–30.
16. Ibid., p.229.
17. *Irish Churchman*, 14 July 1911.
18. *Belfast Weekly Telegraph*, 8 February 1913.
19. Wolffe, *God and Greater Britain*, p.230.
20. Townshend, *Easter 1916*, pp.34–5; A. Jackson, *Home Rule: An Irish History, 1800–2000* (London, 2003), p.120.
21. Report to chief secretary, 15 March 1913 (NA, confidential reports to Dublin Castle, CO/904/27 /694–6).
22. Paul Bew, *Ideology and the Irish Question* (Oxford, 1994), pp.93–4.
23. County inspector reports, July 1913 (NA, CO/904/27/511).
24. Order of service for 1st battalion South Down regiment, 8 March 1914, in St Paul's Castlewellan; order of service for 1st battalion South Down regiment, 5 April 1914, in Clough Presbyterian church (Public Record Office of Northern Ireland (PRONI), Seaforde UVF papers, D/1263/4).
25. T.R.P. McCammond to north Antrim UVF commanders, 29 July 1914 (ibid., O'Neill papers, D/1238/194).
26. Lord Dunleath to Lady Londonderry [?], 1914 (ibid., Lady Londonderry papers, D/2847/1/7/23).
27. *Newtownards Chronicle*, 24 January 1914.
28. *Ulster Gazette*, 28 March 1914.
29. Minute book of UVF County Fermanagh committee, 19 December 1912 (PRONI, Fermanagh UVF papers, D/1402/3/2).
30. County inspector reports, July 1913 (NA, CO/904/27/511).
31. *Fermanagh Times*, 6 November 1913; 4 December 1913.
32. Ibid., 4 December 1913.
33. Ibid.
34. Drill inspection notebook, 30 July 1913 (PRONI, Sir Charles Falls papers, D/1390/19/1).
35. Ibid., 4 August 1913.
36. Ibid., 19 August 1913.
37. Fermanagh UVF membership book (ibid., Fermanagh UVF papers, D/1402/4/1).
38. County inspector reports, July 1913 (NA, confidential reports to Dublin Castle, CO/904/27/511).
39. The rector of Grange headed the nursing corps of his local UVF contingent, *Ulster Gazette*, 11 October 1913; Rev. M. Hogg acted as a sanitary officer at an inspection of the Keady UVF ambulance corps, ibid., 28 March 1914.
40. Canon Clarke presented prizes to the UVF contingent in Dungonnell, *Ballymena Observer*, 20 March 1914.
41. Rev. T. McCreight and his wife won the croquet tournament but lost in the final of the lawn tennis at a UVF fundraising fête in Ballynahinch, *Down Recorder*, 3 January 1914.
42. North Antrim UVF papers, 10 January 1914 (PRONI, O'Neill papers, D/1238/3b).
43. St Thomas' vestry minute book, 11 November 1913 (PRONI, CR/1/36/D/4).
44. *Lisburn Standard*, 1 November 1913.
45. *Northern Constitution*, 14 June 1913.

46. *Belfast Weekly Telegraph*, 19 July 1913.
47. *Northern Constitution*, 4 October 1913.
48. *Belfast Weekly Telegraph*, 11 March 1911.
49. M. Foy, 'The Ulster Volunteer Force: its domestic development and political importance in the period 1913–1920' (Queen's University Belfast, unpublished Ph.D. thesis, 1986), pp.58–9.
50. R.G.S. King, *Ulster's Protest: Her Industrial, Political, Imperial Reasons for Refusing to Submit to Home Rule. An Appeal to Great Britain* (Derry, 1913), pp.20–4.
51. *Northern Constitution*, 31 May 1913; the firework display was an improvement on the 1912 celebration in the town, when the firing of a canon was dispensed with owing to the illness of an elderly resident (ibid., 1 June 1912).
52. P. Buckland, *Irish Unionism II: Ulster Unionism and the Origins of Northern Ireland, 1886–1922* (Dublin, 1973), pp.65–6.
53. R.G.S. King, *Ulster's Refusal to Submit to a Roman Catholic Parliament, Stated and Justified* (Derry, 1914), p.3.
54. Ibid., p.21.
55. *Belfast Newsletter*, 26 September 1913.
56. *Lurgan Mail*, 4 October 1913.
57. For example, at Bangor, Portaferry and Portadown: see *Belfast Newsletter*, 9, 18, 21 February 1914.
58. Ibid., 10 March 1914.
59. Ibid., 5 January 1914.
60. Ibid., 9 March 1914.
61. *Lurgan Mail*, 29 March 1913. Hobson expressed similar sentiments at a Unionist demonstration against Home Rule in Portadown in August: ibid., 16 August 1913.
62. *Lisburn Standard*, 4 October 1913.
63. *Belfast Newsletter*, 5 January 1914.
64. Ibid., 6 January 1913.
65. Ibid., 2 February 1914.
66. *Fermanagh Times*, 19 March 1914.
67. *Lurgan Mail*, 18 April 1914.
68. Ibid., 30 May 1914.
69. Buckland, *Ulster Unionism II*, p.66.
70. Charles Townshend, *Political Violence in Ireland: Government and Resistance since 1848* (Oxford, 1983), p.249.
71. Townshend, *Easter 1916*, p.33.
72. Alvin Jackson, *Sir Edward Carson* (Dublin, 1993), p.36; Jackson, *Home Rule*, p.120.
73. Cyril Falls, *The History of the 36th Ulster Division* (Belfast, 1922), p.2.
74. J.J. Lee, *Ireland 1912–1985* (Cambridge, 1989), p.17.
75. *Northern Constitution*, 25 October 1913.
76. For example, in Kilrea, Camus Juxta, Lower Moville, Donagheady and Culdaff (in Donegal): Kilrea vestry minute book, 7 November 1913 (PRONI, MIC/1/55); Camus Juxta vestry minute book, 2 December 1913 (ibid., MIC/1/307/D/3); Lower Moville and St Columba's vestry minute book, 5 December 1913 (ibid., MIC/1/138/D/1); Donagheady vestry minute book, 9 December 1913 (ibid., MIC/1/35/1); Culdaff vestry minute book, 9 December 1913 (ibid., MIC/1/278/D/4).
77. Drumclamph vestry minute book, 8 December 1913 (ibid., MIC/1/304/D/1).
78. Kilbroney vestry minute book, 2 February 1914 (ibid., MIC/1/88).
79. Ibid., 11 February 1914.
80. Down vestry minute book, 12 June 1914 (ibid., CR/33/DB/2).
81. Lower Moville and St Columba's vestry minute book, 8 December 1914 (ibid., MIC/1/138/D/1).
82. Belleek vestry minute book, 5 May 1914 (ibid., MIC/1/270/D/1).
83. Ibid., 22 September 1914.
84. St Thomas' vestry minute book, 4 February 1914 (ibid., CR/1/36/D/4).
85. Ibid., 11 February 1914.
86. Ibid., 7 March 1914.
87. Mary Magdalene vestry minute book, 26 February 1914 (private possession); St Jude's vestry minute book, 23 March 1914 (private possession).
88. Lisburn Cathedral vestry minute book, 10 March (PRONI, CR/1/35/D/4).
89. Ibid., 7 April 1914.
90. *Lisburn Standard*, 7 August 1914.
91. Lady Spender diary, 2 August 1914 (PRONI, Lady Spender papers, D/1633/2/19).
92. Lisburn Cathedral magazine, September 1914 (private possession).

93. Lisburn Cathedral vestry minute book, 11 August 1914 (PRONI, CR/1/35/D/4). Ironically, in 1911 the Cathedral Literary and Debating Society held a meeting at which 'Women's suffrage' was discussed with the 'greatest calmness', Lisburn Cathedral magazine, January 1911 (private possession).
94. *Newtownards Chronicle*, 7 February 1914; *Lisburn Standard*, 6 March 1914, 17 April 1914; *Ballymena Observer*, 8 May 1914.
95. *Belfast Weekly Telegraph*, 4 October 1913.
96. *Belfast Newsletter*, 30 October 1913.
97. Ibid., 11 February 1914.
98. Ibid., 24 March 1914.
99. Ibid., 30 March 1914.
100. *Lurgan Mail*, 11 April 1914.
101. *The Times*, 23 April 1914.
102. Ibid., 2 May 1914.
103. Ibid., 4 May 1914.
104. Ibid., 7 May 1914.
105. Charles Frederick D'Arcy, *The Adventures of a Bishop* (London, 1934), p.192.
106. Hugh Shearman, *Not an Inch: A Study of Northern Ireland and Lord Craigavon* (London, 1942), p.69.
107. *Ulster Gazette*, 11 October 1913.
108. *Newtownards Chronicle*, 24 January 1914.
109. *Belfast Newsletter*, 23 March 1914.
110. *Lurgan Mail*, 11 April 1914.
111. Wilfred Spender to C. Brett Ingram, 1959 (PRONI, Spender papers, D/1295/2/6).
112. *Belfast Newsletter*, 12 March 1914.
113. Ibid., 16 March 1914.
114. F.B. Meyer to Randall Davidson, 10 October 1913; Davidson to Meyer, 4 December 1913 (Lambeth Palace Library, Davidson papers, vol. 389/70–1; vol. 389/93–5).
115. J. Gough McCormick to Davidson, 18 December 1913 (ibid., vol. 389/122).
116. Davidson circular to English bishops, 19 December 1913 (ibid., vol. 389/129).
117. *Belfast Newsletter*, 1 January 1914.
118. Ibid., 5 January 1914.
119. G.K.A. Bell, *Randall Davidson: Archbishop of Canterbury, vol. I* (Oxford, 1935), p.722.
120. H.H. Henson, *Retrospective of an Unimportant Life, vol. I, 1863–1920* (Oxford, 1942), p.171; although Henson doubted the wisdom of the setting-up of a provisional government in Ulster (ibid., p.170).
121. House of Bishops resolution, January 1914 (Lambeth Palace Library, Davidson papers, vol. 389/209–10).
122. *Belfast Newsletter*, 2 January 1914.
123. Ibid., 4 March 1914.
124. John Baptist Crozier to Davidson, 4 April 1914 (Lambeth Palace Library, Davidson papers, vol. 389/309–12).
125. Crozier to Davidson, Easter Day 1914 (ibid., vol. 389/319–26).
126. J. Smith, 'Federalism, devolution and partition: Sir Edward Carson and the search for a compromise on the third Home Rule bill, 1913–14', *Irish Historical Studies*, 35, 14 (2007), pp.496–518.
127. Ibid., p.518.
128. Davidson to Crozier, 9 April 1914 (ibid., vol. 389/316); Davidson acted as an intermediary between Asquith and Bonar Law in the aftermath of the Curragh Crisis (Bell, *Archbishop Davidson*, pp.726–8).
129. D'Arcy to Davidson, 3 May 1914 (Lambeth Palace Library, Davidson papers, vol. 389/327).
130. D'Arcy to Davidson, 24 May 1914 (ibid., vol. 389/338–9).
131. Crozier to Davidson, 5 August 1914 (Lambeth Palace Library, Davidson papers, vol. 390/72–82).
132. C. O'Leary and P. Maume, *Controversial Issues in Anglo-Irish Relations, 1910–1921* (Dublin, 2004), p.43.
133. *New York Times*, 28 February 1915 (TCD, Hannay papers, Mss/3436/PC 7).
134. *Ulster Gazette*, 14 March 1914.
135. *Belfast Newsletter*, 23 March 1914.
136. *The Times*, 23 April 1914.
137. T. Bowman, 'The Ulster Volunteer Force, 1910–1920: new perspectives', in D.G. Boyce and A. O'Day (eds), *The Ulster Crisis* (London, 2006); also A. Gailey, 'King Carson: an essay on the invention of leadership', *Irish Historical Studies*, vol. 30 (1996), p.79.
138. Wolffe, *God and Greater Britain*, p.236.

139. *Church of Ireland Gazette*, 7 August 1914.
140. Ibid., 14 August 1914.
141. See Chapters 5 and 6, of this volume.
142. Jackson, *Home Rule*, p 141.
143. *Newtownards Chronicle*, 24 January 1914, 14 December 1914.

5

'The seal of lofty purpose and pure patriotism'?
The Church of Ireland and the Outbreak
of the Great War

The Church of Ireland's response to the First World War was similar to Churches across Europe. The war was given the unmistakeable air of a religious crusade by churches in the belligerent states. Clergy and theologians in France and Germany played a 'considerable part' in justifying participation in the war, 'whether in terms of its justness and virtue, or by claiming that God was with their nation's defensive struggle'.[1] More pertinently for a study of the Church of Ireland, most clergy of the Church of England 'unhesitatingly and confidently asserted' that Britain had no option but to declare war on Germany. German militarism had, it was claimed, repudiated the Sermon on the Mount, thus forcing Britain to engage in a 'just and holy war'.[2] However, while the response of the Church of England to the war is relatively well documented, there has been a lack of similar work on the Church of Ireland.[3] Accounts are brief and tend to focus solely on the views of the episcopate and higher clergy.[4] The paucity of Church of Ireland historiography of the war supports Keith Jeffery's assertion that the role of the Irish Churches in supporting or opposing the war, and dealing with the bereavement caused by the war, is a 'largely neglected area of study'.[5] Correcting this neglect shows there were many parallels between how the Anglican Churches in England and Ireland viewed the war. Like the Church of England, the Church of Ireland proved a consistent and vocal supporter of the British war effort. The Church, from archbishops to lower clergy and select vestries, encouraged recruitment and constructed a moral basis for Britain's involvement in the war. However, the political context in Ireland in 1914 and events in Ireland during the war ensured that certain aspects of the Church of Ireland's response to the war were unique.

A 'KRUPP GUN' OR THE CROSS: THE MORALITY OF WAR

Archbishop John Baptist Crozier quickly emerged as a vocal supporter of Britain's war effort, and consistently articulated the righteousness of Britain's participation. Preaching in Armagh shortly after the outbreak of war, Crozier defended the moral integrity of Britain's intervention. England had 'striven hard for peace' but had been forced to 'fight for the weaker nation who relied on England's honour and England's pride'. In contrast to the moral virtue of fighting a 'righteous war', Crozier noted national 'evils a thousand times worse', such as gambling, sexual 'impurity', and drunkenness. In the context of such immorality, Crozier implied that soldiers who died sacrificially in war would atone for the United Kingdom's national sin by restoring the 'nation's character'.[6] In a pastoral, Crozier expressed a similar belief in the morally vivifying benefit of war, which would 'develop all that is noblest and best in our character and conduct'. Crozier's pastoral also emphasised the necessity of constant prayerfulness. The implicit assumption that God would answer their prayers provided further legitimisation of Britain's intervention in the war. As the 'very existence of our Empire and of our homes is at stake', they needed to commit their cause to 'God Almighty, and to pray to Him in humble penitence and faith for His comfort, guidance and protection'.[7] Calls for prayer issued in parish magazines sustained this spiritual view of the war. In late 1914, Bray parish church issued a list of members involved in the war, detailing regiments and places of service, so that parishioners could pray for them by name.[8] A similar concern for focused and committed prayer was displayed in St Peter's in Dublin, where the rector assigned particular days to members of the congregation to attend daily intercessory services.[9]

In addition to asserting the righteousness of Britain's involvement in the war, Crozier painted Germany as a godless, merciless enemy. Preaching a farewell sermon to UVF men who had enlisted for Kitchener's new army, Crozier repeated the commonly accepted explanation of 'England's' participation in the war as a selfless desire to defend 'weaker nations', allowing a contrast to be drawn with Germany: 'on the one hand we have the ideals of Jesus Christ – justice and mercy, honour and truth. On the other a cruel and degraded spirit of militarism, based openly on the conduct of Attila the Hun.' The destruction of Louvain provided evidence of the 'gross materialism' of German philosophy and the 'ever-growing rationalism and atheism' of a once Christian nation. Against such an enemy, the volunteers had the right to 'look for the Divine presence, because you are carrying out God's great law of vicarious sacrifice'.[10] In common with German and British preachers throughout the war, Crozier often employed the rhetoric of sacrifice and comparisons with Christ to grant some degree of sanctity to soldiers' wartime experience.[11] In a sermon at the Clandeboye training camp in October 1914, he asserted that the soldiers who had perished already in the war had 'died that we might live; they have followed in the steps of Christ and have given their lives as a ransom for many'.[12] He repeated these sentiments at the 1915 General Synod, comparing a dead soldier's sacrifice to that of Christ's.[13] Such language and imagery not only conferred glory on the dead soldiers, but attempted to imbue their deaths with some meaning. Crozier may also have employed the Christ comparison to encourage those who had not enlisted by emphasising the inherent righteousness of fighting (and dying) for one's country.

Bishop Charles Frederick D'Arcy also articulated the moral case for war. Preaching at Lambeg church, D'Arcy hoped God would continue to watch over Great Britain so that 'she should continue as a witness for liberty and against all forms of tyranny'.[14] The plight of Belgium also served to illustrate the righteousness of Britain's involvement in the war. At a public meeting in Bushmills, held to discuss the causes of the war, D'Arcy claimed Britain's desire to uphold her treaty obligations required her to participate in the war as, having 'pledged herself' to Belgium, 'Britain was prepared to sacrifice everything that her word might be kept'. Therefore, Britain was engaged in a 'righteous war, and a war of honour'.[15]

D'Arcy and Crozier defended participation in the war as it provided resistance to German aggression and evidence of Britain's moral righteousness. Britain's involvement in the war was interpreted in terms of the British national myth, with its notions of freedom, liberty and fair play.[16] D'Arcy confirmed his Whiggish perception of Britain's role in the war in a sermon in Belfast Cathedral.

Great Britain stood for 'human liberty'; Britain's 'free institutions' served as models for the whole modern world, while Britain had also championed the cause of the oppressed, leading the way in the liberation of slaves and the suppression of the slave trade. Therefore, if Britain was to be 'true for what she stands for in the world', she must be 'ready to give herself and all resources at the present time'. Britain's glorious liberal lineage and contribution to the world naturally contrasted with Germany, which was now possessed by a 'very terrible spirit' of atheism, materialism and greed. He blamed Friedrich Nietzsche for Germany's 'religious decline', as he had been the 'principal teacher' of the philosophy now dominating German thought. Nietzsche's philosophy taught that Christianity was a 'religion for slaves' and that 'might is right'. Such principles guided the German emperor, although he took the name of God 'upon his lips'.[17] At a sermon in St Peter's, Belfast, D'Arcy presented Nietzsche as the 'apostle of force', whose philosophy 'destroyed the Christian graces of mercy and piety' and found its 'logical expression in the barbarities perpetuated in Belgium and France'.[18]

D'Arcy's explanation of Germany's alleged madness and barbarity as the result of immoral thought was to be expected from an aspiring philosopher-bishop. However, it was a common theme in British sermons during the war to posit Nietzsche, among others (the historian Heinrich von Trietschke and General Friedrich von Bernhardi were other oft-cited thinkers and with Nietzsche made up the 'unholy trinity' of German thought), as the harbingers of Germany's fall from grace.[19] Preachers alleged that Nietzsche's philosophy and social Darwinism found fertile ground in Germany due to the drift towards critical rationalism, which had undermined confidence in the reliability of the Bible.[20] In practice, such thought led to what was termed the doctrine of the 'amoral state' – the idea that the state was the judge of its own morality, as it had no body to constrain its action. Preachers saw the amoral state doctrine practised in the early months of the war in the German invasion of Belgium and destruction of Louvain.[21] Germany's practice of *realpolitik* was held to contradict the Bible's claim that nations were responsible to God for their ethical conduct (many Old Testament examples were used to illustrate this critique of Germany). Therefore, if Germany was guilty of flouting God's moral law, Britain was morally obliged to intervene in the war.[22] For the Church of Ireland, as with imperial Anglicanism,[23] it took the outbreak of war to generate this critique – before 1914 there was little evidence in Church of Ireland journals or sermons of opposition to German thought.

D'Arcy further elaborated on his belief in the moral basis of the war in an article entitled 'The ethics of war' published in the Church of Ireland periodical, *Irish Church Quarterly*. D'Arcy considered the morality of war as opposed to 'weak submission' and 'passive endurance' in the light of Christian ethical principles and the Sermon on the Mount.[24] He argued the community was the trustee of the rights of the individual – if the individual was attacked, the community must act in defence. Therefore, there was nothing 'unspiritual' in the use of force 'provided the force be rightly directed. Might is in its place when it is the servant of right.' D'Arcy's defence of the legitimacy of armed force provided support for what he termed 'defensive warfare' – if the community was bound to defend itself and its members from violence from within, it was also obliged to protect itself from violent aggression from without.[25] However, aggressive warfare – of which Germany was guilty – was as 'incapable of moral justification as highway robbery'. War that was purely selfish in origin was always wrong and 'inhuman' because the 'social organisation of man was dependent upon the preservation of morality'.[26] D'Arcy believed the application by Germany of social Darwinian theory to warfare was 'scientifically, a hideous blunder' as the destruction of millions by machinery 'will not tend to the survival of the fittest'.[27] While admitting Christ's teaching of non-resistance in the Sermon on the Mount caused much doubt and hesitation, D'Arcy maintained no moral rule was of 'quite universal application', as moral rules tended to limit one another and were limited in their application by circumstances.[28] The moral rule of non-resistance did not apply in circumstances when an individual or state was forced to act as the 'trustee' of the rights of others, as in the case of Britain towards Belgium.[29]

D'Arcy's article provoked a reply from Sterling Berry, bishop of Killaloe, published in the April 1915 edition of *Irish Church Quarterly*. Berry disagreed with D'Arcy's interpretation of the Sermon on the Mount, as he believed Christ's teaching left no 'loophole' for exceptions.[30] He asked if D'Arcy would apply the same principle of exceptions to other moral laws, such as forgiveness.[31] Berry claimed the attitude towards non-resistance advocated by D'Arcy was adopted by most Christians and made the law of non-resistance in practice a 'dead letter', as illustrated by Christian support for wars that were 'wholly unrighteous' in their aims, such as the Boer War.[32] For Berry, the principle of non-resistance was practical, and was attainable for states if they did not measure greatness in terms of wealth, territory or armaments.[33] His article drew a fairly stinging retort from D'Arcy, who claimed Berry was treating the Sermon on the Mount as legislation rather than parable. Berry's argument amounted to an acceptance that 'submission to violence is an absolute rule for all Christian people. To resist at all is evil.' For D'Arcy, such a 'doctrine' of non-resistance, while consistent logically, was contrary to ordinary conscience and reason.[34] D'Arcy argued that if non-resistance was the correct doctrine to follow, Britain should have left Belgium and France to face Germany alone and in addition was 'wrong in defending the liberties and possessions of her own people by force of arms'.[35] Berry responded by claiming Britain's treaty obligations left no option but to go to war and defend the violated neutrality of Belgium. However, the war was the result of the unchristian principles that had dominated the life of western Christendom, and of which both Church and nation needed to repent.[36]

D'Arcy's articulation of just war theory was similar to preachers in both England and Germany. As D'Arcy himself acknowledged, a 'careful hermeneutic' of the Sermon on the Mount was developed, which cast Jesus' words as parable, proverb or paradox.[37] In addition, as Hoover argues, preachers in Germany and Britain suggested that love of enemies and non-retaliation were ethical principles requiring critical evaluation before application, a point made by D'Arcy in his *Irish Church Quarterly* controversy with Berry.[38] D'Arcy's just war defence may also have been influenced by localised factors. His belief in 'defensive warfare', resting on an assumption that the community was obliged to bind together to resist violent aggression, bore some resemblance to arguments used in support of the Ulster Covenant. On a more general level, D'Arcy's patronage of Ulster unionist militancy since 1912 naturally fed into his *Irish Church Quarterly* articles supporting the 'ethics of war'. Similarly, Berry's opposition to D'Arcy's stance had prewar antecedents. In 1912 Berry opposed the Ulster Covenant on the basis that a Church should not be involved in politics.[39] Such a quiescent view of the Church's role in society was reflected in Berry's advocacy of 'non-resistance'. However, Berry was unusual in opposing intervention in the war – the majority of clergymen, including those in the south who opposed the Church's identification with Ulster Day, or those, like James Owen Hannay who were sympathetic to home rule, supported the British war effort.[40]

As with their episcopal superiors, Church of Ireland parochial clergy supported Britain's entry into the war largely on the basis of the need to defeat the supposed barbarity of Germany. Walter Bentley, who preached at a service of intercession in St George's, Belfast, believed 'a greater case of wanton aggression ... of unnational unrighteousness than that presented by Germany perhaps the world had never known'.[41] S.I. Graham, preaching in Down Cathedral, declared Germany aimed to 'trample on the weak and unoffending with her iron heel after smashing them with her mailed fist'. Graham identified Britain's role in the war with the 'cause of right, that is, the cause of God', which left him confident that they were 'fully justified in depending on and expecting God's aid'.[42] The *Irish Churchman* questioned the sanity of the German emperor for urging his people to 'invoke the blessing of God' on the German army. Such 'effrontery' demonstrated the emperor's 'unsound' mental condition, as 'the war in which he is engaged is a wholly unrighteous and cruel war and deserves to bring down the wrath of Almighty God'.[43] Rev. W.S. Kerr reasoned Germany's declaration of war and conduct during the war was the result of the 'tone of thought that has spread of late in that country'. The 'glorification of naked force' propounded in the philosophy of Friedrich Nietzsche had been applied to 'practical concerns' by German leaders such as General Bernhardi, which ultimately meant Germany's declaration of war was a 'deliberate, scientific assault on Christianity, backed up by the mightiest armed force the world has ever known'. German militarism was attempting to establish a world religion, the symbol of which would be a 'Krupp gun instead of a cross'.[44] The Donnybrook parish magazine posited Britain's involvement in the war as the fulfilment of a bounden obligation to protect weak nations against a Germany that followed the philosophy of Nietzsche, creating a 'cult' in which the 'worship of force is the god to be honoured above all gods'.[45] George Stephenson, rector of Mary Magdalene in Belfast, described the war as a battle for 'true civilisation' against German militarism, the 'supreme ideal of German life'.[46]

The Mary Magdalene parish magazine proved a valuable vehicle for reinforcing a spiritual view of the war. For example, in July 1916 a letter was published from Robert Browning, a parishioner fighting in France. Browning alluded to the connection he felt existed between his Christian faith and involvement in the army. He was glad to have 'signed the pledge to follow Christ faithfully', and was a 'soldier of both Kings' who sought to 'lead others in the same direction'.[47] The thoughts expressed in 1918 by Lewis Crooks, the newly installed rector of Knockbreda, were similar to those of Stephenson at the outbreak of war. Speaking at Knockbreda's annual vestry meeting, Crooks utilised the 'big words' identified by Keith Jeffery as important in motivating participation in the war.[48] Crooks asserted the empire was not fighting in the war for self-aggrandisement, 'but for the sake of justice, mercy, and truth, and we thanked God not only for the superb valour but the patient fortitude' of their troops. The 'Prussian drill sergeant' and British soldier were representatives of 'two diametrically opposed ideas of civilisation'. Germany was the 'moral outcast' of the modern world, while the empire stood for 'progress' and the 'highest and divinest ideals of the human race'.[49]

Besides this setting of the righteousness of Britain alongside Germany's spiritual degradation, the moral aspect of the war was emphasised in the added impetus given to the temperance movement. Early in the war, the *Irish Churchman* lamented the 'treating' of soldiers, as 'nothing is more likely to unfit soldiers for the toils and fatigue of a campaign than strong drink'.[50] In a letter to the clergy of his diocese, D'Arcy pointed to the need for 'some great moral sacrifice on the part of the whole nation', emphasising that it was the 'special duty' of clergy to bring before their parishioners the need for temperance.[51] D'Arcy had drawn attention to a problem that was raising concern among the government. The chancellor, David Lloyd George, asked Randall Davidson (archbishop of Canterbury) to take the lead in appealing for total abstinence.[52] In March 1915 the king gave up alcohol for the duration of the war, a move supported in a signed statement by the archbishops of Canterbury and York and the leaders of the Catholic Church and Free Church council.[53]

At a parish level in the Church of Ireland, clergy and vestries encouraged temperance, probably motivated as much by the king's abstention from alcohol as by the urgings of their bishops. At St Jude's general vestry meeting in 1915, Canon Davis encouraged the congregation to follow the example of the king and refrain from alcohol for the course of the war. Such self-denial demonstrated appreciation for the soldiers, 'who are pouring out their lifeblood like water for us'. A resolution was passed commending the example of the king to the congregation.[54] Mary Magdalene, Willowfield and Holywood passed similar resolutions.[55] St Comgall's in Bangor successfully opposed the sale of alcohol in the town. In May 1915 the select vestry appointed a deputation to meet the urban council in order to ask for restrictions on the sale of alcohol to soldiers.[56] In June 1915 the select vestry was informed that the 'object of the deputation had been achieved'.[57]

Demands for prohibition permeated all levels of Church government. The General Synod passed a resolution calling for 'abstention from alcoholic liquor during the period of the war'. The king was thanked for his 'noble example' and it was hoped there would be 'self-denial on the part of every individual of our race', so energy could be devoted to the war.[58] The House of Bishops passed a resolution calling for the extension to Ireland of the prohibition measures operating in England and Wales, where convictions for drunkenness during the war fell from 3,388 to 449 per annum, partly as a result of increased taxation on alcohol.[59] The resolution was sent to the lord-lieutenant, chief secretary and the MPs for Dublin University.[60]

While leading clergy in England leant their support to calls for prohibition, a number (for example, Hensley Henson and Charles Gore) opposed such moves as puritanical. Wilkinson suggests that in opposing moves for prohibition, such clergy displayed an Anglican distaste for committing to ethical positions closely identified with the politics and culture of dissent.[61] The Church of Ireland's demand for prohibition was probably more fervent than in the Church of England. The resolution of the House of Bishops suggested leading members of the Church were united in favouring prohibition, while the statements emanating from the General Synod and vestries proved that prohibition was supported at all levels within the Church. This more vocal demand may have been due to the lack of any effective legislation enforced in Ireland prohibiting the sale of alcohol. However, Church of Ireland involvement in prohibition may also have reflected the relatively close ties with 'dissenting' Churches. The united opposition to home rule (as well as the temperance movement before the war) had accustomed the Church of Ireland to acting in unison with the Presbyterian and Methodist Churches on political matters. In addition, clerical demands for individual and national moral reform, seen not only in temperance appeals but also in calls for greater self-sacrifice, built on the prewar anti-home rule arguments that God would providentially bless Irish Protestants and save them from home rule if they brought their lifestyle into line with his will, by confession of sin and increased religious observance. Similarly, if Britain relied upon God during the war it would be delivered from the perceived scourge of German militarism.

'A NOBLE ERRAND': ENCOURAGING PARTICIPATION IN THE WAR

A practical corollary of clerical justification for the war was an encouragement of recruitment. Crozier published an appeal for recruits in the *Church of Ireland Gazette* early in the war. For Irishmen to speak only of defending their own shores was, he asserted, 'a policy of cowardly and selfish isolation which must in the long run end in shame and confusion of face, as the war was one 'of self-preservation against barbarism and brutal excess'. Instead, 'brave men' were needed to face 'danger, difficulty, or death' in support of the empire. Crozier was sure that in the hour of trial Irishmen would not 'fail to support the flag'.[62] Crozier's explicit encouragement of recruitment was unsurprising in the context of Irish unionism at the start of the war. Besides unionists' emotional affinity with Britain, the political leaders of unionism realised that their self-designation as patriots and their identification of Ireland (and especially Ulster) with Britain could only be vindicated by active participation in the war.[63]

Crozier's support of recruitment was also unsurprising in the context of imperial Anglicanism at the start of the war. For Anglican bishops in Australia, encouraging recruitment was motivated by 'prudence' (military reality) and the sacred duty of serving the empire.[64] The majority of bishops in the Church of England were also keen advocates of recruitment. In a pastoral published in December 1914, Randall Davidson appealed for recruits.[65] However, although a firm supporter of recruitment, Davidson did not support Lord Derby's call for recruiting sermons as he considered official endorsement unwise.[66] On the other hand, Crozier was not averse to making recruiting appeals from the pulpit. Preaching to a congregation including local contingents of the UVF in Lurgan parish church, Crozier contrasted those who wavered and preferred 'their own comfort at home to their country's call' (whom he 'pitied') with the soldiers and sailors who 'represent to us the priceless value of sacrifice'. The members of the UVF who joined the army were thus going out on a 'noble errand' to give their lives 'if need be that we at home may live'.[67]

In a 1914 Ulster Day sermon, subsequently directed to be read in all the churches in his diocese, the bishop of Clogher, Maurice Day, also encouraged recruitment. Day's call for enlistment was supported by an example of martial fervour from the Old Testament (2 Chronicles 14) – the stand of Judah and Benjamin (an area 'probably not larger than the province of Ulster') against the massed ranks of Zerah, the Ethiopian ruler. Day pointed out that probably every man from the tribe of Benjamin and Judah 'enrolled himself as a soldier'. Although 'not a recruiting sergeant', Day hoped such enthusiasm would be replicated in Ulster. Those who failed to enlist when fit to do so were disloyal and complicit in any German victory, doing their part 'in allowing a mighty and tyrannous foe to prove victorious over our troops, and it might be … to invade and ravage our country'.[68]

As with their episcopal superiors, Church of Ireland parochial clergy actively encouraged enlistment in the army and involvement in the war effort. Recruiting appeals were issued at UVF meetings as well as during church services. Shortly after the outbreak of war, R.G.S. King, rector of Limavady and chaplain to the local UVF, urged the volunteers to join the war effort, at home or at the front. The *Northern Constitution* reported the majority at the meeting opted for home service.[69] At a church service, Rev. A.E. Sixsmith encouraged 700 UVF men to join Kitchener's army.[70] L.G. Pooler, archdeacon of Down, preached a recruiting sermon based on Matthew 25:34 ('how many loaves have ye?'). Pooler urged the congregation to offer the 'loaf' of service, suggesting that Ulster should have no difficulty in forming a division of 10,000 men.[71] The dean of Dromore issued an uncompromising call for recruitment in November. Preaching in Down Cathedral to Orangemen at the annual Gunpowder Plot commemoration service, Dean O'Loughlin claimed the war was a 'glorious opportunity' for younger men. If O'Loughlin had a son, he would tell him it was 'his bounden, his Christian duty to go'. O'Loughlin offered the young men in his congregation glory and 'certain' victory if they joined the army to fight the 'war of God against militarism'.[72] Equally strong support was demonstrated by the Church of Ireland in the south and west of the country. Parish magazines kept parishioners updated on the fate of church members at the front.[73] Rolls of honour erected in church porches or read aloud at services of intercession reminded parishioners of church members who had joined the forces.[74] By December 1914, forty-two members of Donnybrook parish had enlisted, serving 'King and country' as 'sailors, soldiers or medical officers', while seventy members from Taney parish (County Dublin) enlisted in the first months of the war.[75]

Churches proved eager to commend the example of parishioners who enlisted, and expressed sympathy with families who lost loved ones. St Comgall's in Bangor sought to express its support for members who enlisted by giving them a 'testament with suitable inscriptions'.[76] A visible reminder of enlistment from the ranks of Mary Magdalene (Belfast) members was provided by a roll of honour, erected in October 1914. The roll of honour listed all members who had joined the army or navy, and produced a great deal of satisfaction for the rector, George Stephenson. By October 1914, 100 parishioners had enlisted, a 'record of which any parish may be proud, and it bears striking testimony to the patriotism of our men'. Stephenson hoped God would 'strengthen and bless' the men in every way, 'and may the cause of righteousness with which our Empire is now identified be soon crowned with a great and lasting victory'.[77] The following month, the reality of the war was felt as the first condolences were offered to those from Mary Magdalene who had lost loved ones. The families were assured that 'the whole parish is proud of these young soldiers who have so nobly laid down their lives in defence of Empire and of home'.[78] By January 1915, Mary Magdalene's roll of honour had grown to 230 names, made up of men already fighting or in training. Stephenson attempted to boost morale by pointing to the success of Mary Magdalene members on active service. In July 1916, William McCadden had been promoted to first class petty officer; he had already received the Distinguished Conduct Medal. Two other members of the congregation were also noted as having been recently promoted. Such 'heroism and skill in the midst of such great danger by sea and land' from 'so many of our parishioners' was a source of 'pride and gratification to us all'.[79] In July 1917 special mention was made of the family of Anthony White, a parishioner whose six sons had enlisted, and one of whom had been awarded the Russian order of St George and St Stanislaus for gallantry in action.[80] However, tales of heroism were overshadowed by the increasing death toll among members of Mary Magdalene in the army and navy. In February 1917 the parish magazine recorded the death of Sergeant Major Scott, a member of the men's Bible class.[81] At a service held in January 1918, a list of the fifty-five Mary Magdalene members killed in action was read aloud.[82] If Stephenson's claim that up to 500 parishioners had enlisted by April 1918 is correct,[83] just over 10 per cent of those from the church who experienced active service were killed.

The process of remembering church members who had died on active service began during the war. The general vestry of Upper Falls (County Antrim) passed resolutions of sympathy in 1915 and 1916 to parishioners whose family members had been killed in the war.[84] In 1917 a resolution of sympathy was passed to the relatives of the 'gallant men' who had been killed in action. The resolution was passed in silence, the members standing.[85] Five members from St Bartholomew's in Dublin had died at the front by June 1915, but it was recorded that their sacrifice was not in vain as the empire would be 'spiritually stronger' after the war.[86] The impact of the war was felt in rural parishes such as Belleek (County Fermanagh) and Killeevan (County Monaghan), and in urban centres such as Bangor and Lisburn.[87] At Holywood's annual general vestry meeting in 1918, Canon Moore announced that 170 parishioners had enlisted. Thirty had been killed in action, three had been awarded the military cross and one, Lieutenant John Dunville of the Royal Dragoons, had received the Victoria Cross for 'self-sacrificing bravery'.[88]

Besides encouraging recruitment, rhetorically and actively, the Church of Ireland provided practical support for the war in other ways. In Newtownards, the rector of St Mark's (William Twist-Whatham) acted as a secretary of the Soldiers' and Sailors' families association (SASFA), a welfare organisation concerned with caring for families who had 'providers' away at war. Twist-Whatham intended to devote 'nearly all his time' during the war to the SASFA. He offered his services in examining the papers which needed to be sent in order for wives to receive the proper allowances.[89] In a letter published in the local press at Christmas, Twist-Whatham requested information regarding the name, regimental number and regiment of any Newtownards man serving in the war, so that 'no man may be overlooked'.[90] Such practical pastoral concern was paralleled by financial support. Churches held special collections to raise money for various organisations set up to provide relief during the war. One week after Britain declared war on Germany, the select vestry of Knockbreda resolved to hold a special collection for the relief of 'distress', raising £4, 3s, 3d.[91] A similar intention to alleviate any 'distress' caused by the war was seen in Mary Magdalene when Stephenson asked to be informed by women whose husbands had enlisted, so they 'may be helped in the absence of the breadwinners'.[92] The financial resources of Knockbreda were also utilised throughout the war to assist soldiers and their dependents. The £16 given to the Prince of Wales national relief fund was the highest of any special offering from the parish in 1914.[93] In 1916 the biggest special collection was £12, given to the UVF patriotic fund.[94] Collections for war organisations were also larger than average in Killinchy and Willowfield.[95]

Parishes also provided material support for the war effort through organising collections of socks and other 'comforts' for soldiers. The Mothers' Union of St Mark's, Dundela kept up an 'unfailing supply of socks which they knit for the men at the front'. The Girls' Friendly Society followed the example of their seniors and 'embarked upon a great knitting campaign'.[96] By November 1914 the working party of Howth had sent forty shirts and forty pairs of socks to troops at the front; the parish magazine published letters of thanks from a number of the grateful recipients.[97] The working party of St Ann's in Dublin felt 'privileged' in assisting 'in however small a degree those who are devoting themselves to the defence of our country'. By June 1915 the working party had sent 950 items, including shirts, pillows and pillow cases, to the St John Ambulance for distribution in field hospitals.[98] Under the patronage of the Royal Dublin Fusiliers committee, the choir of Donnybrook held a concert to raise money for sick and wounded soldiers.[99] St Peter's in Dublin sent thirty-five Christmas parcels, including plum puddings, woollen comforts, cigarettes and a Christmas card, to parishioners serving at the front. The parish magazine published letters of thanks for the food parcels, one stating 'the weather here is very bad, and I shall be very glad when I am back again in old St Peter's.'[100]

The existence of a pre-war militaristic tradition in Ireland, represented by the UVF and the Irish Volunteers, has been identified as a major factor in shaping Irish participation in the war.[101] It was perhaps inevitable that the pre-war militarism of the Church of Ireland in Ulster would segue into a vigorous defence of involvement in the war. However, it is not evident that Church of Ireland clerical patronage of the UVF in 1913–14 made clergymen more likely to support the war. Of the 109 Church of Ireland military chaplains, sixty-seven came from the southern province (one quarter were clergy based in the diocese of Dublin) and therefore had no prewar connection with the UVF, either as members or chaplains.[102]

Church of England bishops and clergy also demonstrated an affinity with military organisations, deepening their already close relationship with local army regiments.[103] Similarly, the Church of Ireland also supported local army regiments. The dean of Belfast twice preached in Belfast Cathedral at farewell services for army regiments, while the 4th battalion of the Royal Inniskilling Fusiliers deposited their colours in Enniskillen parish church.[104] It is possible clergy saw little difference between offering support to the army and the UVF, as both were viewed as legitimate military organisations. During the war, St Comgall's in Bangor offered the use of its premises to the UVF and army. The select vestry wrote to the war office in September 1914 offering the use of their church hall (the Dufferin Hall) to the army or navy as a military hospital, if required.[105] The outbreak of war caused the select vestry of St Comgall's to adopt a more generous policy in renting out the church hall. In January 1914 the vestry had refused Bangor Unionist Club permission to use the hall for drilling the local battalion of the UVF 'on account of the hall being so frequently required for church purposes'.[106] However, in October the vestry allowed the UVF use of the church hall on Friday evenings for a class in connection with signalling. The cost was negligible, with only caretaker fees required.[107] Such financial generosity was also a change from the prewar period, when the vestry had refused to allow Bangor Unionist Club a reduced rate.[108] By 1915 the Royal Irish Rifles were also using the hall for training, at the cost of a 'minimum charge'.[109]

Besides mirroring the support of the Church of England for the war, clerical involvement in Ulster paralleled that from the Church of Ireland in the south and west of Ireland. The similarity between the Church in Ulster and the rest of Ireland in constructing a moral basis for the war has been noted, along with the practical support offered to the war effort. Therefore, while the UVF undoubtedly contributed to an enthusiastic clerical response to the war, it was one of a number of factors motivating support for Britain's war effort.

'WHERE ARE THE NATIONALIST VOLUNTEERS?': HOME RULE AND THE WAR

There were many similarities between the response of the Church of Ireland and Church of England hierarchies to the war. In both churches, Britain's participation was endorsed, on the basis of Britain's moral righteousness and Germany's moral and religious decline. Recruitment was also actively encouraged – the recruiting fervour and pro-war sympathies of the bishop of London, Arthur Winnington-Ingram, are well documented and stand comparison with the recruiting enthusiasm of Church of Ireland bishops.[110] The bishops of both churches also had a shared experience of loss during the war. The sons of thirteen Church of England bishops were killed at the front by 1916.[111] The son of the bishop of Ossory, John Henry Bernard, was killed at Gallipoli in 1915, while D'Arcy's son was twice seriously wounded.[112]

However, while such similarities existed, the response of the Church of Ireland to the war was coloured by the political situation in Ireland. In a letter to the clergy and laity of his diocese, D'Arcy compared the likely effect of the war on everyday life to the 'grim, elemental facts of life and death' experienced in the previous two years in Ulster. As great sacrifices were made and strong resolutions formed, they had 'felt the bracing influence of contact with the sterner realities of existence'.[113] In addition to this experiential similarity, the dispute over the third Home Rule Bill provided Church of Ireland clergy with a rhetorical framework in which to interpret the war and encourage recruitment. In an analysis of the Church of England's role in recruitment, Albert Marrin claimed many clerical recruiting sermons and speeches were 'masterpieces of the salesman's art', calculated to appeal 'simultaneously to religious feelings, love of country, and the emotions'.[114] Clergy in the Church of Ireland had been selling such sentiments to their parishioners and crowds of unionists since 1910, in sermons aimed at defending the union and attacking home rule. For many in the Church of Ireland, the issues at stake in the war were similar to those at stake in the home rule dispute. The sanctity of the empire would be defended, and Irish unionists hoped their perceived status as integral members of the United Kingdom could be demonstrated by participating in the war. Therefore, wartime sermons and statements often sounded very similar to anti-home rule rhetoric. Church services that had served to reinforce opposition to home rule were, during the war, recast as opportunities to endorse support for the British war effort. The bishop of Derry acknowledged as much in his sermon at the 1914 Relief of Derry service. Two weeks previously, he stated, the commemoration of the relief of Derry would have involved calling on Ulster unionists to 'guard' their 'liberty, the liberty of Ulster'. However, 'today the nation, for our place in which we were ready to risk all, calls to us in a great emergency; and our hearts leap as we behold her, unbound by any pledge, taking an unselfish and a glorious stand for the freedom of Europe'.[115]

The opposition to home rule represented by Ulster Day and the Covenant was associated with the need to join the war effort. In a number of ways, Ulster Day services in 1914 were similar to those held in 1912 and 1913. Rev. F. Matchett, preaching in Christ Church, Lisburn, believed involvement in the war should be characterised by a similar spirit to the fight against home rule, as in both cases 'our first and last line of defence is the strong arm of the omnipotent God of Hosts'.[116] A major theme of 1914 Ulster Day sermons was the alleged iniquity of the government in using the cover provided by the outbreak of war to obtain the king's assent to the Home Rule Bill. Home rule had been placed on the statute book but suspended until after the war, with the promise of an amending bill to deal with the Ulster question. In addition to petitions to God and the expected attacks on the government, another similarity in 1914 with earlier Ulster Day services was the attendance of local UVF contingents. At the Lisnaskea Ulster Day service, the Covenant was read aloud by the rector, R.C. Lapham, as it had been in 1912 and 1913. In 1914 the Covenant provided Lapham with a rhetorical device to encourage participation in a war that threatened 'all of which we vowed our devotion': 'our material well being, our civil and religious liberty, our citizenship of the United Kingdom, the unity of the Empire'. Despite the 'dishonourable means' by which home rule had been placed on the statute book, the UVF should give themselves 'wholly to the task of helping the government … in the prosecution of the war to a successful issue', and then resume their active hostility to home rule. Lapham's Ulster Day sermon sustained opposition to home rule. The fight against Germany 'at the present time' was, he claimed, the fight against home rule. By enlisting, the Ulster Covenanters would witness to the 'British people and the world' that they held as their most prized possession their 'share in the Empire' and the 'flag'.[117] Similar sentiments were expressed by M.B. Hogg, the rector of Keady, in his Ulster Day sermon. Hogg believed Ulster's enthusiastic response to the war proved Ulster 'deserved the best at England's hands'.[118]

The war provided a context for Ulster unionists to prove their loyalty to the United Kingdom, a context given added potency by the alleged iniquity of the government in passing home rule. A common belief, made clear by the archdeacon of Dromore (E.D. Atkinson), was that such loyalty would have to be rewarded after the war. Ulster unionist participation in the war would make it 'absolutely impossible for any government at the close of the war to force upon Ulster any measure of Home Rule to which she objects'. If this was the case, it was crucial that Ulster unionists continued to enlist. Atkinson encouraged recruitment in language reminiscent of appeals to oppose home rule: 'As loyal men, whose loyalty is not for sale; as patriots, whose patriotism is not of the bread-and-butter type, we can't hear our country's call in this day of her sore distress and remain indifferent.'[119] The dean of Belfast believed the war offered Ulstermen the opportunity 'to translate their covenant into action in a way more glorious than they ever anticipated'. Such glorious action made the dean confident of the 'ultimate victory of the cause of Ulster'. During the war, if Ulster unionists continued to do their duty, prepared wisely, showed self-sacrifice and self-restraint, and placed their trust in God, 'there was no danger of the old flag falling from their hands'.[120]

Diocesan synods held in Ulster in 1914 confirmed that the home rule issue affected how the Church of Ireland in the province viewed the war. At the Derry and Raphoe synod, Bishop Chadwick stressed that the war proved Ulster's loyalty to England and commitment to the union, as 'in the hour of her peril we did not stop to make conditions'.[121] Dr Alfred Elliot claimed in his speech to the Kilmore synod that the government passed the Home Rule Bill as it knew Ulster 'in loyalty to the throne was more English than the English themselves'. Elliot also suggested the war was 'indirectly due' to the home rule issue. The arming of Ulster against the policy of the government meant rumours of 'civil war' were often heard in parliament: 'The Kaiser was kept fully informed of this, and from it gathered that England threatened with civil war and a demoralised army dare not interfere with his [the kaiser's] designs.' However, Elliot believed the kaiser's action had instead disarmed the political parties and united the country on the matter of the war. He praised Redmond for his role in encouraging recruitment, with a rather back-handed compliment: 'The Balaam whose mission was to curse Israel now undertakes to bless her by becoming her recruiting agent in Ireland. In this newly found occupation they wished him every success.'[122] At the Armagh synod, Crozier praised the readiness of the UVF to join the war effort despite the passing of home rule. The synod were proud that the 'very flower' of their young men 'largely armed during the last two years to preserve for our land her proud place in the Imperial Parliament' had proved equally ready to 'lay down their lives for the great Empire of which we form a part'.[123] In his 1914 diocesan synod speech, D'Arcy interpreted Ulster unionist support for the war as a continuation of their opposition to home rule and as evidence of the UVF's patriotism during 1913–14:

> After the great sacrifices which they [the UVF] made for Ulster, this fur-
> ther sacrifice sets the seal of lofty purpose and pure patriotism on all that
> they have done hitherto. The men of Ulster have acted nobly now because
> they have acted nobly all through.

A resolution was passed at the Down and Connor and Dromore synod encouraging 'all men and women of our race' to take their share in the 'gigantic struggle' for the liberty of mankind. The 'splendid demonstration of loyalty' by the UVF in supporting the British war effort was hailed as a victory against home rule by 'securing the vindication of the principles for which they stand'.[124]

Taken together with the 1914 Ulster Day sermons, diocesan synod speeches suggested the Church of Ireland in Ulster viewed the war as a continuation of the anti-home rule struggle. Some within the Church of Ireland may have genuinely believed enlistment would demonstrate Ulster's right to remain part of the union. They trusted the integrity of the government would ensure such valour made it impossible to place Ulster under a Dublin parliament. On the other hand, it is possible there was a concern in the Church about the readiness of Ulster unionists to enlist, owing to the passing of the Home Rule Bill. Therefore, clerical sermons and speeches sought to emphasise the need to enlist, in spite of the oft-cited 'betrayal' by the government. It is notable that as the war progressed, clerical calls for voluntary recruitment and praise of Irish enlistment gave way to calls for conscription.[125] For example, in May 1916 Crozier claimed many thousands of Irishmen were 'quite ready to let others do service on their behalf', although they would not refuse to enlist if 'summoned by Parliament'.[126] Four months later, Crozier drew attention to the 'pitiful' need to replenish the Irish divisions with soldiers from England, Wales and Scotland.[127] The downturn in recruiting enthusiasm (noted by Crozier among others) challenged the triumphal recruiting story proffered by, for example, the *Irish Churchman*. Bowman has noted the reliance of the 36th (Ulster) division on non-Irish recruits to fill its ranks and the lack of enlistment in rural areas of Ulster.[128] The early linkage of the need to enlist to defeat home rule offered in clerical recruitment statements was possibly an early example of the later (realised) fear that Ulster Protestant recruitment could be insufficient.

The *Irish Churchman* continued to articulate anti-home rule arguments by perpetuating its prewar attacks on Irish nationalism. Alleged lack of nationalist enthusiasm for the war provided the *Churchman* with an additional reason to oppose home rule. John Redmond received opprobrium for his Woodenbridge recruitment speech, which 'although delivered with all the oratorical arts at his disposal failed lamentably in results'. The paper noted with glee how those attending a Redmond speech in Belfast took shelter in picture houses when it began to rain, proving nationalists' lack of bravery: 'The men who boast of being fireproof against their enemies were not even waterproof.'[129] In November the *Churchman* enquired: '"Where are the Nationalist volunteers?" This is the question which is being asked daily.' Lack of recruitment existed despite the plight of 'gallant little Belgium', which looked 'in vain for the help of Roman Catholic Ireland'.[130] The case of Belgium was treated as a propaganda gift by Ulster unionists. The response of Protestant Ulster in going off to war to fight for Catholic Belgium, with all the moral rectitude attached to such a claim, was contrasted with the lack of engagement from Catholic Ireland.[131] Enlistment rates in Ireland for 1914 lend credence to the *Irish Churchman*'s rhetoric on recruitment. In the early months of the war, Catholics represented a minority of enlisted men, due largely to the high level of Ulster Protestant recruits.[132] However, as Jérôme aan de Wiel points out, the Catholic hierarchy also recognised the propaganda value of Belgium as a recruiting agent. A number of bishops and priests declared it was the duty of Irishmen to join the British war effort in order to prevent Prussian militarism from wreaking the same havoc in Ireland as it had exerted in Belgium.[133] Despite evidence of Catholic (and nationalist) support for the war, the *Irish Churchman*'s belligerent treatment of Catholic recruitment efforts provided an early indication that the war would not provide the panacea to Ireland's divisions.

While large elements of the Church of Ireland in Ulster hoped the war would deliver the province from home rule, in the south a conciliatory attitude was preached. The *Church of Ireland Gazette*'s rhetoric was in marked contrast to the *Irish Churchman*. The *Gazette* called for the rival armies in Ireland to unite in protection of their 'Motherland'; in an editorial entitled 'A new Ireland', the paper commended Redmond's support for the British war effort.[134] The *Gazette* encouraged nationalist recruitment and questioned the patriotism of unionists who assumed nationalist enthusiasm for the war was only 'skin deep'.[135] Ulster's recruiting record was also attacked early on in the war, as was Ulster unionism's perceived focus on home rule. In an editorial, the *Gazette* claimed Ulster, which possessed an 'Imperial tradition', had less justification than nationalist Ireland for failing to enlist. It was presumed that in unionist Ulster there was enough 'business acumen and sufficient patriotism' to realise that until 'the Germans are beaten, the question of Home Rule is of very small importance one way or the other'.[136]

The Church of Ireland in the south offered an alternative narrative of the effect of war on Ireland to that proposed by the Church in Ulster, one in which it was hoped the war would bring unity among Irishmen and signal the end to the bitter home rule dispute. John Henry Bernard, the bishop of Ossory, exemplified this conciliatory impulse. Like the *Gazette*, he praised Redmond as a 'true patriot and wise statesman' and hoped the war would produce a 'real fellowship in national sentiment'.[137] In 1915, Bernard received widespread commendation for a speech made at the Ossory synod that suggested the war had brought a common cause and unity – 'the same grass' grew over the graves of Irishmen, north and south, who had been killed at the front:

> We made no distinction between them, no distinction between Unionists and Nationalists, Roman Catholics and Presbyterians and Churchmen when we spoke with pride through our tears of their brave deeds, of what our children's children should tell their children in the days to come.

Bernard reminded the meeting that the first Irish chaplain killed in the war was the Catholic chaplain of the Dublin Fusiliers. The memory of such events 'must, and ought, to soften the bitterness of political antagonism by and by'. For Bernard, the shared Irish wartime experience made it 'unthinkable that Irishmen should draw the sword against Irishmen, because of political differences, when the war was over'. If the home rule issue were to be settled, both sides would have to abandon 'old party shibboleths'; they should 'hear no more of Irishmen arming against Irishmen'. They were proud of the Irish soldiers 'who fought shoulder to shoulder on behalf of us all. God forbid that any should encourage them to fight with each other.'[138]

Bernard's speech elicited positive comment in the press. An editorial in the *Irish Times* thought every Irishman should 'share the hopes' Bernard derived from his appreciation of Ireland's 'national community of effort and sacrifice'.[139] The *Derry Journal*, a nationalist paper, praised Bernard's speech as 'remarkable' coming from a 'Protestant Conservative'. Bernard's words aimed to achieve 'that spirit of peace and unity for which Mr Redmond on many occasions since hostilities commenced has eloquently pleaded'.[140] The *Ulster Guardian*, a liberal paper, endorsed Bernard's diocesan synod speech in an article entitled 'An open letter to the Bishop of Ossory'.[141]

In private, the press endorsement of Bernard's diocesan synod speech was reflected in praise from a mixture of southern unionists, Liberal-minded Anglicans and nationalist sympathisers. Lord Desart praised Bernard's speech as a 'valuable contribution to war literature' and a pointer to the 'road most likely to lead our distracted country towards some kind of unity'.[142] Rosamund Stephen, a member of the Guild of Witness, hoped Bernard's speech would be reproduced as a tract. Orangemen and members of the UVF should be told in 'very plain language how loyally the Roman Catholics are supporting the army'.[143] Bernard was commended for his 'patriotic address' by R.J. Kelly, a Catholic king's counsel, as it demonstrated there was 'hope for a country that has men who will appeal to these principles and not encourage those narrow views I am sorry in the North so many of your creed do'.[144] Bernard received a further letter in December passing on the admiration of the Irish Party leadership for his diocesan synod speech. Robert Morrow, rector of Billy (in north Antrim) reported a conversation he had had with a leading Catholic politician:

> He says all the leaders seem to be greatly impressed by your speech on the war and Ireland. Mr [Joe] Devlin said you are certainly not a time server seeing you made the speech while the Dublin [archbishopric] election was imminent.[145]

However, while Bernard received praise for his conciliatory attitude from various quarters, his episcopal superior was less impressed. Crozier claimed the war had increased the 'bitterness of party' in Ulster for two reasons. Protestants resented nationalist slurs on the UVF's non-participation in the war, 'as if it were their [the UVF's] fault that they had not gone out until 10 days ago'. Secondly, Protestants were aware that 'only about 1 RC has volunteered for every 20 Churchmen'. In addition, 'we all know' that the priests and Cardinal Logue were trying to keep 'their men' from enlisting: 'You cannot imagine how this intensifies the bitterness – but I think one ought to know the facts which I would not state in public for a King's ransom.'[146] Crozier's admonition was unsurprising in light of his 1914 Armagh diocesan synod speech. Despite the outbreak of war, Crozier was pessimistic about hopes for unity in Irish life. He feared politicians had 'shattered for many long years to come the last hope of burying the religious and political differences in a common grave'.[147] While one year had passed between Crozier's synod speech and his letter to Bernard, it is clear that Crozier did not believe the differences were ready to be buried.

Bernard's Ossory speech may have marked the point, at least publicly, when he graduated to a leading role in Irish politics. Rev. Robert Morrow informed Bernard how his speech had led nationalists to consider submitting 'the difficult question of the Irish difficulty to your judgement'. With a fair degree of pre-science, considering Bernard's future role in the Irish Convention, Morrow suggested Bernard would 'no doubt have great influence when the settlement comes to be made but perhaps you don't realise how much'.[148] Bernard's analysis of how the war changed the Irish question seemed to mirror the apparent (if brief) political conversion of Basil Brooke, then serving as a cavalry officer. H. MacManaway, a clergyman in contact with Brooke, sent Bernard a copy of a letter he had received from Brooke explaining how the war had entirely changed his outlook on Ireland. MacManaway realised Brooke's sentiments coalesced with those expressed in Bernard's diocesan synod speech.[149] Brooke implied the Church of Ireland had failed in its duty before the war by urging 'our side to take up arms and fight' and that after the war it should act as an agent of mediation. He warned that the man who urged others to civil war was guilty of a 'crime against humanity'.[150] While the Easter Rising caused Brooke to revert to his pre-war Ulster unionism, Bernard maintained his advocacy of closer ties with moderate Irish nationalism. The response to Bernard's diocesan synod speech, and his receipt of MacManaway's letter, suggests Bernard was seen as a focus for the conciliatory elements in the Church of Ireland and Irish unionism.

An article by W.S. Kerr in the January 1916 edition of *Irish Church Quarterly* came close to endorsing Bernard's diocesan synod speech. As editor of the *Irish Churchman*, Kerr was a reliable barometer of Ulster Church of Ireland clerical thought on the Irish question. He asserted that once the war began, both sides in Ireland had postponed their traditional differences. Ulster demonstrated its 'traditional loyalty' by enlisting. However, unionists needed to 'frankly recognise' the 'thousands upon thousands' of young southern Catholics 'offering themselves to take the field under the English flag'. Such facts could not be ignored by the 'most ardent – or bigoted if you like – of Orangemen'. Kerr believed the 'unexpected' rush to the colours by Irish Catholics would 'perhaps to a great degree … modify the political situation'.[151] In words reminiscent of Bernard's diocesan synod speech, Kerr claimed no barrier of creed or geography should limit the grief held for the gallant Irishmen who had fought and died for the empire. The result of the war should be a demand for a peaceful settlement in Ireland: 'We cannot feel towards each other as we did in days before fellowship in suffering and valour called out kindly feelings.'[152]

However, at this point Kerr fell back on more conventional Ulster unionist arguments. Unionists could not be blind to the fact that many Irish nationalists were anti-British and pro-German, and many more Protestants, especially in Ulster, had joined the army than Catholics. In addition, the Ulster division had been attacked in the nationalist press. In the face of such 'virulence', Ulster unionists 'cannot conclude that the universal reign of brotherly love has set in'.[153] Kerr proposed any settlement should grant 'autonomy to Ulster as a whole'. Exclusion, if only including six counties, was a 'miserable makeshift', and involved 'serious issues' for the Church of Ireland.[154] Provincial autonomy for

Ulster would deliver self-government and give nationalists in the south and west of Ireland their desired parliament. By leaving 'hostages in both camps', Kerr's plan prevented any 'likelihood of oppression'.[155] Kerr's article suggested the war would not solve the Irish question in the manner hoped for by Bernard. If anything, according to Kerr, the war had hardened his determination that Ulster should be exempted from the rule of a Dublin parliament. Kerr's article also pointed to an issue that would cause tension within Ulster unionism – the area to be excluded from home rule. The question of six or nine-county exclusion was seen by Kerr as equally important for the Church of Ireland as for Ulster unionism.

CONCLUSION

The wartime experience of the Church of Ireland was in a number of ways similar to that of the Church of England (and churches across Europe). Support for the war was encouraged and an attempt was made to sustain enthusiasm by constructing a moral and spiritual argument in support of the conflict. The German theologian, Alfred Uckeley, writing in 1915 claimed:

> Our battles are God's battles. Our cause is a sacred, a wholly sacred matter. We are God's chosen among the nations. That our prayers for victory will be heard is entirely to be expected, according to the religious and moral order of the world.[156]

Such sentiments could equally be applied to the Church of Ireland clergy, who believed God was on the side of the British empire. Clergy attempted to find meaning in the war through recourse to their faith in a providential, benevolent God. George Stephenson, the stridently pro-war rector of Mary Magdalene, summarised this belief at the end of the war:

> Of course, we knew that in the good Providence of God, victory was coming, but few expected so sudden and so complete a collapse as has befallen the Empire's foes.[157]

The war continued the Church of Ireland's influential role in Irish politics. Although difficult to prove empirically, it is likely the Church of Ireland played an important role in encouraging recruitment. Fitzpatrick has noted the power of group loyalties in motivating enlistment – 'those belonging to militias, fraternities or sporting clubs were particularly susceptible to collective pressures'. To this list could be added the parish church, which provided another forum in which 'the power of group loyalties' could be manifested. A 'peer-group' would be influential if key members were persuaded by organisers to enlist.[158] A parish church possessed various tools for persuading members to subordinate individual gratification to collective interest: through sermons, intercessory services, rolls of honour, letters published in magazines from church members serving at the front, resolutions of sympathy, and working parties, the war – and the inherent righteousness of aiding the British war effort – was kept at the forefront of parish life.

There were similarities between the Church of England and Church of Ireland response to the war, both in terms of active participation and rhetoric; comparisons could also be drawn with the Anglican Church in Australia, which believed Australia's future as a secure dominion 'stood or fell with the fate of the Empire'.[159] Therefore, the prewar militarism of the Church of Ireland in Ulster was not crucial in motivating support for the war. Christian militarism was a force in Churches outside Ireland and, as Wolffe argues, was not broken by the conflict but actually served to make sense of the slaughter by making explicit the linkage between Christianity and patriotism.[160] Counterfactually, if there had been no Ulster crisis, it is likely the Church of Ireland's response to the war would have been as enthusiastic as it was in reality.

However, it is possible that without the Ulster crisis and the threat of home rule, the 'holy truce' seen in other belligerent states may have taken hold in Ireland. Home rule complicated the response of the Church of Ireland to the war. Politically, the Church of Ireland was not united in seeking to encourage nation-alist–unionist co-operation. While the increasingly southern unionist *Church of Ireland Gazette* believed the war promised future peace in Ireland, as unionist and nationalist 'sunk their differences in a passionate determination to spend their strength in the crushing of the common enemy of themselves and of all civilisation', the rhetoric of the *Gazette*'s Ulster unionist counterpart, the *Irish Churchman*, suggested such hopes were optimistic.[161] For Ulster unionist clergy, the Irish question provided an additional factor in conceptualising the importance of the war by holding out the possibility of government concessions if Ulster could prove her fealty to the empire on the battlefield.

The war highlighted the divisions within the Church of Ireland on home rule. For the Church in the south and west, the war accelerated the acceptance of a con-ciliatory solution to the third home rule crisis. Bernard's Ossory diocesan synod speech, made shortly before he was elected archbishop of Dublin, demonstrated the gulf opening up with the Church of Ireland in Ulster. The rhetoric of Ulster Day sermons and diocesan synods and Kerr's article in *Irish Church Quarterly* suggested future tensions would exist in the Church, between Ulster churchmen who favoured partition and southern churchmen who sought a settlement based on the kind of post-war unity envisioned by Bernard. Events from 1916 brought these tensions to the surface, as the Easter Rising and subsequent attempts at finding a settlement threatened to splinter the unity of the Church of Ireland.

NOTES

1. Michael Burleigh, *Earthly Powers: Religion and Politics in Europe from the French Revolution to the Great War* (London, 2005), p.439.
2. Kenneth Hylson-Smith, *The Churches in England from Elizabeth I to Elizabeth II, vol. III, 1833–1998* (London, 1998), p.170.
3. For the Church of England, see Albert Marrin, *The Last Crusade: the Church of England in the First World War* (Durham, North Carolina, 1974) and Alan Wilkinson, *The Church of England and the First World War* (London, 1978).
4. See R.B. McDowell, *The Church of Ireland, 1869–1969* (London, 1975), pp.105–9; Alan Acheson, *Church of Ireland, 1691–1996* (Dublin, 1997), pp.227–9; David McConnell, 'The Protestant churches and the origins of the Northern Ireland state' (Queen's University Belfast, unpublished Ph.D. thesis, 1998), ch. 3; Alan Megahey, *The Irish Protestant Churches in the Twentieth Century* (London, 2000), pp.37–43.
5. Keith Jeffery, *Ireland and the Great War* (Cambridge, 2000), p.156.
6. *Belfast Newsletter*, 17 August 1914.
7. *Ulster Gazette and Armagh Standard*, 22 August 1914.
8. Bray quarterly calendar, winter 1914/1915 (Representative Church Body (RCB) Library, Dublin, P.580. 28. 3).
9. St Peter's parish magazine, December 1915 (ibid., P.45. 16. 10).
10. *Ulster Gazette*, 26 September 1914.
11. See A.J. Hoover, *God, Germany and Britain in the Great War: A Study of Clerical Nationalism* (New York, 1989), pp.108–9.

12. *Belfast Newsletter*, 26 October 1914.
13. *Journal of the General Synod*, 1915, p.liii.
14. *Lisburn Standard*, 21 August 1914.
15. *Northern Constitution*, 29 August 1914.
16. Thomas Hennessey, *Dividing Ireland: World War One and Partition* (London, 1998), p.83.
17. *Belfast Newsletter*, 7 September 1914.
18. Ibid., 14 December 1914.
19. Hoover, *God, Germany and Britain in the Great War*, p.37; Moses suggests Anglican bishops of the Australian Church also cited Nietzsche and Bernhardi as part of their wartime critique of Germany: J.A. Moses, 'Australian Anglican leaders and the Great War, 1914–1918: the "Prussian Menace", conscription, and national solidarity', *Journal of Religious History*, 25, 3 (October 2001), pp.314–15.
20. Hoover, *God, Germany and Britain in the Great War*, p.36.
21. Ibid., pp.21–2.
22. Ibid., pp.24–5.
23. See Moses, 'Australian Anglican leaders and the Great War', p.312.
24. *Irish Church Quarterly*, January 1915, p.4.
25. Ibid.
26. Ibid., p.6.
27. Ibid., p.5.
28. Ibid., p.7.
29. Ibid., pp.8–9.
30. *Irish Church Quarterly*, April 1915, p.105.
31. Ibid., p.106.
32. Ibid., pp.106–7.
33. Ibid., p.110.
34. *Irish Church Quarterly*, July 1915, pp.180–1.
35. Ibid., p.185.
36. *Irish Church Quarterly*, October 1915, pp.268–9.
37. Hoover, *God, Germany and Britain in the Great War*, pp.104–5.
38. Ibid., p.106.
39. See Chapter 3, of this volume.
40. Hannay served as a chaplain, *Irish Church Directory*, 1919, p.315; his son, Robert, joined the army in 1914, B. Taylor, *The Life and Writings of James Owen Hannay (George A. Birmingham), 1865–1950* (New York, 1995), p.138.
41. *Belfast Weekly Telegraph*, 15 August 1914.
42. *Down Recorder*, 5 September 1914.
43. *Irish Churchman*, 11 September 1914.
44. *Belfast Weekly Telegraph*, 19 September 1914.
45. Donnybrook parish magazine, September 1914, January 1915 (RCB Library, P.246. 25).
46. Mary Magdalene parish magazine, September 1914 (private possession).
47. Ibid., July 1916.
48. See Jeffery, *Ireland and the First World War*, p.10.
49. Knockbreda vestry minute book, 4 April 1918 (Public Record Office of Northern Ireland (PRONI), CR/1/24D/3).
50. *Irish Churchman*, 21 August 1914.
51. *Belfast Newsletter*, 23 November 1914.
52. Wilkinson, *Church of England and the First World War*, p.102.
53. Ibid.
54. St Jude's vestry minute book, 7 April 1915 (private possession).
55. Mary Magdalene vestry minute book, 8 April 1915 (private possession); Willowfield vestry minute book, 9 April 1915, 28 April 1916, 13 April 1917 (private possession); Holywood vestry minute book, 16 February 1916 (private possession).
56. St Comgall's vestry minute book, 3 May 1915 (PRONI, CR/1/87/D/3).
57. Ibid., 7 June 1915.
58. *Journal of the General Synod*, 1915, p.ci.
59. Wilkinson *Church of England and the First World War*, p.102.
60. Minutes of the House of Bishops, 16 March 1916 (RCB Library).
61. Wilkinson, *Church of England and the First World War*, p.104.
62. *Church of Ireland Gazette*, 4 September 1914.
63. See Jeffery, *Ireland and the Great War*, pp.14–16.
64. Moses, 'Australian Anglican leaders and the Great War', p.319.

65. Wilkinson, *Church of England and the First World War*, p.32.
66. See Marrin, *Last Crusade*, p.180; Wilkinson, *Church of England and the First World War*, p.32.
67. *Lurgan Mail*, 19 September 1914.
68. *Fermanagh Times*, 1 October 1914.
69. *Northern Constitution*, 15 August 1914.
70. Ibid., 19 September 1914.
71. *Down Recorder*, 12 September 1914.
72. *Lurgan Mail*, 21 November 1914.
73. For example, St Ann's parish magazine, January 1915, June 1915 (RCB Library, P.344. 25).
74. Howth parish magazine, October 1914 (ibid., P.373. 25); St Bartholomew's parish magazine, November 1915 (ibid., P.64. 25. 1).
75. Donnybrook parish magazine, December 1914 (ibid., P.246. 25); Taney annual report, 1914 (ibid., P.609. 21. 3).
76. St Comgall's vestry minute book, 5 October 1914 (PRONI, CR/1/87/D/3).
77. Mary Magdalene parish magazine, October 1914.
78. Ibid., November 1914.
79. Ibid., July 1916.
80. Ibid., July 1917.
81. Ibid., February 1917.
82. Ibid., January 1918.
83. Mary Magdalene vestry minute book, 14 April 1918.
84. Upper Falls vestry minute book, 9 April 1915, 27 April 1916 (PRONI, CR/1/69/D/2).
85. Ibid., 13 April 1917.
86. St Bartholomew's parish magazine, June 1915 (RCB Library, P.64. 25. 1).
87. Belleek vestry minute book, 7 September 1915 (PRONI, MIC/1/270/D/1); Killeevan vestry minute book, 10 April 1917 (ibid., MIC/1/154/C/1); St Comgall's vestry minute book, 5 June, 3 July, 2 October 1916 (ibid., CR/1/87/D/3); Lisburn Cathedral vestry minute book, 3 October 1916, 2 January 1917 (ibid., CR/1/35/D/4).
88. Holywood vestry minute book, 4 April 1918.
89. *Newtownards Chronicle*, 12 September 1914.
90. Ibid., 26 December 1914.
91. Knockbreda vestry minute book, 12 August 1914 (PRONI, CR/1/24D/3); Knockbreda preacher book, 30 August 1914 (ibid., CR/1/24G/6)
92. Mary Magdalene parish magazine, September 1914.
93. Knockbreda vestry minute book, 6 April 1915 (PRONI, CR/1/24D/3).
94. Ibid., 10 April 1917.
95. Killinchy preacher book, 16 August 1914, 29 September 1916 (ibid., CR/1/16F/6); Willowfield preacher book, 19 August 1914, 31 December 1916.
96. St Mark's Dundela parish magazine, December 1914 (private possession).
97. Howth parish magazine, November 1914, February 1915 (RCB Library, P.373. 25).
98. St Ann's parish magazine, December 1914, June 1915 (ibid., P.344. 25).
99. Donnybrook parish magazine, December 1915 (ibid., P.246. 25).
100. St Peter's parish magazine, January 1916, February 1916 (ibid., P.45. 16. 10).
101. One third of recruits to the 36th (Ulster) Division came from the UVF, see D. Fitzpatrick, 'The logic of collective sacrifice: Ireland and the British army, 1914–1918', *Historical Journal*, 38, 4 (December 1995), p.1027.
102. *Irish Church Directory*, 1919, pp.315–315b.
103. Wilkinson, *Church of England and the First World War*, pp.33–4.
104. *Belfast Newsletter*, 10, 14 August 1914; *Fermanagh Times*, 13 August 1914.
105. St Comgall's vestry minute book, 7 September 1914 (PRONI, CR/1/87/D/3).
106. Ibid., 5 January 1914.
107. Ibid., 5 October 1914.
108. Ibid., 2 October 1911.
109. Ibid., 22 February 1915.
110. For Winnington-Ingram, see Burleigh, *Earthly Powers*, p.449; Wilkinson, *Church of England and the First World War*, pp.35–6; John Wolffe, *God and Greater Britain: Religion and National Life in Britain and Ireland* (London, 1994), p.239.
111. Burleigh, *Earthly Powers*, p.448.
112. Megahey, *Irish Protestant Churches in the Twentieth Century*, p.41; Charles Frederick D'Arcy, *The Adventures of a Bishop* (London, 1934), pp.196, 204. The son of the bishop of Kilmore was killed in action in 1916 (*Fermanagh Times*, 22 June 1916).

113. *Irish Churchman*, 14 August 1914.
114. Marrin, *Last Crusade*, pp.181–2.
115. *Belfast Newsletter*, 13 August 1914.
116. *Lisburn Standard*, 2 October 1914.
117. *Fermanagh Times*, 1 October 1914.
118. *Ulster Gazette*, 3 October 1914.
119. *Lurgan Mail*, 3 October 1914.
120. *Belfast Weekly Telegraph*, 3 October 1914.
121. *Belfast Newsletter*, 14 October 1914.
122. Ibid., 26 October 1914.
123. *Ulster Gazette*, 31 October 1914.
124. *Belfast Weekly Telegraph*, 31 October 1914.
125. See Chapter 7, of this volume for a discussion of the Church of Ireland's support for conscription.
126. *The Times*, 9 May 1916.
127. *Ulster Gazette*, 7 October 1916.
128. T. Bowman, 'The Ulster Volunteer Force and the formation of the 36th (Ulster) division', *Irish Historical Studies*, 32, 128 (November 2001), pp.505–8.
129. *Irish Churchman*, 30 October 1914.
130. Ibid., 13 November 1914.
131. Ibid., 4 December 1914, 18 December 1914.
132. D. Fitzpatrick, 'Logic of collective sacrifice', pp.1024–5.
133. J. aan de Wiel, *The Catholic Church in Ireland: 1914–1918* (Dublin, 2003), p.26.
134. *Church of Ireland Gazette*, 7, 14 August 1914.
135. Ibid., 2 October 1914.
136. Ibid., 20 November 1914.
137. Ibid., 14 August 1914; at the Ferns diocesan synod, Bernard stated that Protestant and Catholic, Unionist and Nationalist, would fight side by side 'like brothers' (ibid., 9 October 1914).
138. *Irish Times*, 25 September 1915.
139. Ibid., 25 September 1915.
140. *Derry Journal*, 29 September 1915.
141. *Ulster Guardian*, 2 October 1915.
142. Lord Desart to John Henry Bernard, 25, 28 September 1915 (TCD, J.H. Bernard papers, Mss 2388/96, 98).
143. Rosamund Stephen to Bernard, 28 September 1915 (British Library, J.H. Bernard papers, Add. Ms 52782/40–1). The Guild of Witness sought to promote the Church of Ireland's 'Irish' character; Oonagh Walsh (ed.), *An Englishwoman in Belfast: Rosamund Stephen's Record of the Great War* (Cork, 2000), p.4.
144. Richard John Kelly to Bernard, 29 September 1915 (ibid., Add. Ms 52782/42).
145. Robert Morrow to Bernard, 21 December 1915 (ibid., Add. Ms 52782/48–9). Bernard was elected ahead of D'Arcy in the election to the archbishopric of Dublin (he was appointed on 7 October 1915).
146. John Baptist Crozier to Bernard, 11 October 1915 (ibid., Ms 52782/44–6).
147. *Ulster Gazette*, 31 October 1914.
148. Morrow to Bernard, 21 December 1915 (ibid., Add. Ms 52782/48–9).
149. H. MacManaway to Bernard, 19 February 1916 (TCD, J.H. Bernard papers, Mss 2388/100).
150. Basil Brooke to H. MacManaway, 6 November 1915 (British Library, J.H. Bernard papers, Add. Ms 52782/47).
151. *Irish Church Quarterly*, January 1916, p.109.
152. Ibid., p.110.
153. Ibid., p.112.
154. Ibid., p.117.
155. bid., p.118.
156. Burleigh, *Earthly Powers*, p.445.
157. Mary Magdalene parish magazine, December 1918.
158. Fitzpatrick, 'Collective sacrifice', pp.1029–30.
159. Moses, 'Australian Anglican leaders and the Great War', p.309.
160. Wolffe, *God and Greater Britain*, p.244.
161. *Church of Ireland Gazette*, 2 October 1914.

6

'A counsel of lunacy'?
The Church of Ireland, the Easter Rising,
and Partition

> Treason is openly preached in Dublin and in many parts of the country, and
> no one objects. The weakest spot in the Cabinet is the place that is still kept
> for Birrell. This is no time for jokes and humbug – we want a *man* here to
> rule us, and we have not got him.[1]

John Henry Bernard's words, written in May 1915, seem prophetic in light of
events in Dublin and other parts of Ireland in April 1916. The Easter Rising was
an attempt to raise the cause of Ireland from a British domestic concern to an
international issue, and to revive the Irish separatist ideal.[2] Many unionists held
Dublin Castle, under the leadership of the chief secretary, Augustine Birrell, to
be largely responsible for the breakdown of law and order at Easter 1916. In
words reminiscent of Bernard's almost one year earlier, John Baptist Crozier
termed the Rising the 'inevitable insurrection' that 'everybody knew would
come sooner than later, except the … professional humorist, Mr Birrell'.[3]

Despite the prophetic and retrospective claims about the inevitability of the
Rising from Bernard and Crozier, the Church of Ireland, like the government and
Ireland as a whole, was surprised by events in Dublin. Attention in the Church was
probably turning from the celebration of Easter towards the forthcoming general
vestries, or the installation of the rector of Bangor, J.I. Peacocke, as bishop of
Derry on Easter Tuesday. John Gwynn wrote to Peacocke from Trinity College
on Easter Monday, (presumably) mere hours before the Rising began, offering
prayers and best wishes on the eve of his installation.[4] However, Peacocke's day
was completely overshadowed by events in Dublin and elsewhere in Ireland.
While the history of the Easter Rising has been comprehensively told and retold,
the reaction of the Church of Ireland to the Easter Rising has been under-
explored.[5]

The significance of the Easter Rising for the Church of Ireland lay not only
in the Rising itself, but in what followed. The apparently rebellious state of
Ireland persuaded the government that wartime necessity meant an attempt
should be made to solve the Irish question. The result was David Lloyd George's
abortive attempt at a settlement based on partition. The tension this scheme
caused between Ulster and southern unionists was mirrored in the Church of
Ireland. The House of Bishops passed a resolution against the Lloyd George plan
that proved one of the most controversial statements of the decade within the
Church. The resolution opposed the line taken by Ulster unionists in supporting
partition; in addition, on the back of the resolution a number of southern bishops
began advocating a home rule solution to the Irish question, culminating in the
Logue Manifesto of May 1917. This forced northern bishops, such as Charles

Frederick D'Arcy, to publicly break with their southern counterparts and advocate partition.

The war continued to colour the political situation in Ireland. In the midst of debates over the Lloyd George proposal, the Somme offensive reinforced the growing partitionist mindset of Ulster unionism. Like the Easter Rising, the Somme was quickly incorporated into the rhetorical offensive practised by Church of Ireland clergymen in Ulster against home rule.

ULSTER ANGLICAN REACTION TO THE EASTER RISING AND THE SOMME

There was in Crozier and D'Arcy's public reaction to the Easter Rising an underlying assumption that it offered a positive opportunity for Ulster to demonstrate its loyalty to the empire. Speaking at the opening of a Palestine exhibition in Portadown, Crozier urged his listeners to do nothing by word or deed 'to kindle the embers of similar fires in Ulster'. As 'loyalists', they should continue to focus on the war, in order to save the empire. However, they wanted 'please God, to save their own country too', and Crozier hoped the Rising would finally demonstrate to England the danger of home rule.[6] D'Arcy also urged restraint in his first public remarks on the Rising, in a sermon preached at Belfast Cathedral on 30 April. D'Arcy chose 1 Thessalonians 4:11 as his text ('Study to be quiet, and to do your own business') to reinforce his call for Ulster unionists to practise 'firm self-control' in order to give the 'authorities' 'great moral support'. Like Crozier, D'Arcy emphasised that the main danger Ireland faced remained the war, to which 'every personal and local consideration should be subordinated'.[7] The reaction of Crozier and D'Arcy was very much in line with that of the *Belfast Newsletter*, which urged its readers to remember the 'Imperial necessity' they were under as 'loyal subjects of the King' to maintain law and order. If peace was preserved in Ulster, 'it will redound to the credit of the Imperial Province'.[8] The Easter Rising presented Crozier and D'Arcy with an opportunity to reverse the negative images of loyalist resistance embodied in the 'Ulster crisis' by contrasting peaceable Ulster with the supposedly rebellious south and west of Ireland.

However, in private Crozier grew concerned at the effect the Easter Rising could have on Ulster. In a letter and attached memo to Edward Carson, Crozier outlined his fears that the government was planning to disarm the UVF in the aftermath of the Rising, a move he feared could mean 'civil war'.[9] Crozier opposed disarming for two reasons. First of all, he claimed the presence in Belfast of the UVF, armed and ready, had reassured loyalists in the 'Northern outposts' of their safety during the Easter Rising. To remove such an assurance by disarming the UVF would 'spread terror amongst these scattered loyal folk – whose only fault is their loyalty!' Secondly, to disarm the UVF would harm the British war effort. Disarmament would be looked upon by the Ulster division serving in France, largely composed of UVF men, as a 'hideous travesty of justice'. The Ulster division had left their wives and children 'trusting to the faith of their comrades who stay behind to look after and protect them … men who would sacrifice their lives in their defence'. Crozier feared to 'disturb' the 'only confidence' of the Ulster division 'would be to run a risk no sane man ought to dare to face'.[10] Carson forwarded Crozier's letter and memo to the prime minister. Carson hoped nothing would be done to 'create any risk' in Ulster, claiming Crozier knew 'the North of Ireland probably better than any living man'.[11] Asquith assured Carson that the government was not responsible for the rumour about disarming the UVF.[12] It is unclear from Crozier's letter why he believed the UVF so strenuously felt the need to remain armed. Perhaps it was due to a fear that disarmament would leave the volunteers vulnerable to attacks from the kind of militant Irish republicanism seen in Easter Week. Alternatively, he may have reasoned that the UVF held on to their weapons in order to resist the passing of home rule once the war had ended. Crozier's warnings of the dire consequences of any forced loyalist disarmament goes some way to explain his tacit endorsement of the 'armed and ready' UVF in Belfast, which seemed incongruous in light of his strong support for army recruitment; in addition, his belief that the Ulster division relied on the UVF in Ulster to protect their families implied a lack of confidence in the regular army garrison in Ireland, despite the recent suppression of the Easter Rising. The apparent contradictions, expressed in private, suggested Crozier's public appeals for order in Ulster were not merely attempts to claim the moral high ground over Irish nationalism, but the product of a genuine fear concerning the volatility of Ulster unionism.

The speeches of clergy at annual general vestry meetings demonstrated a belief that the Rising could reflect favourably on Ulster unionism. In reviewing the life of the parish in the previous year, clergymen frequently contrasted, explicitly or implicitly, their parish's war work with events in Dublin. The rector of Knockbreda claimed the Easter Rising demonstrated the difference between 'loyal Ulster' (which remained 'as ever on the side of King') and the rest of Ireland.[13] At Trinity's meeting, Rev. Bedell Stanford juxtaposed the example of the 100 men from the parish who had enlisted with the 'horrors' witnessed in Dublin.[14] The rector of St Comgall's drew a contrast between the parochial women's war working party and the Easter Rising.[15] R.H.S. Cooper, rector of Christ Church in Lisburn, believed the 'unshaken loyalty and patriotism' of that congregation would remain conspicuous no matter what resulted from the Easter Rising.[16] The parish magazine of Mary Magdalene also emphasised the contrast between the Easter Rising and the war effort of Ulster. In its 'special wants' section, 'earnest prayer' was called for so that 'the fires of rebellion and strife in our home land may be soon completely stamped out'. In the 'thanksgiving' section, thanks were offered for the self-control of Ulster during the Rising: 'Ulster has always professed to be loyal and we are proud to say that she has never more strikingly vindicated that title.'[17]

Clergymen also hoped the Easter Rising would convince the government of the danger that would be posed to life and property in Ireland under home rule. In a letter to the *Newsletter*, the dean of Dromore acknowledged it was 'no surprise' that rumours of home rule were circulating. However, he believed the Easter Rising had revealed to the 'dullest mind' the great danger of weakening the 'central authority' of the United Kingdom. In the dean's opinion, the Easter Rising had thus 'killed Home Rule as dead as Julius Caesar'.[18] Similar sentiments were expressed by Canon Pounden in the Lisburn Cathedral parish magazine. Pounden hoped the eyes of the 'English government and people' were opened to the 'unmistakeable impossibilities' of peace in Ireland 'if there should be separation of our country from its neighbouring ally'.[19]

The alacrity with which the Easter Rising was woven into the rhetoric of Ulster clerical opposition to home rule demonstrated a readiness to assume that home rule would either lead to separatist violence or be unable to contain it. A corollary of this assumption was a belief in the perceived advantage the Rising could bring to Ulster unionism. Ulster's peacefulness and concentration on the war effort while Dublin was in chaos was viewed as a vivid demonstration of Ulster's loyalty to the empire and was held to reinforce the iniquity of placing Ulster – and, for some clergy, Ireland as a whole – under home rule.

This belief was only strengthened by the tragic events of the Somme. The 36th (Ulster) division suffered huge casualties during an assault on Thiepval Ridge and the supposedly impregnable Schwaben Redoubt. In the first two days of the offensive, over 5,500 men (out of 15,000) from the division were killed, wounded or missing.[20] According to Crozier, the empire owed a great debt to the UVF – the men of the Ulster division had died 'doing their duty for King and country', an example it was hoped would inspire 'fresh generations of Irishmen'.[21] Likewise, in his tribute to the Ulster division, D'Arcy claimed the UVF had willingly sacrificed itself 'for the sake of those great ideals of liberty and progressive humanity which belonged to all that is best in the British race'. This sacrificial spirit had inspired Ulster 'throughout all her recent struggles'.[22] The Somme was also quickly incorporated into the Ulster unionist narrative of resistance, providing in some ways a loyalist counterpoint to the Catholicised rhetoric of blood sacrifice preached by Patrick Pearse and fulfilled in the Easter Rising. The fact that the Somme offensive began on 1 July allowed a link to be drawn with the Battle of the Boyne in 1690, which had occurred on the first day of July. At an Orange service in St Matthew's church on the Shankill Road, the preacher asserted 'those words "Derry!", "the Boyne", "No Surrender!" were the watchwords with which the Ulstermen stormed the trenches'.[23] Preaching in Armagh, Canon Tichborne claimed the men from the Ulster division who fought at the Somme 'were worthy of the great ancestors who fought at Derry and the Boyne'.[24] The casualty lists and rolls of honour were a witness to the bishop of Derry 'that the spirit which held the walls of Derry long ago still lived in their midst'.[25] The patriotism of Ulster was demonstrated, claimed the Mary Magdalene magazine, at the Somme. The example of the Ulster division was seen (implicitly) as a reminder to Britain of Ulster's place in the union as 'neither we … nor the nation which give us birth, can ever forget the renown and glory which have been won for Ulster by the bravery of her sons'.[26]

The Somme carried clear political implications. Bew claims the Ulster division's involvement at the Somme represented an 'Ulster Unionism Britain could identity with; it was all the more difficult at such a moment for Britain to "betray" it'.[27] Whether or not this is true – the British public suffered equal or indeed greater sacrifices than Ulster unionism during the war – is perhaps not the issue. The significance of the Somme lay in how it was perceived in Ulster. Clerical statements suggest that the Somme was viewed as the Ulster division's distinctive, unique sacrifice for the empire, thereby securing her position in that empire free from the rule of a home rule parliament. The equation of the UVF with the Ulster division may have been misleading – the Ulster division was reliant on non-Irish recruits to fill its ranks. However, this does not minimise the reality that large numbers of Ulstermen were killed at the Somme or the fact that, when juxtaposed with the Easter Rising, the Somme was spun by Ulster unionists (including Church of Ireland clergy) as a blood sacrifice by the Ulster division, providing a vivid demonstration of Ulster's growing psychological partition from Ireland.[28] The Somme confirmed unionist Ulster's self-perceived loyalty to the empire and her place in that empire through the sacrifice of the Ulster division. Church of Ireland clergy were quick to identify this element of the Somme and were at the forefront of attempts to integrate it into the loyalist tradition.

However, the Somme was above all a human tragedy. The archdeacon of Down impressionistically tried to convey its full horrors in a sermon at Hollymount Church:

> I see the Ulster Division stationed in a wood that is raked by shell fire. At a word of command they come out … I can visualise the scene but I cannot describe it. Words fail me. I see the earth torn with shells … I see man after man, sometimes whole companies, swept away: the ranks of Ulster thinned, but still invincible.[29]

The effect of the Somme is recorded in parish records. At Knockbreda's July 1916 select vestry meeting, condolences were sent to Mrs Cleland on the death of her son, Captain F.L. Cleland, during the battle.[30] In July 1918 the vestry agreed to erect a memorial tablet to Cleland.[31] At the 1917 general vestry meeting it was noted that three parishioners had died at the Somme, 'when the men who went out from Ulster served so valiantly'.[32] In September 1916 the parish magazine of Mary Magdalene mentioned that a parishioner, Stewart McWilliams (a soldier with the Royal Inniskilling Fusiliers), had died at the Somme. A number of others were missing after the 'great push of 1 July when the men of the Ulster Division won such imperishable renown'.[33] The harsh reality of the Somme offensive was recorded in the preacher book of Armoy parish. Near the end of July 1916, the church held a special intercessory service for 'our soldiers and sailors in the war, and in memory of three local men [parishioners] recently killed'. The collection of £8 was distributed by the rector and churchwardens among the mothers of the dead soldiers.[34]

SOUTHERN ANGLICAN REACTION TO THE EASTER RISING

The Church of Ireland in Ulster was not practically inconvenienced by the Easter Rising – services could still go ahead and there was no danger to life or property. Obviously, matters were different in Dublin, where clergy were caught up in the fighting and commended by General John Maxwell for 'services rendered' during the Rising.[35] Bernard suggested to Maxwell the names of a number of clergy who deserved special mention for 'helping the wounded, passing dangerous areas to reach hospitals, and helping the poor'.[36] Examples of the effect of the Rising on the everyday running of the Church in Dublin are seen in the fact that two weeks following the outbreak, those wishing to attend services in St Patrick's Cathedral still had to show military permits before being allowed to approach the building;[37] the annual general vestry of St Stephen's was postponed to May as the parochial hall was occupied by the 'Sinn Féin rebels' during Easter week,[38] while there was no May issue of the St Peter's magazine as the premises at which it was printed had been destroyed.[39] In Kingstown, the parochial school of the Mariners' Church was turned into a military hospital.[40]

John Henry Bernard informed the Dublin diocesan synod in October that little damage was done to the material fabric of church buildings during the Rising, although the chapel of the Mission to Seamen was destroyed.[41] The lack of physical damage to church property contrasted with the psychological effect the Easter Rising exerted on the Church of Ireland in Dublin. The principal interpretation expressed was that the Rising represented a 'stab in the back' by fellow Irishmen during the war. St Bartholomew's parish magazine claimed that the Rising was a deliberate attempt to betray the Irishmen who were fighting to protect

Irishwomen from the 'brutalities prepared for them by Prussian militarism'. The leaders of the 'insurrection' were 'agents of Germany' who tried to hand Ireland over to 'German rule'.[42] The Howth parish magazine believed the Easter Rising would 'live in history' as an attempt by 'Ireland's worst enemies to stab England in the back' during a 'titanic struggle for right against the forces of might'.[43]

John Henry Bernard's episcopal residence in St Stephen's Green afforded a ringside seat to some of the fiercest fighting of Easter week, and Bernard unsurprisingly became one of the leading critics of the Rising. He reacted vigorously to the outbreak and repeated the 'stab in the back' interpretation of the Rising. He encouraged a Dublin rector to hold morning services as usual on 30 April and urge his parishioners 'from the pulpit to help the forces of the Crown in every possible way'.[44] Bernard expressed similar sentiments in a sermon at St Anne's church in Dublin on 30 April. He asked the congregation to 'be steady and quiet during these days of stress' and to help the army 'by keeping at home and leaving the streets clear'. Bernard's sermon was notable for the uncompromising measures he advocated in dealing with the rebels. Any attempts to 'quell this rebellion … must be of tremendous severity if they are to have permanent efficacy. I hope that we shall not be so weak as to encourage any half measures.' He believed the rebellion was the result of the 'mad treason of unprincipled men, whose leaders were in German pay'. It was the duty of everyone to insist on the 'strongest measures' of repression against 'friends' of the rebels.[45] Bernard's uncompromising calls for punishment reached a wider audience through a letter he had published in *The Times*, in which he appealed for the government not to dispense with martial law as Dublin was still in a perilous state: 'Many armed rebels are at large in Dublin still … As I write there are snipers on the roofs trying to shoot any officers that they may see.' In the light of such disorder, Bernard emphasised 'this is not the time for amnesties and pardons; it is the time for punishment, swift and stern.'[46] This letter to *The Times* provoked a response from A.J. Balfour, a member of the wartime coalition cabinet, who wrote privately to Bernard to reassure him that the penalties on the rebels fixed by General Maxwell would be fully carried out.[47]

Bernard's strongly worded rhetoric reflected a belief among southern unionists that law and order had broken down in the aftermath of the Rising. In a resolution passed on 18 May, the Standing Committee of the General Synod of the Church of Ireland called for the maintenance of martial law. The committee believed the 'seditious spirit' was widespread and 'is not yet over'. Consequently, it urged the government 'to be slow to abandon the exercise of the powers which they have put in force for the maintenance of order in this country'. The committee decided to send the resolution to the prime minister in a private letter, but not to the press.[48] The Donnybrook parish magazine called for the exaction of 'necessary penalties' in order that 'solid foundations are laid for the restoration of law and order'.[49] At the end of May, the bishop of Tuam apologised to Crozier for his failure to attend a meeting of the House of Bishops. He explained that the 'very unsettled state here in the West' meant 'my place is for this moment among my clergy and people and so I am not leaving home this week', adding that they were on the verge of 'great trouble in the West'.[50]

Bernard's biographer has explained his call for such drastic security measures as proceeding from the 'wounded pride of a member of the caste the dominance of which was threatened'.[51] However, Bernard's detestation of the Rising was similar to John Redmond's belief that it was the 'wicked move' of men who 'have tried to make Ireland the cat's paw of Germany' (although unlike Bernard, Redmond urged a degree of leniency in punishing the rebels).[52] It is possible that the severity of Bernard's rhetoric was less the result of 'wounded pride' than the product of a genuine fear that the Easter Rising represented a 'German plot'. Bernard's revulsion at the idea of a 'German plot' was given added potency by the fact that his son had been killed around one year earlier while fighting at Gallipoli.[53] Personal bereavement thus gave Bernard a deep personal emotional commitment to the war, and it is likely that his immediate reaction to the Easter Rising, which he perceived to be perpetrated by Britain's wartime enemies, arose from something more visceral than 'wounded pride'.

However Bernard's reaction to the Rising is interpreted, it appeared to be a temporary hiatus in his moderate, consensual unionism. Such an assessment is reinforced by two sermons he preached in May 1916. In one given at the chapel of the Female Orphan House, he asked that 'there be no bitterness'. While the guilty must be punished 'for the sake of the innocent and the generation to come', there should be a 'strong resolve on our own part that there shall be no more playing with fire'.[54] The following Sunday, Bernard applied 1 Peter 2:17 ('Honour all men. Love the brotherhood. Fear God. Honour the King') to the situation in Ireland, insisting that the command to honour all men still held. In a further softening of his rhetoric from Easter week, he told the congregation to honour even those men whose principles and words were 'abhorrent' to them.[55]

THE LLOYD GEORGE PARTITION PLAN

While Bernard quickly returned to his conciliatory tone towards moderate Irish nationalism, the Easter Rising made him doubt the legitimacy of any ministerial attempts to settle the Irish question. At the start of June, Bernard informed David Lloyd George that unionists were 'as fully convinced as ever that separatist legislation for Ireland will injure Ireland's highest interests', bringing neither prosperity nor peace. Bernard feared that any attempt to give Ireland an independent parliament in the aftermath of the Easter Rising would be a 'direct incentive to lawlessness in the future on the part of the discontented'.[56] Similar sentiments were expressed in public by the bishop of Limerick, R. Orpen, in his speech to the Limerick diocesan synod. Orpen protested 'most strongly' against the principle that change in government should be made as a result of 'violence and rebellion'. Such a course only served to encourage 'discontent and disorder'.[57]

However, the government appeared ready to implement the plan devised by Lloyd George to settle the 'Irish question' for the duration of the war. The deal Lloyd George struck with Edward Carson and John Redmond was that home rule would come into operation immediately, with the exclusion of the six north-eastern counties of Ulster. The excluded area would remain under the control of the imperial parliament; crucially, in the interests of 'political salesmanship', the time period of exclusion was kept ambiguous.[58] Lloyd George informed Carson that the six-county 'Ulster' would not, after the war, 'whether she wills it or not, merge in the rest of Ireland', as there would be no automatic inclusion of the territory into a home rule parliament after the war – 'in other words, there must be further negotiations after the war to clear up this point'.[59] Acceptance of Lloyd George's proposals meant that both Carson and Redmond had made concessions – Carson in effect accepted temporary exclusion, while Redmond accepted the exclusion of six counties instead of the four he was prepared to cede at the

Buckingham Palace conference in 1914. Carson also confirmed he was prepared to sacrifice the three Ulster counties of Donegal, Monaghan and Cavan to secure the exclusion of the remaining six counties from home rule. Any unionist opposition Carson received for accepting the Lloyd George deal was largely due to this decision to jettison the three counties, which some held to revoke the terms of the Ulster Covenant. However, while the 1916 negotiations involved Carson and Redmond making compromises that may have been distasteful to their supporters, the Lloyd George plan failed due to opposition from southern unionists and disaffected Tories, led by Walter Long and Lord Lansdowne. Southern unionists opposed any revival of the home rule question during the war as they believed this would reward the disorder of the Easter Rising. In addition, the 'Imperial necessity' argument used by Carson to defend the deal was deemed illusory.

Arguments for and against the Lloyd George deal raised tensions within the Church of Ireland, as southern Anglicans feared their northern counterparts were prepared to abandon them to a Dublin parliament. An 'Irish Churchman', writing to the *Irish Times*, questioned the patriotism of the UUC in supporting partition. The Lloyd George plan would result, he claimed, in the Church of Ireland losing 'half the force of her title', leaving its members living under two legislatures. 'Irish Churchman' believed Anglicans in Ulster would be in a better position 'to speak for their fellow Churchmen' as members of an all-Ireland parliament than as citizens of an excluded Ulster.[60] T.C. Hammond, a leading evangelical and rector of a Dublin parish, opposed the Lloyd George plan, as it would isolate small minorities in both parts of Ireland. The result, he prophesised, would be a decline in the number of Protestants in the south and west of Ireland and a decline in the number of Catholics living in Ulster. Such demographic change would lead to the establishment of 'two hostile camps' in Ireland. The partition of Ireland thus represented 'not a counsel of despair, but a counsel of lunacy'. Hammond's solution to such political madness was to preach the gospel, urging Protestants to 'proclaim the truth fearlessly' as during the Reformation 'and win the country'. He wanted his congregation, largely composed of Orangemen, to 'live up to their reputations; let them be bigots, but bigots for God'.[61]

The *Church of Ireland Gazette* carried out a concerted campaign against the Lloyd George plan, believing partition to be 'an aggravation of the Irish problem'. The possibility of partition meant 'the position of our church as a vital force in Ireland has never been more seriously threatened'.[62] The *Gazette* proposed that Ulster should be united with the rest of Ireland under some form of provisional government, which would be the starting point for a more 'ambitious' settlement after the war.[63] As it became apparent that Lloyd George's partition plan would fail, an editorial in the *Gazette* commended southern unionists for giving expression to the anti-partition views of their own constituency and the great majority of moderate nationalists. On the other hand, it continued, Ulster unionism had retreated from the Covenant, leaving Protestants in the three excluded counties and three southern provinces to take their 'chances outside'. Southern unionists were imbued with moral legitimacy when compared with their 'increasingly parochial' Ulster counterparts: 'They are today the only party in Ireland which can properly be called constitutional – the only party which does not reinforce its arguments with rifles.' If southern unionists succeeded in convincing the government of their views, it would be a 'signal triumph of moral influence over the pernicious doctrine of physical force'.[64] The *Gazette* feared the

Lloyd George plan could scupper hopes for a new Ireland engendered by the paper's rather different interpretation (to that of Ulster-based clergy) of the meaning of the Somme. In words reminiscent of Bernard's 1915 Ossory synod speech, the periodical asserted that the Somme presented evidence of the 'real Ireland – that Ireland of the future, proud and united, which Ulstermen and Nationalists side by side are fashioning upon the anvil of war'. In contrast, at home was the 'false Ireland', 'degraded and divided', where the UUC and IPP conspired 'behind the backs of our Irish soldiers' to destroy the hopes and ideals for which they were fighting.[65]

In Ulster there was a smaller degree of clerical opposition to the Lloyd George plan, based largely on the assumption that partition involved breaking the Ulster Covenant. Rev. TLF Stack, rector of Drumquin in Tyrone, believed the Covenant had been 'torn up' by the UUC and called for public meetings to be held throughout Ulster to reaffirm the Covenant.[66] Stack continued his opposition to the Lloyd George plan in a sermon based on 2 Kings 19:10 ('The children of Israel have forsaken thy covenant') in which the Ulster Covenant was posited as a solemn vow made before God and 'an absolute oath – no conditions were introduced whereby we could absolve one another by mutual consent.' If Ulster accepted the Lloyd George plan and abandoned the Covenant in its entirety, they would be 'acting as atheists' and disowning 'God for Baal – for compromise and for the world'. He again called for meetings to be held throughout Ulster, disowning the action of the UUC.[67] In a later sermon, Stack claimed the heroism of the Ulster division at the Somme served as a contrast to the UUC: 'While our heroes were shouting "No Surrender!", our council surrendered, cast them to the dogs, let them go under Home Rule, what matter so long as our precious skins escape.'[68] Hugh de Fellenburg Montgomery, a leading layman and member of the UUC, criticised Stack's 'frothy denunciations' and claimed Crozier had reprimanded Stack for his sermons. Montgomery was sure the 'rock of common sense' in the minds of most Ulster unionists ensured Stack would have no success in his attempts at 'doing very wide-spread mischief'.[69]

Montgomery was correct that Stack's arguments made little impression, at least in the proposed six excluded counties of Ulster. The *Newsletter* established the Ulster unionist party line on the Lloyd George plan. While acceptance of Lloyd George's terms meant dispensing with the Ulster Covenant, the 'sacrifice' of the three counties was made 'on the sole grounds of the war necessity'. The UUC did not have the freedom of action of prewar days 'for our patriotism forbids us putting our own interests before the vital interests of nation and Empire'.[70] After the UUC voted to accept the Lloyd George proposals, the *Newsletter* praised the 'splendid self-sacrifice and self-abnegation' of the three excluded counties, and reiterated that 'it was a supreme sacrifice laid on the altar of the Empire's necessities'.[71] In a letter to *The Times*, the archdeacon of Down (L.A. Pooler) argued that as the UUC had accepted the 'clean cut of the six counties', Ulster would 'abide by its decision'. Pooler criticised Lord Lansdowne's attempts to scupper the Lloyd George plan. Lansdowne had failed to block reform of the House of Lords in 1911, 'and our troubles in Ulster became acute from the moment he yielded. I fear he will not do better for us than he did for the House of Lords, and I would rather he let us alone.'[72]

THE 1916 GENERAL SYNOD AND THE LLOYD GEORGE PLAN

The potential for public division within the Church of Ireland as the 1916 General Synod debated the Lloyd George plan was recognised by Hugh de Fellenburg Montgomery. Montgomery unsuccessfully advised Crozier to postpone the General Synod for twelve months, 'before any undesirable talk takes place', as it would be difficult to prevent discussion of the proposals there. Montgomery, an Ulster unionist, was concerned the increasingly southern unionist editorial line of the *Church of Ireland Gazette* underestimated 'the absolute impossibility of placing Belfast under an Irish Parliament'.[73]

At an 'emergency meeting' held the evening before the General Synod, the House of Bishops drew up a resolution on the Lloyd George plan.[74] Read to the synod by Crozier, the resolution stated the bishops' opposition to 'the introduction of a new system of administration, until opportunity has been given of considering its bearing upon the interests of the Church'. Demonstrating Bernard's influence, the resolution stated that the bishops were ready to 'make great sacrifices' in favour of a settlement 'calculated to unite our countrymen'.[75] Bernard had made a similar statement to Lloyd George in his 3 June letter, claiming that many in the south of Ireland were prepared to 'make great sacrifices to secure any stable form of government, under which life and property shall be secure'.[76] However, the resolution maintained that the bishops were not satisfied that imperial necessity was

> sufficiently well founded to justify the hasty adoption of a policy of dismemberment with which no Irishman is content, and which does not give the promise of permanence of unity, or of the impartial administration of common law.[77]

While Crozier had not followed Montgomery's advice to postpone the synod, he did ensure that no debate took place on either the bishops' resolution or the Lloyd George plan. The resolution was not debated as Crozier believed 'it was impossible … to discuss such a question with any prospect or hope of doing any real good in the present crisis'.[78]

The bishops' resolution was welcomed by the *Irish Times*. Its editorial on the matter pointed out the iniquitous results of partition to the Church – three dioceses would have to divide their allegiance between Westminster and Dublin, questions of finance and education would be enormously complicated, while the position of the scattered Protestant communities in the south and west was yet to be adequately safeguarded. The editorial concluded by claiming the resolution would strengthen the hands of cabinet members who opposed Lloyd George's plan.[79] Equally, the curtailment of debate at the synod was not questioned by the *Irish Times* or *Church of Ireland Gazette*. Any discussion was deemed unnecessary as no member could disagree with the resolution, which spoke in the authentic voice of the Church of Ireland.[80] The *Belfast Newsletter* merely quoted the resolution, without any additional comment.[81]

The resolution may not have had the influence leant it by the *Irish Times* and *Gazette*. It is difficult to substantiate whether the resolution increased the likelihood of the Lloyd George plan failing, although it may have strengthened the arguments of the southern unionists and Tories opposed to the proposals. However, the true significance of the bishops' resolution lay in how it illuminated the internal politics of the Church of Ireland. The resolution, with its strong opposition to 'dismemberment', suggested a southern unionist position was becoming predominant within the episcopate. This was not surprising. Bishops of southern dioceses outnumbered those from northern dioceses by eight to four. In addition, D'Arcy, apparently the most forceful and articulate Ulster unionist bishop, was not present at the meeting that drew up the resolution.[82] The implied criticism of Carson's position contained in the resolution meant that Crozier, and to a lesser extent D'Arcy, was initially obliged to defend the position of the House of Bishops in relation to the Lloyd George proposals. However, D'Arcy soon came to oppose the resolution and attempted to reinterpret its meaning.

In a letter to Edward Carson (affectionately addressed to 'My dear Ned'), Crozier justified the bishops' stand by claiming that they looked at the plan 'simply from the standpoint of its effect on the Church all over Ireland'. The bishops protested against the Church of Ireland not having been consulted by the government despite representing 'the best part of the population all over Ireland'. In addition, Crozier claimed the bishops were 'utterly in the dark as to any Imperial necessity for such an appalling change of government as is contemplated'. Crozier assured Carson that the bishops' resolution was 'in no sense a criticism on, or a condemnation of, the action of the Ulster Covenanters'.[83] D'Arcy also clarified to Carson the position of the northern bishops. Although not present, he informed Carson he knew what had happened at the meeting that drew up the resolution. According to D'Arcy, the southern bishops were determined to pass a resolution protesting against both the revival of the home rule question during the war and the exclusion of Ulster ('which most of them do not like'). 'Being a majority', the southern bishops 'could pass any resolution they pleased', he observed. It was only due to the influence of Crozier that the resolution 'took the shape it did, and not one which would have been much more unfavourable to the proposed settlement'.

D'Arcy also believed that, if the Lloyd George proposals were accepted, the exclusion of Ulster would 'certainly ... receive the support of the Bishops in the excluded area'.[84] In thus pledging the support of the northern bishops to exclusion, D'Arcy echoed a claim made by Crozier to Carson in a postscript to his letter of 26 June. The primate had informed Carson 'that we northern Bishops do feel that if Home Rule were bound to come even now, that you plainly found the only possible solution so far as Ulster is concerned'. However, Crozier's statement should not necessarily be taken as a firm endorsement of Ulster exclusion. Arguably, he was merely acknowledging that Carson had obtained the best possible deal for Ulster unionism – this would explain Crozier's claim that if he was present at the UUC meeting that ratified the Lloyd George deal, he would not have opposed it '*as a Covenanter*' (emphasis in original).[85] This apparent support of Ulster exclusion should be read in the context of the rest of his letter, which made clear his view that the partition of Ireland envisaged by the Lloyd George deal would be bad for the Church of Ireland as a whole.

Crozier's tentative acceptance of the legitimacy of partition and D'Arcy's more wholehearted support for exclusion suggests that the public show of unity represented by the bishops' resolution was fallacious. In July D'Arcy explained this rather contradictory position to Carson by claiming that 'the resolution was really a most ambiguous statement and I have not met anyone who knows exactly what it means'. Clearly backtracking on his 28 June letter to Carson, D'Arcy was now openly critical of the resolution. He was 'sorry' not to have been at the meeting when it was drawn up, he told Carson, 'but, as you know, I did not receive the summons and knew nothing of its doings until afterwards. It would have been impossible to secure any modification afterwards and I felt it was wiser to say nothing.' The reason for D'Arcy's change in tone was the increasing opposition of southern unionists to the Lloyd George proposals. He claimed the southern unionists who were trying to 'wreck' the settlement were either 'clinging to a hope of wrecking Home Rule altogether, or are bitterly vexed at what seems to them the privileged position of Ulster'. D'Arcy was 'ashamed' of the efforts being made to prevent a settlement, especially from the *Church of Ireland Gazette*, which was 'mischievous and is showing a very bad spirit'. D'Arcy was sure the line taken by Carson was 'perfectly right': 'If Home Rule is coming, as seems certain, the only possible way of securing any peace or security in Ireland is to exclude the six counties.' In a probable allusion to the Somme, D'Arcy asserted that 'the Ulstermen cannot be forced in. Now, more than ever, this has become impossible.'[86] D'Arcy's support for the Carsonite position on the Lloyd George scheme was in direct opposition to the stance articulated by the House of Bishops in their resolution to the synod.

The speeches of three southern bishops to their diocesan synods in July 1916 served to highlight their divergence from D'Arcy on the issue of partition. Sterling Berry, bishop of Killaloe, wanted members of the Church of Ireland in the south and west of Ireland to unite with the 'vast majority of our fellow countrymen'. Irish nationalists had proved themselves loyal to the empire by joining the war effort. Therefore, 'all sides should unite in allowing bygones to be bygones, and that with one heart and soul we should work together for the welfare of our native land.'[87]

Similar sentiments were more forcibly expressed by B.J. Plunkett, bishop of Tuam, at his diocesan synod. Plunkett welcomed the failure of the 'wretched compromise' represented by the Lloyd George scheme, as it had seemed 'the price they were to pay for the crime of Easter week was the dismemberment of their country, the permanent mutilation of their national life.' He hoped a 'fresh start' would be made towards national unity as the 'only secure basis on which their future government could ever rest'. The Church of Ireland should take the 'God given opportunity' to spread throughout Ireland 'a spirit of love, and so prepare a bond of unity on which a happier Ireland might yet be built'.[88] Plunkett confirmed his views in a letter to Bernard at the end of August, in which he stated it was the Church of Ireland's 'duty' to 'labour for unity and to prepare the way for some united action when we are faced with the actual fact of Home Rule'.[89] The bishop of Ossory (J.A.F. Gregg) also criticised the Lloyd George scheme in a speech to the Leighlin and Carlow diocesan synod. Gregg claimed a 'settlement must rest on something more substantial than an ambiguous phrase'. He hoped members of the Church of Ireland would take part in any attempt at 'conciliation' in Ireland, 'and make it plain that if their home is in Ireland their heart is in Ireland to[o]'.[90]

An editorial in the *Irish Times* praised Plunkett and Berry's diocesan synod speeches for continuing the 'wisdom and foresight' demonstrated in the bishops' resolution. Plunkett and Berry, in accepting self-government and trying to make it 'fair and just for the whole Irish people', had vindicated the 'mission and the patriotism of the Church of Ireland' by pointing out a path to peace.[91] Ulster unionist newspapers were less complimentary than the *Irish Times* about the new-found spirit of episcopal independence emanating from Tuam, Killaloe and Ossory. The *Newsletter* criticised the bishops for appearing to assume that the 'Unionists of this province have taken their stand with insufficient consideration, and that it will be easy to persuade them to depart from it'. The *Newsletter* insisted

Ulster had not proposed to divide Ireland; rather, the rest of Ireland wished to break away from Ulster.[92]

The three bishops' diocesan synod speeches articulated the kind of conciliatory sentiments towards Irish nationalism characteristic of Bernard before the Easter Rising. Indeed, Lord Monteagle recognised this similarity, writing to Bernard that 'I am glad to see your mantle has fallen on your successor at Ossory and his brethren of Killaloe and Tuam.'[93] Despite his initially angry reaction to the Rising, Bernard remained in the vanguard of those southern unionists urging a settlement.[94] In an article in the *National Review* in October, he confirmed his opposition to Ulster exclusion. Indeed, he was now sure that those 'who used to be Unionists' were ready to make 'great sacrifices in their endeavour to make great friends with their Nationalist fellow-countrymen'.[95] In addition, the bishop of Cork believed to see the 'North and South rent asunder' would sadden all those who hoped 'for a prosperous and peaceful future for Ireland'.[96]

When seen in the context of Crozier and D'Arcy's correspondence with Carson, and the statements of southern bishops after the General Synod, the bishops' resolution obscured rather than revealed the true position of the episcopate on an Irish settlement. It could be argued the resolution had been carried to its logical conclusion by Gregg, Plunkett and Berry, and by Bernard in his *National Review* article. The resolution stated the bishops' desire to make 'great sacrifices in favour of any scheme for the future government of Ireland calculated to unite our countrymen'. The proximity of the Lloyd George scheme to the Easter Rising perhaps made it unlikely that the House of Bishops were prepared to make such a sacrifice at the time of the resolution. However, once the dust had settled in Dublin and civilisation did not break down, southern bishops seemed prepared to make concessions in the interests of Irish unity, by advocating some form of all-Ireland home rule.

D'Arcy's anger at southern unionist attempts to scupper the Lloyd George deal implied he would have little sympathy with the all-Ireland conciliatory statements emanating from bishops of southern dioceses. It is possible, as Buckland claims, that the southern bishops 'forced' the bishops of the Church of Ireland to pass the General Synod resolution.[97] D'Arcy's claim (although impossible to substantiate) that he was not told about the House of Bishops meeting that drew up the resolution implied that he had been deliberately excluded. This in turn suggests that D'Arcy was seen as the figurehead of the Ulster unionist section in the Church of Ireland, a position established by his involvement in Ulster Day and endorsement of the UVF. However, while D'Arcy may indeed have been outmanœuvred by his southern unionist episcopal counterparts, it is doubtful that Crozier was 'forced' into signing the resolution. Crozier's ambiguous attitude towards Ulster exclusion was actually well represented by the resolution. While undoubtedly sympathetic towards Ulster unionism (as suggested by his letters to Carson after the Easter Rising), Crozier was nevertheless concerned at the effect partition could have on the Church of Ireland. The resolution claimed to represent the Church of Ireland's view of the Lloyd George plan, allowing Crozier to avoid explicitly identifying the Church with either Ulster or southern unionism. However, in practice, Crozier's desire to develop a particularly 'Church of Ireland' position on partition was challenged by the statements made by Plunkett, Berry and Gregg, articulating views on an Irish settlement that were anathema to the majority of Ulster Anglicans (and to D'Arcy).

THE LOGUE MANIFESTO

The conciliatory moves of Gregg, Berry and Plunkett culminated in their support of the Logue Manifesto, published in May 1917. Composed by the Catholic bishop of Derry, Charles MacHugh, and named after the primate, Cardinal Logue, the manifesto expressed in unmistakeable terms opposition to partition. Eighteen Catholic bishops signed the document, along with Gregg, Berry and Plunkett. The manifesto, addressed to the people of Ireland, stated:

> An appeal to the National conscience on the question of Ireland's dismemberment should meet with one answer and one answer alone. To Irishmen of every creed and class and party the very thought of our country partitioned and torn, as a new Poland, must be one of heart rending sorrow.[98]

Gregg's biography reveals that MacHugh wrote to him on 2 May asking him to sign the manifesto.[99] Gregg lent his signature as he believed it expressed the same sentiment as the 1916 bishops' resolution; he therefore did not believe there was a problem in confirming similar sentiments along with the Catholic bishops.[100] The Logue Manifesto has been largely overlooked in accounts of the period. Jérôme aan de Wiel correctly interprets the manifesto as an attempt to undermine Redmond's position ahead of a forthcoming by-election in South Longford (subsequently lost by the Irish Parliamentary Party).[101] However, the Logue Manifesto carried implications for the Church of Ireland and revealed the growing divisions within the episcopate on the future settlement of Ireland.

There was a decidedly hostile reaction to the manifesto from the Ulster unionist press. The *Newsletter* and *Belfast Telegraph* both opposed it, and questioned why the three Church of Ireland bishops had leant their name in support. By accepting the 'Romanist' view on home rule, the bishops would not, it was alleged, earn the respect of the Catholic majority in their dioceses, 'and it is certain that it will not alter the attitude of Ulster'.[102] The bishops had allowed themselves 'to be made the foolish instrument of the subtlety of others' – the others being the Catholic bishops, who were out to 'have Ireland converted into the sanctuary of their faith, a place where their church will be supreme in politics and in religion'.[103]

In contrast to the view taken by the Ulster unionist press, the *Church of Ireland Gazette* praised the Logue Manifesto as 'one of the most remarkable documents in Irish political history'. The manifesto's commitment to 'the ideal of an Ireland "one and undivided"' expressed the 'only common ground' between nationalist Ireland and southern unionism. All that the three bishops had asserted in the manifesto, it noted, was the principle that 'under any form of government, there shall be no partition, temporary or permanent'.[104] Both the *Gazette* and *Irish Times* believed the manifesto carried added significance due to the three Anglican bishops' signatures. *The Irish Times* claimed the bishops stood 'for the absolutely solid hostility of the Unionists of the South and West of Ireland to a scheme which would doom them to social and political isolation of the most helpless kind'. The manifesto brought the two churches together in a commitment to an Ireland 'one and undivided', a 'portent that is almost unique in Irish history'.[105] The London *Times* also welcomed the manifesto. While it could be seen as a 'knock out blow' to any settlement based on partition, the manifesto was also 'a portent of the most hopeful kind. It ends a chapter in Irish history but promises to open another and far better chapter.' The paper pointed out that any Irish settlement must be limited by two strict negations – no partition and no coercion of Ulster. However, 'in other directions true statesmanship may find its possibilities'.[106]

The difference in how the Ulster unionist and southern unionist press interpreted the manifesto was mirrored by division within the Church of Ireland episcopate. On the day the Logue Manifesto was published, D'Arcy wrote to Gregg asking him if 'dismemberment' was a fair word to use regarding partition. With a hint of irony, D'Arcy admitted 'if those who sign this document are thinking of complete separation from England, I grant that [dismemberment] may be used.'[107] Of course, Gregg was not thinking of complete separation from England, although the Catholic bishops may have been, a difference in motivation D'Arcy was keen to point out. In addition to private criticism of the manifesto, D'Arcy carried out a public dispute in the pages of *The Times* with Sterling Berry. D'Arcy maintained that the three bishops' support for the Logue Manifesto did not signal a change in the Church of Ireland's attitude to home rule. The Church had 'never given any sign' that her opinion towards home rule had changed from that expressed at the three special General Synods (held in 1886, 1893 and 1912). D'Arcy also called on more recent history to illustrate his point by referring to the 1916 resolution:

> Last year our House of Bishops passed a resolution against a 'policy of dismemberment' but, as I understood, our reference was to the policy which would dismember the United Kingdom and divide Ireland at the same time.[108]

Berry replied by claiming D'Arcy's interpretation of the 1916 House of Bishops resolution 'cannot be maintained', as it was evident that the phrase 'policy of dismemberment' referred to Ireland, not the United Kingdom. It was this position, 'unanimously adopted by the House of Bishops last June' that Berry claimed he had reaffirmed by signing the manifesto.[109]

The Logue Manifesto provoked the northern bishops to articulate publicly what at least D'Arcy appeared already to believe privately – that partition was the most attractive option available to Ulster unionists. Gregg was secretary to the House of Bishops and it was his job, on the instructions of Crozier, to summon the bishops to a special meeting to discuss the manifesto. Crozier wanted the bench to be aware of the action the northern bishops proposed to take in relation to the Logue Manifesto:

> The joint action of three bishops of the Church of Ireland with the Roman hierarchy compels the Ulster bishops, alas, to take some public action, as I hear incalculable injury is being done to the Church in the north.[110]

Crozier's letter to Gregg was an edited version of his true opinion on the actions of the three bishops. Writing to Hugh de Fellenburg Montgomery, Crozier stated:

> I am indeed *horrified* at the joint action of three bishops of our Church with the Roman hierarchy. I expected better things of Ossary [Gregg]. *Nothing* done by Tuam [Plunkett] or Killaloe [Berry] would surprise me. I think the action of the three is utterly *disloyal* to their Episcopal brethren and I shall tell them so.[111]

The action taken by the northern bishops involved issuing a statement, signed by Crozier, D'Arcy and the three other bishops of Ulster dioceses. The statement quoted the 1916 resolution by reaffirming that the division of Ireland 'does not give the promise of permanence of unity'. It also emphasised the northern bishops were still of the opinion that the only way to secure the unity of Ireland was to preserve the union. However, in one major way the northern bishops' statement differed from the 1916 resolution. It stated explicitly that no policy of home rule could be put into operation 'without the exclusion of part or the whole of the province of Ulster'.[112] This seemed rather at odds with opposition to the division of Ireland, an ambiguity D'Arcy lamented in a letter to Montgomery. D'Arcy believed the quotation from the 1916 resolution (that 'unhappy resolution') spoiled the statement, but pointed out 'no one signatory to a composite document can ever get his own wishes carried out.' However, he believed the quotation from the 1916 resolution should be interpreted in light of the rest of the document, which was 'perfectly clear' on the matter of partition.[113] However, the *Gazette* believed the northern bishops' statement had come to the same conclusion as the Logue Manifesto – that no viable settlement could involve partition.[114] It is likely the ambiguity in the northern bishops' statement was due to the influence of Crozier. As primate, he wanted to minimise the public rupture within the episcopate and present as far as possible a show of unity. This interpretation is supported by Crozier's desire that Montgomery reply to Sterling Berry's letter in *The Times*. Crozier feared it would be unwise for D'Arcy to 'embark on a newspaper controversy with a brother bishop'.[115]

The publication of the Logue Manifesto stimulated Hugh de Fellenburg Montgomery to compose his own version, closely parodying the original. Montgomery's manifesto opposed partition on the basis of wartime necessity, although he (like D'Arcy) defined partition as the division of the United Kingdom. The safety of the realm, secured in the face of Napoleonic aggression by the Act of Union, would be protected from German aggression by the repeal of the Home Rule Act.[116] Montgomery produced his document as he feared the Logue Manifesto 'will injure the Church in Ulster and also weaken the Ulster Unionist position by creating the impression that we are a very lonely lot of reactionary obstructionists'.[117] The bishops of Derry and Clogher, along with D'Arcy, supported Montgomery's manifesto.[118] D'Arcy commended the document, as 'it puts the case with absolute clearness, and it will be a real reply to the humbug, real downright humbug, which *The Times* and *Daily Mail* have been circulating'.[119] However, John Henry Bernard declined to support Montgomery's manifesto. He interpreted the 1916 resolution in the same way as Gregg, although unlike Gregg the resolution did not provide Bernard with sufficient justification to permit him to sign the Logue Manifesto: 'I think that the partition or dismemberment of Ireland is a wrong headed policy and unlikely to promote peace. But I thought that the opposition of our bishops to partition had been sufficiently indicated in the resolution which they read to the General Synod in June 1916.'[120]

This lack of clarity over the interpretation of the 1916 resolution was a feature of the episcopate's attitude to partition and signified the tensions between northern and southern bishops. The resolution proved a very malleable document, used to justify both the signing of and opposition to the Logue Manifesto. The southern bishops' interpretation of the resolution was more accurate. Produced as a result of Lloyd George's plan to partition Ireland, it seems natural to assume that the 1916 resolution referred to the partition of Ireland. D'Arcy's interpretation of the resolution was flawed – home rule was placed on the statute book in 1914, so it was unlikely the House of Bishops would wait until 1916 to record their opposition to the partition of the United Kingdom. D'Arcy's revisionist interpretation of the 1916 resolution should be seen as an attempt to justify his opposition to the Logue Manifesto, which may have appeared unreasonable in light of the 1916 resolution he gave his name to. The lack of clarity was also expressed in the northern bishops' statement against the Logue Manifesto, which simultaneously opposed the division of Ireland yet called for Ulster exclusion in the case of home rule being enacted. The northern bishops' resolution fulfilled Crozier's desire to maintain unity within the Church, as it was probably Crozier who inserted the reference from the 1916 resolution to water down D'Arcy's call for exclusion.

CONCLUSION

The Easter Rising and the Somme acted as a catalyst for future political developments in Ireland. For southern unionists, the Easter Rising had a short-term but hugely significant impact by hardening the spirit of rapprochement with Irish nationalism already generated by Redmond's response to the war.[121] The effect of the Rising on the Church of Ireland in Dublin, recorded in vestry minutes and parish magazines as well as sermons and other public statements, largely explained the negative reception to Lloyd George's proposed settlement. The rejection of partition in the summer of 1916 has been described as a spectacular example of 'political masochism'.[122] The Lloyd George scheme might have prevented the spread of Sinn Féin and the revolutionary republicanism that ultimately proved destructive for southern unionism as well as the moderate nationalism represented by John Redmond. In addition, the southern unionists' foiling of Lloyd George's proposal angered those Ulster unionists content with the proposed deal, thereby strengthening their partitionist impulse – as seen in the reaction of D'Arcy to the southern bishops' apparently Machiavellian management of the House of Bishops before the 1916 General Synod.

If the Easter Rising placed a temporary brake on southern unionism's positive evaluation of moderate nationalism, and clouded their tactical judgement, the Rising, in conjunction with the Somme, accelerated Ulster unionist acceptance of some form of settlement based on 'Ulster' exclusion. For Ulster Protestants, the Rising demonstrated Ulster's distinctiveness from the allegedly lawless and treacherous south of Ireland. Thanks in part to clerical sermons, the Somme quickly emerged as a narrative of Ulster unionist loyalty and devotion to the empire and confirmation of unionist Ulster's right to remain free from the rule of a Dublin parliament.

The tensions and disagreements between the political representatives of Ulster unionism and southern unionism were manifested in the Church of Ireland. The 1916 bishops' resolution demonstrated the influence of southern bishops (led by Bernard) by pledging opposition to partition. However, while the Lloyd George scheme was rejected, it ultimately convinced the more forward-looking southern bishops that in the absence of support from the British government and Ulster unionism, southern unionism should seek an agreement with moderate Irish nationalism on the future government of Ireland. Plunkett, Berry and Gregg's desire to build a new Ireland out of the ashes of the war, expressed in their 1916 diocesan synod speeches, found formal expression in the Logue Manifesto. The idealism of the three bishops, labouring under an assumption that Ulster could be won to some future vision of an Ireland united and at peace, blinded them to the wider political implications of the Logue Manifesto, with its negative effects on Redmondism and on relations between the Church of Ireland in Ulster and the rest of Ireland. Bernard, pragmatic and politically astute, opposed partition without endorsing the Logue Manifesto and confirmed his position as a leading southern unionist at the forthcoming Irish Convention (1917–18).

D'Arcy's torturous attempts at reinterpreting the meaning of the 1916 bishops' resolution reflected his impression of the political reality of the situation in Ireland – some form of home rule could not be avoided, and therefore Ulster unionism should seek the best it could get – six-county exclusion. In accepting Ulster exclusion, D'Arcy probably had the support of a majority of clergy in the north-east of Ulster, as demonstrated by the 1916 Easter vestries and lack of opposition to the Lloyd George scheme. However, the ambiguous nature of the northern bishops' response to the Logue Manifesto demonstrated their lack of unanimity on exclusion. Such confusion was not unexpected: in 1916, Bishop Day of Clogher told diocesan synod members that they should stand by the terms of the Ulster Covenant and resist home rule for all of Ireland.[123] The *Gazette* praised the 'honesty and courage' of Day's speech, suggesting Ulster unionism had two options – revert to the Covenant and oppose home rule for all of Ireland, or work for a 'real' settlement. There was no middle way, as partition had passed out of the realm of practical politics.[124] The bishop of Derry and Raphoe expressed similar sentiments in May 1917, after the northern bishops' statement. He believed it was 'unwarranted' to assume the 'old Unionist standpoint, i.e. the union as it is and was' had ceased to exist as a viable political position.[125] Such views were in line less with D'Arcy and more with those held by southern unionists still opposed to any form of compromise, who stood for 'the union, the whole union and nothing but the union'.[126] Significantly, Clogher (based in Fermanagh but including much of Monaghan) and Derry and Raphoe (which included County Donegal) had large areas on the 'outer' fringes of any proposed excluded area and would have been 'cross-border' dioceses under six-county exclusion. While clergy (including D'Arcy) in east Ulster appeared willing to countenance six-county Ulster exclusion, the reaction of Day and Peacocke to events in 1916–17 suggested they were tempted to revert to an all-Ireland unionism to preserve intact the integrity of their dioceses.

The dynamic of the political divisions in the Church of Ireland episcopate in 1916–17 was similar to that established in 1912. D'Arcy still represented the Ulster unionist viewpoint, Bernard was still the leading southern unionist figure, although both men replicated the political journeys of the leaders in Irish unionism. D'Arcy followed Carson into an acceptance of six-county Ulster exclusion, while Bernard, if anything, led southern unionists in a conciliatory, home rule, direction. The antagonistic implications of these positions produced the contradictory and confusing statements of 1916 and 1917.

However, Archbishop Crozier attempted to provide, as he had done since 1912, a potential solution to the growing divisions in the episcopate. While Bernard influenced the 1916 resolution, Crozier certainly ensured the northern bishops' response to the Logue Manifesto was as ambiguous – and inoffensive to southern members of the Church of Ireland – as possible. Crozier's position of adopting a kind of halfway house – between opposition to home rule and opposition to Ulster exclusion – was understandable from the head of an all-Ireland Church. To support the line taken by Gregg, Berry and Plunkett would have angered members of the Church of Ireland in Ulster; to support exclusion would have alienated members in the south and west. Therefore, beneath the apparent confusion and contradictory statements on partition from the episcopate in 1916 and the first half of 1917, it is possible to discern some consistency, provided by Crozier's desire to maintain unimpaired the unity of the Church of Ireland, a unity lacking in 'secular' Irish unionism. However, the Irish Convention, called by Lloyd George in May 1917, was to test Crozier's ability at balancing the competing factions within the Church of Ireland.

NOTES

1. John Henry Bernard to Edward Carson, 29 May 1915 (Public Record Office of Northern Ireland (PRONI), Carson papers, D/1507/A/12/27).
2. See Thomas Hennessy, *Dividing Ireland: World War One and Partition* (London, 1998), p.158.
3. *Belfast Newsletter*, 27 April 1916.
4. John Gwynn to Joseph Irvine Peacocke, 24 April 1916 (PRONI, Peacocke papers, MIC/87).
5. See Charles Townshend, *Easter 1916: The Irish Rebellion* (London, 2005) for a recent account of the Rising.
6. *Belfast Newsletter*, 27 April 1916.
7. Ibid., 1 May 1916.
8. Ibid., 26 April 1916.
9. John Baptist Crozier to Edward Carson, 7 May 1916 (PRONI, Carson papers, D/1507/A/16/11).
10. Crozier memo to Carson, 7 May 1916 (ibid., D/1507/A/16/12).
11. Carson to Herbert Asquith, 9 May 1916 (ibid., D/1507/A/16/9).
12. Herbert Asquith to Carson, 10 May 1916 (ibid., D/1507/A/16/10).
13. Knockbreda vestry minute book, 26 April 1916 (PRONI, CR/1/24D/3).
14. Trinity vestry minute book, 27 April 1916 (ibid., CR/1/3/5/2).
15. St Comgall's vestry minute book, 28 April 1916 (ibid., CR/1/87/D/3).
16. *Lisburn Standard*, 5 May 1916.
17. Mary Magdalene parish magazine, May 1916 (private possession).
18. *Belfast Newsletter*, 22 May 1916.
19. Lisburn Cathedral magazine, June 1916; reproduced in *Lisburn Standard*, 2 June 1916.
20. Keith Jeffery, *Ireland and the Great War* (Cambridge, 2000), p.56.
21. *Belfast Newsletter*, 8, 11 July 1916.
22. Ibid., 8 July 1916.
23. *Belfast Weekly Telegraph*, 15 July 1916.
24. *Ulster Gazette*, 22 July 1916.
25. *Belfast Newsletter*, 14 August 1916.
26. Mary Magdalene parish magazine, July 1916.
27. P. Bew, *Ireland: The Politics of Enmity, 1789–2006* (Oxford, 2007), p.382.
28. See Hennessey, *Dividing Ireland*, p.198–200.
29. *Down Recorder*, 15 July 1916.
30. Knockbreda vestry minute book, 12 July 1916 (PRONI, CR/1/24D/3).
31. Ibid., 31 July 1918.
32. Ibid., 10 April 1917.
33. Mary Magdalene parish magazine, September 1916.
34. Armoy preacher book, 23 July 1916 (PRONI, MIC/1/334/E/2–3).
35. General Sir John Maxwell to Bernard, 8 May 1916 (British Library, J.H. Bernard papers, Add. Ms 52782/71); *Irish Times*, 11 May 1916.
36. Bernard to Maxwell, 10 May 1916 (British Library, J.H. Bernard papers, Add. Ms 52782/72).
37. *Irish Times*, 8 May 1916; there was only one route open to the cathedral and the congregation did not number more than 100.
38. St Stephen's vestry minutes, 12 May 1916 (Representative Church Body (RCB) Library, P.46. 5. 2).
39. St Peter's parish magazine, June 1916 (ibid., P.45. 16. 10).
40. Mariners' Church parish magazine, June 1916 (ibid., P.368. 25. 1).
41. *Irish Times*, 17 October 1916.
42. St Bartholomew's parish magazine, July 1916 (RCB Library, P.64. 25. 1).
43. Howth parish magazine, May 1916 (ibid., P.373. 25).
44. Bernard to Rev. Mr Thompson, 28 April 1916 (British Library, J.H. Bernard papers, Add. Ms 52782/50).
45. Handwritten notes of sermon delivered by Bernard in St Anne's, 30 April (ibid., 52782/14–15).
46. *The Times*, 5 May 1916.

47. A.J. Balfour to Bernard, 11 May (British Library, J.H. Bernard papers, Add. Ms 52782/75–6).
48. Minutes of the Standing Committee of the General Synod, 18 May 1916 (RCB Library, Dublin).
49. Donnybrook parish magazine, July 1916 (ibid., July 1916).
50. B.J. Plunkett to Crozier, cited in G.F. Stewart to W. Long, 31 May 1916 (House of Lords Library, Lloyd George papers, D/14/1/45).
51. Robert H. Murray, *Archbishop Bernard: Professor, Prelate and Provost* (London, 1931), p.236.
52. S. Gwynn, *John Redmond's Last Years* (London, 1919), pp.223–5.
53. See A. Megahey, *The Irish Protestant Churches in the Twentieth Century* (London, 2000), p.41.
54. *Irish Times*, 8 May 1916.
55. Ibid., 15 May 1916.
56. Bernard to Lloyd George, 3 June 1916 (House of Lords Library, Lloyd George papers, D/14/2/7).
57. *Irish Times*, 7 June 1916.
58. Alvin Jackson, *Home Rule: An Irish History, 1800–2000* (London, 2003), p.159.
59. David G. Boyce, 'British opinion, Ireland, and the war, 1916–1918', *Historical Journal*, 17, 3 (1974), p.580.
60. *Irish Times*, 8 June 1916.
61. Ibid., 3 July 1916.
62. *Church of Ireland Gazette*, 2, 16 June 1916.
63. Ibid., 2 June 1916.
64. Ibid., 30 June 1916.
65. Ibid., 7 July 1916.
66. *Irish Times*, 17 June 1916.
67. Sermon preached by Rev. T.L.F. Stack in Lower Langfield Church, 25 June 1916 (PRONI, Montgomery papers, D/627/429/33).
68. Sermon preached by Rev. T.L.F. Stack in Lower Langfield Church, 9 July 1916 (ibid., D/627/429/91).
69. Montgomery to Sinclair, 20 September 1916 (ibid., D/627/429/66).
70. *Belfast Newsletter*, 7 June 1916.
71. Ibid., 13 June 1916.
72. *The Times*, 24 June 1916.
73. Montgomery to Crozier, 18 June 1916 (PRONI, Montgomery papers, D/627/429/41).
74. Minutes of the House of Bishops, 19 June 1916 (RCB Library).
75. *Irish Times*, 21 June 1916.
76. Bernard to Lloyd George, 3 June 1916 (House of Lords Library, Lloyd George papers, D/14/2/7).
77. *Irish Times*, 21 June 1916.
78. Ibid.
79. Ibid.
80. Ibid.; *Gazette*, 23 June 1916.
81. *Belfast Newsletter*, 21 June 1916.
82. See minutes of the House of Bishops, 19 June 1916 (RCB Library).
83. Crozier to Carson, 26 June 1916 (PRONI, Carson papers, D/1507/A/17/26).
84. D'Arcy to Carson, 28 June 1916 (ibid., D/1507/A/17/31).
85. Crozier to Carson, 26 June 1916 (ibid., D/1507/A/17/26).
86. D'Arcy to Carson, 7 July 1916 (ibid., D/1507/A/18/7).
87. *Irish Times*, 26 July 1916.
88. Ibid., 27 July 1916.
89. B.J. Plunkett to Bernard, 28 August 1916 (British Library, J.H. Bernard papers, Add. Ms 52782/122–3).
90. *Irish Times*, 29 July 1916.
91. Ibid., 27 July 1916.
92. *Newsletter*, 15 August 1916.
93. Monteagle to Bernard, 31 July 1916 (British Library, J.H. Bernard papers, Add. Ms 52782/95–8).
94. P. Buckland, *Irish Unionism I: The Anglo-Irish and the New Ireland, 1885–1922* (Dublin, 1972) p.83.
95. *Belfast Weekly Telegraph*, 7 October 1916.
96. *Church of Ireland Gazette*, 27 October 1916.
97. Buckland, *Irish Unionism I*, p.63.
98. *Irish Times*, 8 May 1917.
99. George Seaver, *Gregg: Archbishop* (Dublin, 1963), p.86.
100. Ibid., p.87.
101. Jérôme aan de Wiel, *The Catholic Church in Ireland: 1914–1918* (Dublin, 2003), p.174.
102. *Belfast Newsletter*, 8 May 1917.
103. *Belfast Telegraph*, 8 May 1917.

104. *Church of Ireland Gazette*, 11 May 1917.
105. *Irish Times*, 8 May 1917.
106. *The Times*, 10 May 1917.
107. Seaver, *Gregg: Archbishop*, p.90.
108. *The Times*, 14 May 1917.
109. Ibid., 16 May 1917.
110. Seaver, *Gregg: Archbishop*, p.90.
111. Crozier to Montgomery, 11 May 1917 (PRONI, Montgomery papers, D/627/431/14).
112. *Belfast Newsletter*, 17 May 1917.
113. D'Arcy to Montgomery, 18 May 1917 (PRONI, Montgomery papers, D/627/431/38).
114. *Church of Ireland Gazette*, 18 May 1917.
115. Montgomery to Stronge, 18 May 1917 (ibid., D/627/431/41).
116. Montgomery to Bernard, 10 May 1917 (TCD, Convention papers, Mss 2986–7/273).
117. Montgomery to Bagwell, 9 May 1917 (PRONI, Montgomery papers, D/627/431/9).
118. Peacocke (bishop of Derry) to Montgomery, 11 May 1917 (ibid., D/627/431/7); Maurice Day (bishop of Clogher), 12 May 1917 (ibid., D/627/431/26).
119. D'Arcy to Montgomery, 11 May 1917 (ibid., D/627/430/6).
120. Bernard to Montgomery, 11 May 1917 (ibid., D/627/431/6).
121. Buckland, *Irish Unionism I*, p.51.
122. Jackson, *Home Rule*, p.170.
123. *Belfast Newsletter*, 30 September 1916.
124. *Church of Ireland Gazette*, 6 October 1916.
125. Joseph Irvine Peacocke to Montgomery, 12 May 1917 (PRONI, Montgomery papers, D/627/431/29).
126. Richard Bagwell to Montgomery, 15 May 1917 (ibid., D/627/431/34).

7

'A potent instrument of national unity'?
The Church of Ireland Episcopate and the
Irish Convention, 1917–18

The failure of the Lloyd George negotiations at the end of July 1916 appeared to signal a lull in attempts at achieving an Irish settlement. However, the issue of home rule remained on the agenda, and was debated six times in the House of Commons between July and December 1916.[1] Privately the government, pressured largely by wartime exigencies into seeking a settlement, worked to keep the negotiating spirit alive. In May 1917 David Lloyd George (who had succeeded Asquith as prime minister in December 1916) offered Redmond the immediate implementation of home rule with the exclusion of the six north-eastern Ulster counties, or, as a 'last resort', 'a convention of Irishmen of all parties for the purpose of producing a scheme of Irish self-government'.[2] Redmond plumped for the convention, which was subsequently announced by Lloyd George in a speech to the Commons on 21 May 1917. An Irish Convention 'fully representative' of Irish opinion was promised, tasked with producing a form of Irish self-government 'within the Empire'.[3] The Convention first met at Trinity College Dublin on 25 July 1917 and continued to meet intermittently until April 1918. Chaired by Horace Plunkett, membership was composed of ninety-five members, including five from the Irish Parliamentary Party, led by John Redmond, five southern unionists, led by Lord Midleton, and five Ulster unionist delegates, led by Hugh Barrie (MP for North Londonderry). Among other representatives were chairmen of county councils and fifteen government appointees. Members of the three main churches also attended. John Baptist Crozier and John Henry Bernard acted as representatives of the Church of Ireland.

In the opinion of its chairman, the Irish Convention 'laid a foundation of Irish agreement unprecedented in history'.[4] Such optimism was misplaced. The Convention *did* produce a proposal with majority support – but failed to obtain the support of the Ulster unionist delegation and a significant number of nationalists, and from outside was opposed from the start by Sinn Féin. A proposal put forward by Lord Midleton formed the basis of the majority report produced by the Convention. The southern unionist delegation conceded the establishment of an Irish parliament (with an executive responsible to it) for the whole of Ireland, with control over internal legislation, administration and direct taxation.[5] Two minority reports were proposed. The Ulster unionist delegation insisted on Ulster exclusion, while a number of nationalists angered at the lack of 'fiscal autonomy' embodied in the majority report called for an Irish parliament to have control of customs and excise. Ultimately, the Convention report did not represent the 'substantial' majority hoped for by the government.[6]

Midleton's proposal almost obtained 'cross-party' support – and possibly would have succeeded had the chairman, Horace Plunkett, not intervened by initiating a debate on land purchase instead of seeking a prompt agreement of the essentials of the proposed deal. Plunkett's failure as a chairman is a theme of the historiography of the Convention.[7] Of relevance for this chapter, the Convention is also seen as solidifying the growing divergence between Ulster and southern unionism.[8] Despite initially appearing interested in the Midleton proposal, the Ulster unionists came to oppose the deal because the doubts of their extremists hardened during the 'lost time' of the land purchase debate. Midleton had hoped to work with the Ulster unionists, but retrospectively claimed co-operation between 'ten men who were bent on finding a solution to this age-long problem and twenty-one men who were determined to frustrate any settlement for Ireland as a whole was soon found to be hopeless'.[9]

The Convention broke up early in April 1918 amid growing unrest at proposals to introduce conscription to Ireland. The *Irish Churchman* despondently noted that 'so far from making an approach to unity [the Convention] has increased the differences and bitterness of Irish life'.[10] The differences and bitterness created by the Convention between Ulster and southern unionism were replicated within the Church of Ireland. The effect of the Convention on the Church has played a minor role against the backdrop of the larger drama of Ulster unionist–southern unionist in-fighting. However, the differing parts played by Crozier and Bernard at the Convention highlighted the potentially debilitating effects of the political divisions within the Church. Bernard's clear articulation of southern unionist sympathies contrasted with Crozier's rather hapless attempts at establishing a distinctively 'Church of Ireland' position. In the absence of firm leadership from Crozier of the Ulster unionist elements in the Church of Ireland, Charles Frederick D'Arcy forcefully opposed Bernard's growing influence. The interaction of these positions threatened a split within the Church of Ireland episcopate.

Any study of the Church of Ireland and the Convention is bound to focus on Bernard and Crozier, and a few prominent bishops and laymen who had access to what was going on – the debate caused by the Convention was largely carried on out of the glare of public opinion, as restrictions were imposed on the reporting of the proceedings. As far as the public was concerned, their role was to pray that during the Convention 'trust and justice, religion and piety, peace and unity, might be restored to their land'.[11]

EPISCOPAL SUPPORT FOR THE CONVENTION

It is unsurprising that John Henry Bernard welcomed the Irish Convention. In March 1917 he had written to *The Times* calling for a conference of Irish leaders and representatives of Irish opinion to consider the Irish question. Bernard's desire for a conference was driven by a fear of partition, which was 'hateful to Irishmen'. If partition was to come, Bernard believed those who 'know Ireland best' should have the opportunity of considering its details before it was embodied in legislation.[12] The bishop of Tuam, Benjamin Plunkett (one of the signatories of the Logue Manifesto), pointed out that even if the Convention achieved nothing practical, it would have succeeded by getting 'men of various creeds and politics together'.[13] Charles Dowse, bishop of Cork, expected 'great things' from the Convention 'if men come to it with open minds and with an earnest endeavour to make it a success'.[14] Such relatively idealistic notions contrasted with the more pragmatic position articulated by northern bishops. John Baptist Crozier (like Carson) realised that with the third Home Rule Bill on the statute book, it was 'absolutely necessary ... for us to take part in the Conference'.[15] Charles Frederick D'Arcy feared that if there was no Ulster unionist representation at the Convention the government would force upon Ulster a Redmondite scheme 'which will seem plausible to England'.[16]

D'Arcy's motivation for supporting Ulster unionist participation in the Convention was borne of a desire to prevent any semblance of Irish self-government. D'Arcy posited an acceptance of Irish conscription by all parties as a key precondition in establishing Ulster unionist tractability at the Convention.[17] In D'Arcy's opinion, the extension of conscription to Ireland would allow the Ulster unionist delegation to 'go into the Convention with real good-will and desire for settlement'. However, D'Arcy must have been aware of the widespread opposition to conscription among even moderate Irish nationalists. While all shades of unionist opinion were supportive of extending compulsory service to Ireland, it is likely D'Arcy's linking of the Convention and conscription was a deliberate wrecking tactic intended to lend justification to Ulster unionist intransigence. If conscription was not accepted, D'Arcy believed Ulster unionists should participate in the Convention 'in order to protect imperial interests and safeguard Irish unionists, and for no other reason'.[18]

D'Arcy's linkage of the Convention and conscription highlighted the difference between the interpretative framework he had constructed towards the war's effect on home rule with that of moderate southern bishops (such as Bernard and Plunkett). Rather than encouraging a new consensual approach to the Irish question, the war emphasised the importance of eschewing any tampering with the constitution. In his diocesan synod speech in October 1917, D'Arcy linked the Convention with Irish participation in the war by claiming that any settlement should secure Ireland against the possibility of being made 'a base for German operations against England and France'. The imperial nationalism of Redmond (the likely beneficiary of any settlement at the Convention) made it unlikely an Irish government of which he was in charge would countenance assisting Germany. Therefore, D'Arcy may have been alluding to the weakness of any settlement that did not take into account Redmond's weakness in the face of an increasingly confident and popular separatist movement headed by Sinn Féin. For D'Arcy, the union provided a crucial bulwark against the supposed designs of radical separatists and their German allies. Again, the implication was that the unionist delegations, in the interest of the war effort, should resist Irish self-government. D'Arcy maintained Ireland and England were and should remain inseparable:

> We cannot realise the best that is within us as a people except through association with England. We are not a separate race from the English, nor are our traditions separate from theirs ... The British Empire is an Irish Empire as well as English Empire.

Ireland would validate this imperial connection if it was more active in the war, a war that was bringing about 'marvellous unity among the free peoples of the world'.[19]

D'Arcy's desire for conscription, as well as a referendum in Ulster on any settlement achieved at the Convention, revealed his partitionist sympathies.[20] In his 1917 diocesan synod speech D'Arcy emphasised his perception of the exclusivity of Ulster from the rest of Ireland. Ulster as a 'great industrial and commercial community' needed peace and security more than the south and west of Ireland (an 'agricultural and pastoral people'). Therefore, if the Convention could 'arrive at a settlement which will be a real settlement, and which will not barter away our birthright, we shall rejoice'.[21] However, the conditions that D'Arcy believed needed to be met for an acceptable settlement made such rejoicing unlikely, certainly in unionist Ulster.

Of significance is how D'Arcy's views differed from the representatives of his Church at the Convention. The *Church of Ireland Gazette* believed Crozier and Bernard

> will conceive themselves ... to be entrusted at the Convention with a mission not merely to safeguard the interests of the Church, but to invoke all the Church's latent resources as a potent instrument of national unity.

Anticipating accusations that Crozier would be sympathetic to Ulster unionism at the Convention, the *Gazette* claimed 'he would be the first to repudiate the suggestion that his selection merely adds one more to the Ulster unionist delegation'. Bernard was equally impervious to the pull of political loyalties, bringing to the Convention 'an unpledged gift of statesmanship'.[22] However, Bernard's 'unpledged' statesmanship was promised to the southern unionist delegation at the Convention and he played a key role in articulating and defending the Midleton proposal. Crozier's attempted neutrality was challenged by Ulster unionist voices outside the Convention such as Hugh de Fellenburg Montgomery and D'Arcy, concerned that Bernard would be seen as representative of Church of Ireland opinion on self-government.

CROZIER AND BERNARD'S INVOLVEMENT AT THE CONVENTION

Soon after the Convention was announced, Lord Midleton expressed a 'strong desirability' among southern unionists that Bernard should be chosen as a representative of the Church of Ireland. His membership would add 'immense weight' to the Convention and provide the southern unionist delegation with a 'really impartial opinion to appeal to'.[23] Bernard's subsequent involvement as a leading figure in the southern unionist delegation was demonstrated by his presence at meetings between the delegation and members of the Irish Parliamentary Party and the government.[24] In addition, in an echo of D'Arcy and Crozier's earlier attempts to influence government opinion towards the UVF, Bernard effectively lobbied the archbishop of Canterbury with his concerns at the Convention's proceedings. Davidson complied, forwarding Bernard's correspondence on to leading figures in the cabinet, such as Lord Curzon.[25]

An insight into Bernard's decision to act as a representative of the southern unionists as opposed to the Church of Ireland was provided in his first speech to the Convention. Bernard declared himself an 'impenitent Unionist', although he was open to conversion 'if cause is shown'. However, Bernard identified himself more particularly with southern unionism, the only side in Ireland not to have resorted to violence:

> We have been content, and are content, and shall be content in the future to obey the laws made by the people for the people, even though we do not like them. And a democracy which has not learnt that lesson is ill fitted for political responsibility.

Bernard's affinity with southern unionism, a reaction to militant Ulster unionism and Irish separatism, does not fully account for his willingness to compromise with moderate Irish nationalists at the Convention. An explanation is provided by his belief that the 'coming struggle' in Ireland would not be between unionists and home rulers or Protestants and Catholics. Rather, it was the 'great struggle' between the 'forces of order and good government on the one hand, and the forces of anarchy and revolution on the other'. Bernard believed political, social, moral and religious anarchy was 'a very real danger at this hour' and hoped, in a gesture likely aimed at the Catholic bishops attending the Convention, that the 'forces of religion will co-operate to resist it'.[26]

Bernard's fear of the 'anarchy' threatened by Sinn Féin, and possibly militant Ulster unionism, provided an intellectual and emotional rationale for his support of the Midleton proposal that conceded an Irish parliament. Despite his self-confessed impenitent unionism, Bernard ultimately feared Sinn Féin more than home rule. Bernard wanted the government to treat the 'Irish Republican party' as 'treasonable and seditious' and a hindrance to 'the allies in the prosecution of the war'.[27] In a meeting of the southern unionist delegation with Lloyd George in December 1917, Bernard claimed that in the event of a German invasion of Ireland, the 'fuller organisation of Sinn Féin' meant '200,000 men could be collected in aid of Germany within 24 hours'.[28] While Bernard may have over-hyped the strength of Sinn Féin in order to emphasise the need for a settlement, there is no doubt his fears were genuine. Bernard's opening speech at the Convention and subsequent remarks on Sinn Féin demonstrated that the increasing popularity of Irish republicanism provided an impetus for his growing willingness to reach a settlement with Redmond. In a speech before the Convention on 3 January 1918, Bernard defended the Midleton proposal by claiming 'Imperial and domestic necessities alike call for some united policy among Irishmen'. A settlement would help the war effort and arrest the growth of unrest in Ireland.[29] The instinctive reaction of southern unionism (and to some extent, Bernard) to the Easter Rising was to recede from any nascent conciliation with moderate Irish nationalism. However, the Convention proved Bernard's return to his pre-Rising spirit of compromise, influenced as before by the effect of war and in addition by the recent recrudescence of Irish republicanism, which Bernard realised was as inimical to Redmondite home rulers as it was to southern unionism.

Bernard's desire to reach a settlement contrasted with what he perceived as the intransigence of the Ulster unionist delegation. Such unwillingness to 'put forward any positive proposals' was partly the fault of the government by refusing to force Ulster to accept a settlement 'which she does not like'. Bernard explained to Archbishop Davidson:

> I am satisfied that Ulster will not move until awakened from her dream of security. But her people are too sensible not to see the situation if it is explained to them by the Government.

Bernard clearly intended, through Davidson's contacts, to exhort the government to place pressure on the Ulster unionist delegation to compromise. He also sought to influence the government's dealings with Redmond. It would be 'pitiable' if the Convention failed, especially as the difference between the southern unionists and nationalists had been reduced to the one point of fiscal autonomy. Bernard emphasised the southern unionist delegation was 'ready to agree to the provisions for an Irish Parliament put forward by the Nationalists, with the necessary Imperial safeguards'.[30] Bernard repeated his desire for government pressure on Redmond and the Ulster unionists during a meeting with Lloyd George in December 1917.

He believed Redmond would compromise on the customs issue if the government put pressure on the Ulster unionist delegation to adopt a more conciliatory attitude. When Lloyd George refused to promise to coerce Ulster into accepting a settlement which they did not want, it seemed to Bernard 'the disappointing conclusion to the whole matter, and to the break up of the Convention'.[31]

Bernard's 3 January speech in support of the Midleton plan attempted to expose the objections of the Ulster unionist delegation and fiscal autonomists. The settlement did not repeal the union, as Ireland was to remain an 'integral' part of the United Kingdom. Instead, the deal represented a full measure of home rule 'and we Unionists propose to accept it for the sake of Irish unity'. The demand for control over customs should not be met, as Ireland was not a colony and the 'analogy between Ireland and the Dominions is wholly misleading. And simple facts of geography are sufficient to show that the parallel between Ireland and Canada is quite fallacious.' Bernard concluded his speech by welcoming the compromises made by the pro-Midleton nationalists and querying: 'We have not yet heard what concession is offered by Ulster.'[32]

In contrast to Bernard's high level of involvement in the inner councils of the Convention, Crozier had difficulty exerting any influence. This was largely due to Ulster unionist concerns over Crozier's reliability. In August, Hugh de Fellenburg Montgomery outlined to Hugh Barrie various discussions he had held with southern unionists, including Archdeacon Buler and J.A.F. Gregg, bishop of Killaloe. Buler had suggested a form of home rule within home rule, in which a Dublin parliament and a nominally subordinate Ulster parliament would be established. Crozier 'with his usual caution' had agreed with Buler's proposal. Anticipating Barrie's suspicions concerning Crozier's Ulster unionist credentials, Montgomery attempted to bolster Crozier's standing by referring to the Logue Manifesto dispute: 'At that time he [Crozier] was an uncompromising Ulster Unionist though his position as Primate of All Ireland obliged him to take a very cautious line.'[33] His defence obviously failed: three weeks later Montgomery informed Crozier that the Ulster delegates were 'getting rather uneasy and suspicious about you, fearing you might take some line which would weaken the line of defence they have adopted'. Montgomery, as a member of the Church of Ireland, was able to acknowledge how Crozier's position as Primate of All Ireland obliged him to take a 'detached position' and not to identify with any 'provincial group'. However, from an Ulster unionist viewpoint, Montgomery counselled Crozier that 'it would be a great calamity if the confidence of the Ulster Protestants in you were weakened'.[34]

Crozier thanked Montgomery for his 'hint', but defended himself by claiming 'all I thought of saying was that "I had no idea whether Provincial Parliaments would be acceptable or not, but it was worth consideration."' However, in a further indication that Crozier's aim at the Convention differed from the Ulster unionist delegation, Crozier considered it worthwhile to try and 'hammer out something acceptable to Ulster other than partition and comparative safety for other Counties', which he feared could be left to the 'wolves'.[35] Crozier's lack of enthusiasm for partition set him apart from the decision of the Ulster Unionist Council in 1916 concerning the Lloyd George plan and contrasted with D'Arcy's endorsement of Ulster exclusion in May 1917.

Crozier's spirit of independence culminated in his exclusion from the Grand Committee (a representative committee intended to streamline the Convention's proceedings), a move which angered Crozier as Bernard was included as a southern unionist representative. Crozier's exclusion represented an 'insult' to the Church of Ireland and a 'serious injury' to the Convention, leaving the Church of Ireland unrepresented on the committee as Bernard had 'rightly more than once spoken of himself as the representative of Southern Unionists'. In a revealing comment, Crozier called for his inclusion on the Grand Committee as 'one Diocese in the Northern Province, alone, has more Church people in it than the whole Southern Province including Dublin!!'[36] However, this argument was illogical – Crozier had already admitted that Bernard was acting as a representative of the southern unionists, not the Church of Ireland, so it was ultimately of little consequence if his diocese had fewer members than Crozier's. Bernard was not chosen because he was a Church of Ireland archbishop, but because he had allied himself clearly with the southern unionist delegation. Crozier had failed to obtain similar confidence from the Ulster unionist delegation, wary of his earlier flirtation with home rule within home rule – it was his unwillingness to toe the Ulster line that led to Crozier not being chosen by the Ulster delegates. Montgomery explained to Crozier that the Ulster strategy was to ensure none of their members voted 'of his own' or conferred with 'other groups or individuals without consultation with the committee'. Crozier, for 'perfectly good reasons', decided to 'stand aloof':

> Your position was respected, but when it came to nominating members of committees the group was bound to prefer one of its own sworn men to any one else whatever. You could not have it both ways![37]

Crozier's complaints about his exclusion from the Grand Committee had an effect – Horace Plunkett 'entirely on [his] own responsibility' worked to obtain Crozier's membership.[38] Plunkett viewed Crozier as an independent, neutral voice, who had a 'broader outlook' than other members of the Convention.[39] Plunkett hoped this 'broad outlook' would influence the Ulster unionist delegates. In a summary of the events leading to Crozier's inclusion on the Grand Committee, Plunkett presented Crozier as a figure of consensus, able to bring the differing sides in the Convention together:

> In this erstwhile militant prelate we might soon find the badly needed mediator between the country over which his primacy extends and that Ulster community which he truly says must be converted and not coerced.[40]

Plunkett assumed Crozier's track record of militant Ulster unionist support yet determination to act independently at the Convention would make him acceptable to both the Ulster unionist representatives and those representing all aspects of southern opinion. Having someone play such a role at the Convention would have been important for Plunkett, who as a Protestant home ruler had little political capital with Ulster unionists.

However, Crozier was rebuffed when he attempted to influence the Ulster unionist delegation. At a crucial early stage of the Convention, Plunkett sent an 'exam paper' to the unionist and nationalist delegations questioning them on their financial arguments. On 7 November Plunkett informed Crozier that Barrie 'said he would have to bring the whole matter before his advisory Committee and Monday was the first day on which they could be assembled'.[41] Two days later Crozier informed Plunkett of 'a pressing invitation from the Ulster Representation to meet them on Monday in Belfast – and *I will now do it*'. Crozier reassured Plunkett that he had reminded the Ulster unionist delegates of his independence and how he was 'not an Ulster representative in any sense but the representative of the Church of Ireland' and that the interests of 'all Ireland' were his 'real and chief concern'.[42] Plunkett urged Crozier to exert his influence on the Ulster unionists to insure they stayed 'on board' the Convention.[43]

Crozier was confident he could play a mediating role. He informed Bernard of his invitation to meet the Ulster unionist delegation and his desire to 'avert a deadlock' claiming: 'I think I may say I am about the only person who occupies an independent position and who could have any influence just now.' In a barely concealed criticism of Bernard's position, Crozier maintained he was not an Ulster delegate, as 'I feel my position and office was to represent the church. From this position I do not intend to recede.'[44] However, the Ulster unionist delegation rescinded its invitation: to his 'utter grief' the Ulster unionists would not expect Crozier to meet them in Belfast.[45] There is no confirmation of why Crozier was cold-shouldered by the Ulster unionists.[46] A likely explanation is that it was precisely what made Crozier useful to Plunkett – his 'neutrality' – that made him unwelcome in the inner councils of the Ulster delegates, especially as the Ulster unionist Presbyterian moderator was present at the meeting.[47] The fact Crozier was not chosen to sit on the Grand Committee indicated his precarious hold on Ulster unionist patronage. Believing he could be the equivalent of a unionist free spirit while maintaining a position of influence with the Ulster unionists revealed Crozier's political naïvety. The Ulster unionist–Crozier relationship also revealed Plunkett's mismanagement of the Convention – he clearly miscalculated in believing Crozier could play a 'mediating' role despite the precedent of the Grand Committee incident.

THE CONVENTION'S EFFECT ON THE CHURCH OF IRELAND EPISCOPATE

The Midleton proposal was set before the Convention on 3 January 1918, two weeks before a tumultuous special meeting of the Standing Committee of the General Synod of the Church of Ireland held to discuss the Convention. Four accounts of the meeting exist. The minutes of the standing committee merely state, with judicious (and frustrating) understatement, that 'His Grace [Crozier] made a statement with reference to the work of the Irish Convention and a discussion ensued thereon.'[48] Bernard's papers include a report of the meeting, written in his handwriting, although in the third person. The report declared Bernard's support for the Midleton proposal and his belief that 'this course was the best for the Church'. If a vote had been taken, the standing committee would have been divided into two sections of nearly equal strength. Crozier did not commit himself 'explicitly' but left an impression 'that he disapproved of the suggested line of settlement, and was still prepared to oppose a Dublin Parliament'.[49] A third account came from Sterling Berry, bishop of Killaloe and a signatory to the Logue Manifesto, who commended Bernard for realising 'that it is infinitely better by a settlement to kill the Sinn Féin movement than to join hands with the Sinn Féiners in wrecking the Convention'. Illuminating the tension between northern and southern sections of the Church of Ireland, Berry claimed the meeting made many 'sick at heart', and questioned the 'Ulster party' tactics at the Convention.[50]

Hugh de Fellenburg Montgomery, a member of the standing committee, provided Hugh Barrie with a report of the meeting. Unsurprisingly, the speeches made in support of Bernard were 'very drivelling' and those made in support of the 'Ulster case' (by D'Arcy, among others) were 'admirable and forceable'. Richard Bagwell, a prominent southern unionist, attacked Bernard's position by claiming that 'he [Bagwell] was too old to turn his coat' but 'the Archbishop of Dublin was now a Home Ruler' who 'advocated the acceptance of Home Rule'. D'Arcy opposed the Midleton settlement by pointing out how Ulster unionism, during 1912–14, 'had saved the Country and the Empire from the great danger in which the setting up of a Irish Parliament before the war' posed. According to Montgomery, Bernard 'protested that he was still a unionist in as much as he would prefer to maintain the Union were it possible to do so'. Crozier feared a settlement that would partition Ireland, as this could weaken the Church of Ireland's claim to be an 'all-Ireland' Church, and 'expressed his dread of any-thing that would divide the Church of Ireland which is now the Church of the whole country'. Montgomery's account substantiated Bernard's claim that the standing committee was fairly evenly divided over the Midleton proposal, with the majority supporting the 'Ulster case' – five speeches against the southern union-ist position were mentioned, with four in support.[51] However, D'Arcy evidently disagreed with Bernard's assessment that Crozier had rejected Midleton's plan, asserting that Crozier 'seemed to be acting with the Archbishop [Bernard], more or less definitely'.[52]

In January, under pressure from the Catholic Church and fiscal autonomists, Redmond had been unable to support Midleton's compromise settlement, a move that threatened the imminent failure of the Convention. However, Crozier, together with Joe Devlin (a prominent nationalist from Ulster) combined to com-mit the Convention to send a representative deputation to Lloyd George in an attempt to salvage an agreement. Crozier's role angered the Ulster unionists. They would have welcomed a breakdown of the Convention due to the failure of the southern unionists to reach an agreement with the nationalists over the Midleton deal, as this would have left the Ulster delegates innocent of any blame for the collapse. Montgomery rebuked Crozier for agreeing to the deputation, claiming: 'The impression made on me is that you are not possessed with a suf-ficiently long spoon to sup safely with the Devil or the Devlin!'[53] Apparently, Crozier's acceptance of the invitation to send members to see Lloyd George made it difficult for the Ulster group to oppose the proposal 'actively'. Montgomery warned Crozier that 'I have a feeling that you had "better not do it again".'[54]

Besides confirming his isolation from the Ulster unionist delegation, the dep-utation controversy placed pressure on Crozier to speak out publicly against Bernard, a member of the southern unionist deputation to see Lloyd George. Bernard's inclusion angered D'Arcy, who pointed out: 'Steps should be taken to let it be known that he [Bernard] does not represent the opinions of Churchmen.'[55] Montgomery asked Crozier what was being done to make it clear that Bernard 'does not represent the collective opinion of Irish Churchmen in the matter discussed with the Prime Minister'.[56] Crozier agreed that Lloyd George should know Bernard did not represent the views of 'three quarters of Church people in Ireland'. However, in relation to making a public statement against Bernard, Crozier claimed '*I can't move.*'[57] Montgomery probably accurately interpreted Crozier's reluctance to make a public statement against Bernard as a desire to avoid a potential split in the Church over home rule.[58] In the absence of Crozier taking firm action, Montgomery and D'Arcy led the move to ensure Bernard was not seen as a representative of the Church of Ireland by lobbying

Ulster unionist members of the deputation 'to see that [the] Archbp. only speaks for himself'.[59] A sermon preached by D'Arcy in Belfast Cathedral on 3 February 1918 (three days before the deputation) should be seen in this context. Taking Matthew 6:22 as his text ('if thine eye be single, thy whole body shall be full of light') D'Arcy urged the 'Ulstermen' to 'Stand Firm. Be true to your principles' to ensure that a 'pro-German state' would not be established in Ireland. D'Arcy saw Ulster's duty as being to guard the 'Fortress of Liberty here at home'. Nothing would induce them to accept any arrangement 'which would betray the people of Great Britain to their cruel foes'. Significantly, considering his desire to undermine Bernard's standing as a Church of Ireland representative, D'Arcy claimed to be speaking for the clergy and people of the Church of Ireland, of which nearly three fourths were in Ulster.[60] Such views emphasise, like his diocesan synod speech of 1917, D'Arcy's linking of the war and the Convention. The underlying theme was that while 'our Gallant sons fight abroad' (to protect the empire) those at home must do all they can to avoid weakening the empire by political compromise over home rule. The *Irish Churchman*, a Church of Ireland newspaper sympathetic to Ulster unionism, recognised this theme of D'Arcy's sermon, claiming he 'used strong and justified words about the world importance of the Irish question'.[61]

The standing committee meeting and deputation controversy revealed the weakness in the neutral stance Crozier adopted at the Convention. Crozier's unwillingness to either endorse or criticise Midleton's plan at the standing committee convinced Bernard that the primate maintained his sympathy with Ulster unionism. Equally, in D'Arcy's opinion, Crozier's prevarication implied his complicity with Bernard. Montgomery interpreted Crozier's involvement in securing the deputation as an attempt to exercise some form of influence over the Convention. In this reading, Crozier was moved to act because Bernard was 'exerting a powerful influence over a very large section of Churchmen' while he was not.[62] According to Montgomery, Crozier had tried to play a more prominent role at the Convention than 'his position rendered practicable, and has got himself into rather a mess ... Of course the line the Archbishop took has greatly multiplied the Primate's difficulties.'[63] Montgomery suggested to Crozier that 'a closer understanding with the Ulster Unionists might exist, without actual membership'. He realised that Bernard – 'a very complete Lundy' – had made Crozier's position more difficult, but cautioned him to 'avoid doing anything calculated to create doubts in the minds of your Unionist friends in these parts'.[64] D'Arcy had less sympathy for the primate's position, commenting rather patronisingly: 'How clear the position would be if he had stuck by the Ulstermen, and that we know would have been his own real mind.' He believed Crozier's fears of a division in the Church to be 'groundless' as 'in the long run, the Southern Churchmen will respect us all the more for sticking by the principles which they really hold.'[65]

The 'doubts' in the minds of Crozier's Ulster unionist 'friends' were shared by members of the southern unionist delegation at the Convention. It appears Crozier did in fact attempt, through Walter Long, to influence the government to reject the Midleton plan. Lloyd George informed the southern unionist deputation (including Bernard) that Crozier denounced Midleton's plan as 'mad' and that if 'anything of the kind were passed into law the artisans of Ulster would "down tools"'. Midleton responded by claiming Crozier 'had not impressed the Convention with the belief that he knew his own mind clearly, and that he doubted if the Primate was empowered to make so grave a threat'.[66] Midleton's damning assessment confirmed that Crozier's desire to remain politically unaligned at the Convention while maintaining a degree of influence over its proceedings had backfired. Ultimately, Crozier's neutrality made him irrelevant to the Ulster unionist and southern unionist delegations, thereby forfeiting any influence he may have possessed.

The fact that Crozier chose to criticise the Midleton plan in private (to Walter Long) rather than in public at the standing committee meeting or in the Convention revealed his intention to maintain his position as a Church of Ireland representative. After the deputation controversy, Crozier informed Montgomery that 'I represent chiefly the Northern *Province* in which (and outside of which) are some of our most devoted Church people.'[67] Part of the northern province was outside Ulster, so even nine-county exclusion lacked appeal if Crozier considered it from a purely Church of Ireland viewpoint. Aside from the threat posed to the external unity of the Church of Ireland by any proposed political deal, Crozier was also likely to be troubled by the threat posed to the unity *within* the Church by the Convention controversy. The standing committee revealed the lack of harmony among important figures in the Church concerning a settlement – Crozier held the unenviable position of trying to balance the competing factions. The conflicting pressures on Crozier – of representing the northern province as opposed to Ulster unionism, and the Church of Ireland as opposed to Irish unionism – resulted in support of Barrie's amendment to the Convention report as well as defence of a federal settlement. In voting for Barrie's amendment (which insisted Ulster should be excluded from the Home Rule Act of 1914), Crozier stated his abhorrence of partition. He only supported Barrie's amendment as he could not accept Ulster's coercion into a self-governing Ireland, which the settlement reached by the Convention would entail. In a speech on 14 March 1918, Crozier urged the Convention to consider the federalist proposal of James Mahaffy (provost of Trinity College Dublin), which offered Ireland a central parliament along with 'absolute provincial autonomy'. This scheme would 'unite rather than divide Irish interests', giving 'vast scope for each province to develop along its own lines'. From his 'absolutely independent position of representing the Church of Ireland', Crozier defended the Ulster delegates' behaviour. However, Crozier's aim at the Convention was to consider what would 'work well' for Ireland, thinking not only of fellow members of the Church of Ireland but 'of all my fellow countrymen from Cape Clear to the Giant's Causeway'.[68]

In supporting Mahaffy, Crozier rather ingeniously sidestepped the possibility of committing to either the southern unionists or Ulster unionists at the Convention. Crozier and Mahaffy stated they could not vote for the final settlement reached by the Convention as it entailed either the coercion of Ulster, 'which is unthinkable', or the partition of Ireland, 'which would be disastrous'.[69] Crozier consistently, in public and private, articulated his independence and position as a representative of the Church of Ireland. As Primate, he believed his role was to preserve the unity of the Church, which made him unwilling to support publicly at the Convention any position he felt could lead to the division of Ireland. However, this aim of being an independent voice at the Convention was shown to be flawed by Bernard's support for the southern unionists. Bernard's views would have carried little or no support in Ulster, where the majority of Church of Ireland members lived, placing pressure on Crozier to articulate the position of this majority – the fear of D'Arcy and Crozier himself was that Bernard could come to be seen as articulating the position of the Church of Ireland towards an Irish settlement. But for Crozier to oppose Bernard would mean advocating a partisan political position – the opposite of what he intended to do at the Convention.

When Crozier's difficulties are considered, it is unsurprising he supported the relatively inoffensive proposals of Mahaffy. The federalist proposal allowed Crozier to claim he had fulfilled his Convention aims – acting in the best interests of Ireland and the Church of Ireland, by seeking to reach a settlement that would not divide Ireland. The *Irish Churchman*, edited by the staunch Ulster unionist W.S. Kerr, lauded Crozier's support of the Mahaffy plan:

> It is a very gratifying thing that the Primate, whose position was so obviously difficult, has given his influence to this plan, and has strongly opposed the disastrous policy of forcing Home Rule on Ulster as well as the Partition of Ireland.[70]

Crozier and Mahaffy were not alone in their support of federalism – leading figures in the cabinet, particularly Walter Long, pushed a federal solution to the Irish question throughout the first half of 1918 (without success).[71] A more immediate influence on Crozier may have been the views of Edward Carson, who urged Lloyd George (while the Convention was still sitting) to reach a federal settlement. Crozier was also in contact with the seventh Marquess of Londonderry, the one member of the Ulster unionist delegation who held federalist sympathies.[72] Londonderry's desire to table a federalist motion at the Convention in November 1917 had been scuppered by his Ulster unionist colleagues, and he grew uncomfortable with the obstructionist tactics of the delegation.[73] Londonderry and Carson, in supporting a federal solution, were both out of step with the 'governing counsels' of Ulster unionism.[74] Crozier's support for a federalist policy can be seen, therefore, as the final confirmation of his rejection of the exclusionary policy of Ulster unionism.

CONSCRIPTION

In the midst of the Convention's impending closure, the success of the German offensive on the western front in March 1918 made the extension of conscription to Ireland seemingly inevitable.[75] A new military service bill raised the maximum age of conscripts from 40 to 51 and proposed to apply compulsory service to Ireland, with Lloyd George intending to introduce conscription simultaneously with some form of home rule based on the Convention's final report.[76] However, due to intense opposition from all sections of Irish nationalist opinion, the dual policy of conscription and devolution was a failure: 'A constitutionalist strategy that was struggling for the oxygen of political support was now connected to, and suffocated by, the military draft.'[77] A contemporary Irish Anglican view supports this assessment: the *Gazette* believed hopes for a settlement in Ireland were prejudiced 'very gravely' by conscription.[78] However, the conscription crisis held out the possibility of breathing new life into the unity of the Church of Ireland, producing an issue on which there was almost universal agreement.

Conscription offered Crozier and Bernard the opportunity to gloss over the divisions that characterised their participation at the Convention. Both men had been long-standing advocates of increased Irish recruitment and, if necessary, conscription. Crozier had objected to Ireland's exclusion from the Compulsory Service Bill in January 1916, and in the aftermath of the Easter Rising called for 'equality with the rest of the United Kingdom' through the extension of conscription to Ireland.[79] As early as May 1915, in the aftermath of his son's death at the front, and stung by the apparent 'apathy of the 'farming classes' who were 'making money as they never did before', Bernard had written to Carson calling for compulsory service to be extended to Ireland.[80] In November 1916, Bernard supported the imposition of compulsory service to Ireland by claiming that the 'sacrifice of 500 or 1,000 lives (I do not anticipate it would cost this much)' involved in implementing conscription was 'worthwhile, if we can thereby shorten the war by a single day'.[81] Therefore, it was unsurprising that the two archbishops welcomed Lloyd George's intention to extend conscription to Ireland. On 17 April, just over one week after Lloyd George introduced the Military Service Bill, Crozier and Bernard issued a joint appeal calling for voluntary recruitment from members of the Church of Ireland. They also lamented that conscription had not been applied to Ireland two years previously, when it would have been 'readily obeyed'. If the Military Service Bill was applied to Ireland, the two archbishops hoped it would be 'cheerfully … accepted by our fellow countrymen as imperatively demanded in the awful crisis through which Ireland and the rest of the Empire alike are passing'.[82] The contrast in the archbishops' attitude to conscription with that of nationalist Ireland was highlighted by the Mansion House conference. Intended as a protest against the right of England to conscript Irishmen, the conference was attended by members of the Irish Parliamentary Party, independent nationalists and Sinn Féin. Following the conference a 'national pledge' against conscription was signed at chapel doors around Ireland in scenes similar to those surrounding the Ulster Covenant.[83]

A.W. Samuels, a prominent southern unionist, praised Bernard and Crozier for rendering 'inestimable service' by their 'lofty appeal to our Young Churchmen in this hour of universal danger to the world, our Empire and our … greatly misguided Ireland'.[84] The *Gazette* was rather more circumspect, claiming the archbishops' appeal had not explicitly endorsed conscription and had merely called for voluntary recruitment. The *Gazette* feared that as Irish nationalists were intent on opposing compulsory service, any attempt to enforce conscription would use as many soldiers as it would recruit.[85] This position was actually not too far from that held privately by Bernard, who informed the archbishop of Canterbury that conscription risked the loss of many lives in Ireland, although it could have been imposed 'with no trouble' two years previously.[86] However, the *Gazette* went further than Bernard in its doubts over the viability of conscription, and reasoned that Irish churchmen could, without disloyalty to their archbishops, sign the 'Protestant protest against conscription', which, it was held, demonstrated conscription was not a religious issue.[87] The protest, supported by the Irish Guild of the Church, asserted that conscription was a 'violation of the law of God' as it was an attempt to force men to act contrary to their will and conscience.[88]

The *Gazette*'s ambivalent position on conscription aroused opposition from the *Irish Churchman* – the *Gazette* did not represent the Church of Ireland and voiced the views of a 'fatuous little clique that pretends it does not know what the allies are fighting for'.[89] The *Churchman*'s attack on the *Gazette* was unsurprising in the context of the contrasting positions the two Church of Ireland papers held on an Irish settlement. Perhaps more surprising was Bernard's strong attack on the 'Protestant protest', and by implication the *Gazette*'s position on the protest. Bernard termed the protest a 'mischievous and misleading manifesto', and claimed that if conscription was a violation of the law of God, he could not ask churchmen to 'cheerfully accept compulsory service, if put into force'. The protest implied that 'defiance' of the law may become a 'duty', and would 'certainly damage voluntary recruiting'.[90] Bernard's argument echoed his private upbraiding of Henry Barbor, the rector of Castledermott, who had publicly supported the Catholic 'national pledge' against conscription. Bernard asserted that to associate with those who '*resist* the law' went beyond what was legitimate for a 'Christian clergyman'. Anticipating that Barbor may point to Ulster unionism's intention to resist 'the law' (i.e. Home Rule), Bernard stated that Ulster resistance 'was … a very wrong decision'.[91]

Bernard's reference to Ulster's prewar militarism was a reminder that the conscription crisis would not engender the unity glimpsed in the archbishops' recruitment appeal. The *Irish Churchman* linked conscription and the Convention, claiming that the 'unquestioned control' of the Catholic bishops manifested in the anti-conscription campaign would be replicated in the 'Dublin parliament that Archbishop Bernard and his Southern colleagues voted for'.[92] There was an unintended (and unforeseen) irony in this criticism. At the height of the conscription crisis at the end of April, the archbishop of Canterbury asked Bernard for his (private) opinion on the position of the Catholic bishops 'in case I am asked to give private counsel to anybody: and this is not impossible'.[93] Bernard advised Davidson that the 'Roman hierarchy' placed themselves at the head of the anti-conscription campaign to regain 'the confidence of all Roman Catholic Ireland'. The bishops were 'intensely anti-British at heart, thoroughly disloyal to the King, to Great Britain, and to the Empire. That is in their blood.' However, except in 'two or three instances', Bernard did not believe the Catholic bishops were 'positively pro-German'.[94] Bernard's vigorous criticism of the Catholic bishops contrasted with the *Irish Churchman*'s allegation that his stance at the Convention would have made him complicit in any Catholic domination of a home rule parliament. Therefore, despite the apparently widespread unity in the Church of Ireland on the need for Irish recruits – or conscripts – the 'Irish question' continued to breed a degree of suspicion and tension between northern and southern elements in the Church. In the late spring and early summer of 1918, the aftermath of the Irish Convention overshadowed the unanimity between Bernard and the Church of Ireland in Ulster on the war. The fact that the conscription issue ultimately failed to banish the disunity caused by the Convention highlighted how the war failed to produce any form of 'truce' on political issues in the Church.

Any possibility that the southern unionist stance at the Convention would prove durable, or successful, was shattered by the conscription crisis. The support of moderate nationalists for the anti-conscription campaign demonstrated the impossibility of establishing a settlement in Ireland based on the kind of unity envisaged by Bernard and Midleton.[95] The conscription crisis also failed to gloss over the tensions between Ulster unionism and the position held by the supporters of the southern unionist delegation to the Convention. While such north–south disagreement was an increasingly familiar feature of Irish unionism, the Convention also opened up a rupture within southern unionism. The Midletonite position was opposed with increasing success throughout 1918 by the irredentist Southern unionist Committee, pledged to preserving the union and resisting any form of home rule.[96] The bishop of Cashel doubted any 'practical result' would come from the Convention, and believed the only hope for the 'future prosperity of Ireland' was in the 'maintenance of the legislative Union with Great Britain and in the firm and just administration of the law'.[97]

CONCLUSION

According to the *Irish Churchman*, the Irish Convention was 'likely to leave a sad memory of division and resentment among Irish Protestants'.[98] The Convention maintained the divisions within Irish unionism, and the Church of Ireland, on an Irish settlement. By advocating a home rule settlement, the southern unionist delegation confirmed Ulster unionist suspicions of their southern counterparts and alienated a large number of unionists in the south and west of Ireland. Bernard's brand of consensual, moderate unionism, although demonstrating a willingness to engage constructively with moderate Irish nationalism, reflected the increasingly fissiparous nature of southern unionism. The conscription crisis invalidated the Convention report, and although it was not a panacea to the divisions in Irish unionism, the crisis at least allowed Crozier and Bernard, at an archiepiscopal level, to demonstrate a public show of unity.

Crozier's role at the Convention has suffered in comparison with Bernard. His contemporaries at the Convention believed Crozier's connection with Ulster impaired his participation: Horace Plunkett believed Crozier's support for the Ulster unionist amendment revealed that he, 'no more than Lord Londonderry, could be deaf to the "rumble of the distant drum"'.[99] Midleton informed Bernard's biographer that Crozier, was 'handicapped by the Ulster surroundings'. However, Bernard was able to speak with 'absolute detachment from his surroundings, and was willing to go as far as any fair-minded man could to meet his opponents'.[100] R.B. McDowell's analysis of the bishops' roles mirrored that of Plunkett and Midleton. McDowell assigned 'great dignity, exquisite manners and abundant good will' to Crozier but correctly noted that 'his dual position as the senior prelate of the Church of Ireland and bishop of a diocese in the Ulster Unionist zone put him in an awkward position.' On the other hand, Bernard's 'patience, lucidity and decisiveness … inspired confidence and gave him immense weight in council'.[101] These assessments are persuasive. Crozier was hampered by his Ulster connection, and in addition exhibited a damaging combination of political naïvety and pride in believing he could remain neutral and exert influence over the Ulster unionist delegation. Crozier's apparent inadequacy as a forceful delegate was in stark contrast to Bernard, who played a leading role in the southern unionist delegation, providing intellectual and rhetorical support to Midleton's proposal.

However, Bernard did not, as Midleton claimed, speak with 'absolute detachment' from his surroundings. Instead, it was Bernard's deliberate eschewing of his Church of Ireland identity at the Convention in favour of a clear alignment with Midletonite southern unionism that created his 'statesmanlike' reputation.[102] Bernard did not represent a distinctively Church of Ireland position at the Convention, but a political position that happened to mirror the views of (some) of the members of the ecclesiastical province of which he was archbishop. Crozier was not so fortunate. In considering what was best for the Church of Ireland, he had to balance the interests of Church members in Ulster with those in the rest of Ireland. The Convention suggested Crozier's ability at reconciling the conflicting opinions among the episcopate was nearing failure. The standing committee meeting confirmed the division between Bernard and D'Arcy over an Irish settlement, a division Crozier had sought to minimise by holding a form of *via media* between exclusion and all-Ireland unionism. In this context, Crozier's support of Mahaffy's federalist proposal was a tactical master stroke, surprising considering his earlier political ineptitude at the Convention. The plan allowed Crozier to appear as consensual, leaving him untarnished from any allegations of being a 'wrecker' or a compromiser over home rule. Crucially, it also avoided the division that would have been caused in the Church of Ireland if he had supported the Ulster unionists against the southern unionist delegation composed of a fellow archbishop.

Perhaps most significantly for the Church of Ireland, the Convention cast doubt on the Church's potential to exert any form of meaningful influence on Irish politics. This seems counter-intuitive, given Bernard's crucial role in the southern unionist delegation. However, as already stated, Bernard's prominence was due to his political, not ecclesiastical, affiliation. Crozier's apparently sincerely, and consistently, held desire to articulate an authentically 'Church of Ireland' position at the Convention rendered him largely irrelevant to the Ulster unionist delegation. The 'increasingly absolute demand for exclusion' from Ulster unionism 'rode roughshod' over those who had 'all-Ireland and broader British sensibilities', such as Londonderry and Carson.[103] Crozier's position as primate of all-Ireland placed him in a similar position. Ultimately, he could not offer Ulster unionism the requisite support on the issue of partition.

NOTES

1. D.G. Boyce, 'British opinion, Ireland and the war, 1916–1918', *Historical Journal*, 17, 3 (1974), p.584.
2. A. O'Day, *Irish Home Rule: 1867–1921* (Manchester, 1998), p.279.
3. T. Hennessy, *Dividing Ireland, World War 1 and Partition* (London, 1998), p.202; C. O'Leary and P. Maume, *Controversial Issues in Anglo-Irish Relations, 1910–1921* (Dublin, 2005), p.59.
4. Sir H. Plunkett *et al.*, *Report of the Proceedings of the Irish Convention, 1918* (London, 1918), p.3.
5. Hennessy, *Dividing Ireland*, p.206.
6. O'Leary and Maume, *Controversial Issues*, p.63.
7. R.B. McDowell, *The Irish Convention, 1917–18* (London, 1970), p.147; P. Buckland, *Irish Unionism I: The Anglo-Irish and the New Ireland, 1885–1922* (Dublin, 1972), p.126; T. West, *Horace Plunkett: Co-operation and Politics, and Irish Biography* (London, 1986), p.147; A. Jackson, *Home Rule: An Irish History, 1800–2000* (London, 2003), p.184.
8. A. Jackson, *Ireland 1798–1998: Politics and War* (Oxford, 1999), p.241; P. Buckland, *Irish Unionism II: Ulster Unionism and the Origins of Northern Ireland 1886–1922* (Dublin, 1973), p.113.
9. W. St John Brodrick (Lord Midleton), *Records and Reactions, 1856–1939* (London, 1939), p.235.
10. *Irish Churchman*, 18 April 1918.
11. *Church of Ireland Gazette*, 3 August 1918.
12. *The Times*, 21 March 1917.
13. Benjamin Plunkett to John Henry Bernard, 19 May 1917 (TCD, J.H. Bernard papers, Ms 2388/120).
14. Charles Dowse to Bernard, n.d. (ibid., Ms 2388/122).
15. John Baptist Crozier to Hugh de Fellenburg Montgomery, 2 June 1917 (Public Record Office of Northern Ireland (PRONI), Montgomery papers, D/627/430/29); Carson claimed that as Home Rule 'has now become the law of the land' Ulster Unionists should attend the convention aiming to obtain a 'compromise' 'compatible with the principles for which we stand'. Edward Carson to Montgomery, 28 May 1917 (ibid., D/627/430/22).
16. D'Arcy to Montgomery, 6 June 1917 (ibid., D/627/430/37).
17. D'Arcy to Montgomgery, 21 May 1917 (ibid., D/627/430/15).
18. D'Arcy to Montgomery, 6 June 1917 (ibid., D/627/430/37).
19. *Belfast Newsletter*, 31 October 1917.
20. D'Arcy to Montgomery, 6 June 1917 (PRONI, Montgomery papers, D/627/430/37); D'Arcy to Montgomery, 13 June 1917 (ibid., D/627/430/44).
21. *Belfast Newsletter*, 31 October 1917.
22. *Church of Ireland Gazette*, 15 June 1917.
23. Lord Midleton to Bernard, 23 May 1917 (British Library, J.H. Bernard papers, Add. Ms 52781/46–8).

24. Memo of meeting between Bernard, Midleton and Joe Devlin, 12 October 1917 (ibid., Add. Ms 52782/179–81); memo of meeting between Bernard, Midleton and John Redmond, 12, 13 December 1917 (ibid., Add. Ms 52782/194–8); memo of meeting between southern Unionist delegation and David Lloyd George, 5 December 1917, (ibid., Add. Ms 52781/19–21).

25. Randall Davidson to Bernard, 15, 18 October 1917 (ibid., Add. Ms 52782/182–3); Lord Curzon to Davidson, 17 October 1917 (ibid., Add. Ms 52782/184); Buckland, *Irish Unionism 1*, p.121.

26. Handwritten copy of speech delivered by Bernard to Convention, 29 August 1917 (British Library, J.H. Bernard papers, Add. Ms 52784/31).

27. Bernard to Lord Midleton, 22 October 1917 (National Archives, Midleton papers, PRO 30/67/33/1741).

28. Memo of meeting between southern Unionist delegation and Lloyd George, 5 December 1917 (British Library, J.H. Bernard papers, Add. Ms 52781/19–21).

29. Handwritten copy of speech delivered by Bernard to Convention, 3 January 1918 (ibid., Add. Ms 52784/39–43).

30. Bernard to Davidson, 28 November 1917 (ibid., Add. Ms 52782/190–2).

31. Memo of meeting between southern Unionist delegation and Lloyd George, 5 December 1917 (ibid., Add. Ms 52781/19–21).

32. Handwritten copy of speech delivered by Bernard to Convention, 3 January 1918 (ibid., Add. Ms 52784/39–43).

33. Montgomery to Barrie, 18 August 1917 (PRONI, Montgomery papers, D/627/430/76).

34. Montgomery to Crozier, 6 September 1917 (ibid., D/627/430/90).

35. Crozier to Montgomery, 10 September 1917 (ibid., D/627/430/92).

36. Crozier to Plunkett, 20 October 1917 (Plunkett Foundation, Plunkett papers, Arm 3)

37. Montgomery to Crozier, 8 February 1918 (PRONI, Montgomery papers, D/627/433/40).

38. Plunkett to Crozier, 22 October 1917 (Plunkett Foundation, Plunkett papers, Arm 4).

39. Ibid.

40. Confidential Report (TCD, Convention papers, Mss 2986–7/177).

41. Plunkett to Crozier, 7 November 1917 (Plunkett Foundation, Plunkett papers, Arm 9).

42. Crozier to Plunkett, 9 November 1917 (ibid., Arm 10).

43. Plunkett to Crozier, 10 November 1917 (ibid., Arm 11).

44. Crozier to Bernard, 9 November 1917 (TCD, J.H. Bernard papers, Ms 2388/129).

45. Crozier to Plunkett, 12 November 1917 (Plunkett Foundation, Plunkett papers, Arm 12).

46. The minute book of the Ulster Unionist delegation avoided recording anything of a controversial (or detailed) nature: minute book of the Ulster Unionist delegation to the Irish Convention, 12 November 1918 (PRONI, Ulster Unionist Council papers, D/1327/2/17).

47. See list of attendance at 12 November meeting, ibid., 12 November 1918.

48. Minutes of the Standing Committee of the General Synod of the Church of Ireland, 17 January 1918 (Representative Church Body (RCB) Library, Dublin).

49. Handwritten account of meeting of Standing Committee, 17 January 1918 (British Library, J.H. Bernard papers, Add. Ms 52784/39–43).

50. Sterling Berry to Bernard, 18 January 1918 (ibid., Add. Ms 52783/3).

51. Montgomery to Barrie, 21 January 1918 (PRONI, Montgomery papers, D/627/433/11).

52. D'Arcy to Montgomery, 31 January 1918 (ibid., D/627/433/19).

53. Montgomery to Crozier, 8 February 1918 (ibid., D/627/433/40).

54. Montgomery to Crozier, 10 February 1918 (ibid., D/627/433/44).

55. D'Arcy to Montgomery, 29 January 1918 (ibid., D/627/433/15).

56. Montgomery to Crozier, 30 January 1918 (ibid., D/627/433/16).

57. Crozier to Montgomery, 31 January 1918 (ibid., D/627/433/20).

58. Montgomery to D'Arcy, 1 February 1918 (ibid., D/627/433/22).

59. Montgomery to Lord Londonderry, 3 February 1918 (ibid., D/627/433/25); Montgomery to Crozier (reporting D'Arcy's contact with Pollock, a member of the Ulster Unionist deputation), 3 February 1918 (ibid., D/627/433/27).

60. Printed copy of sermon preached by D'Arcy in Belfast Cathedral, 3 February 1918 (ibid., D/627/433/24).

61. *Irish Churchman*, 7 February 1918.

62. Montgomery to D'Arcy, 7 February 1918 (PRONI, Montgomery papers, D/627/433/37).

63. Montgomery to Bagwell, 8 February 1918 (ibid., D/627/433/38).

64. Montgomery to Crozier, 8 February 1918 (ibid., D/627/433/40).

65. D'Arcy to Montgomery, 9 February 1918 (ibid., D/627/433/43).

66. Memorandum of meeting between southern Unionist deputation and Lloyd George, 6 February 1918 (National Archives, Midleton papers, PRO/30/67/36/2056–8).

67. Crozier to Montgomery, 5 February 1918 (ibid., D/627/433/34).
68. Speech by Crozier at Convention, 14 March 1918 (TCD, Convention papers, Mss 2986–7/159).
69. 'Note by the Provost of Trinity College and the Archbishop of Armagh', in Plunkett, *Report of the Proceedings of the Irish Convention*, p.35.
70. *Irish Churchman*, 18 April 1918.
71. Jackson, *Home Rule*, p.192.
72. Crozier to Lady Londonderry, 27 February 1918 (PRONI, Lady Londonderry papers, D/2846/2/27/28) recounted to Lady Londonderry a conversation Crozier had had with her son.
73. N.C. Fleming, 'Old and new unionism: the seventh Marquess of Londonderry, 1906–21', in D.G. Boyce and A. O'Day, *Ireland in Transition, 1867–1921* (London, 2004), pp.235–6.
74. Jackson, *Home Rule*, p.191.
75. Between 21 March 1918 and the end of April the British army lost 300,000 men: McDowell, *Irish Convention*, p.185.
76. Ibid., p.186.
77. Jackson, *Home Rule*, p.183.
78. *Church of Ireland Gazette*, 12 April 1918.
79. Ibid., 7 January 1916; *The Times*, 9 May 1916.
80. Bernard to Carson, 27 May 1915 (PRONI, Carson papers, D/1507/A/12/27).
81. Bernard to Wimborne, 24 November 1916 (British Library, J.H. Bernard papers, Add. Ms 52782/139–42).
82. Archbishops' joint appeal on recruiting, 17 April 1918 (TCD, J.H. Bernard papers, Mss 2388/137); the appeal was published in the *Gazette*, 19 April 1918.
83. Maume and O'Leary, *Controversial Issues*, p.67.
84. A.W. Samuels to Bernard, 18 April 1918 (TCD, J.H. Bernard papers, Add. Ms 2388/138).
85. *Church of Ireland Gazette*, 19 April 1918.
86. Bernard to Davidson, 30 April 1918 (TCD, J.H. Bernard papers, Mss 2388/142).
87. *Church of Ireland Gazette*, 26 April 1918.
88. 'Protestant protest against conscription', Irish Guild of the Church: loose papers (RCB Library, RCB 131). The Irish Guild of the Church was a pressure group within the Church of Ireland that aimed to promote the Gaelic revival in the Church.
89. *Irish Churchman*, 25 April 1918.
90. *Church of Ireland Gazette*, 3 May 1918.
91. Bernard to Henry Barbor, 23 April 1918 (British Library, J.H. Bernard papers, Add. Ms 52783/14–15).
92. *Irish Churchman*, 25 April 1918.
93. Davidson to Bernard, 29 April 1918 (British Library, J.H. Bernard papers, Add. Ms 52783/16)
94. Bernard to Randall Davidson, 30 April 1918 (TCD, J.H. Bernard papers, Mss 2388/142).
95. See Buckland, *Irish Unionism I*, pp.165–6, 170.
96. Ibid., p.147. SUC nominees to the general council of the Irish Unionist Alliance were elected by an overwhelming majority, 7 June 1918: ibid., p.161.
97. *Irish Churchman*, 2 May 1918.
98. Ibid., 9 May 1918.
99. Confidential Report (TCD, Convention papers, Mss 2986–7/177).
100. R.H. Murray, *Archbishop Bernard: Professor, Prelate and Provost* (London, 1931), p.315.
101. McDowell, *Irish Convention*, p.91.
102. White claims the convention offered proof of Bernard's 'exceptional gifts as a statesman.' N.J.D. White, *John Henry Bernard, Archbishop of Dublin: Provost of Trinity College Dublin. A Short Memoir* (Dublin, 1928), p.12.
103. Fleming, 'Old and new unionism', p.238.

Conclusion
'Warring for the Promised Land':
The Church of Ireland and Irish Politics, 1910–18

The anxiety of their Church was so aroused that in all her assemblies from the General Synod to the parish vestry voices had been raised against the peril.[1]

Alfred Elliot, bishop of Kilmore, 1912 Kilmore diocesan synod

A united Ireland is the first 'postulate' of all Irish churchmen 'who are churchmen first; for a divided Ireland means death to their Church'.[2]

Editorial, *Church of Ireland Gazette*, 22 November 1918

The bishop of Kilmore's 1912 diocesan synod speech and the 1918 editorial from the *Church of Ireland Gazette* tell two different stories, revealing the change in the Church of Ireland's relationship with Irish unionism. Involvement on the unionist side in the 1910 general elections, and opposition to *Ne Temere* in 1911, revealed a church united politically on the basis of an 'all-Ireland' unionism. The 1912 General Synod confirmed that in a campaign permeating every level of church government, the Church of Ireland largely spoke with one voice in opposing the 'peril' of home rule. However, the ruptures in 'secular' Irish unionism caused by the Ulster unionist drift towards partition were replicated within the Church of Ireland. The 1918 editorial from the *Gazette* confirmed that members of the Church of Ireland in the south were prepared to accept that Irish self-government was preferable to any settlement based on the division of the island. If a fear of partition was the catalyst for southern Anglicanism's relatively positive view of home rule, in Ulster the Church of Ireland was prepared to countenance the exclusion of all or part of the province from a home rule settlement. The tensions inherent between these differing opinions on an Irish settlement raised questions concerning how the Church of Ireland viewed its role in Irish politics – as did its involvement in the various machinations of the third Home Rule Bill period in general. Perhaps most significantly, the increasing probability of partition challenged the Church of Ireland's ability to influence the differing shades of unionist opinion.

I

Within the Church, opposition to home rule was expressed in various forums. Church services played an important part in the Church of Ireland's contribution to the unionist cause and carried clear political implications. Preacher books and newspaper reports demonstrated that 'unionist' or Orange religious services were generally well attended, suggesting the local parish church was valued as a forum through which opposition to home rule could be expressed. An illustration of how such services could, at the least, give the impression of binding the Ulster unionist community together was seen in Newtownards at the start of 1914. The service, in St Mark's, was attended by the elite of Ulster unionism, including Edward Carson, Sir George Richardson, Captain Frank Hall and the Duke and Duchess of Portland, who had all been enjoying a house party at Mount Stewart. Archbishop Crozier preached at a service that brought together Presbyterian and Anglican, temporal and spiritual lords, political and quasi-military leaders, and landowners and volunteers.[3]

As well as potentially binding together the differing elements of Irish unionism, church services provided a visible demonstration of the apparent unity of Irish Protestantism against home rule by often consciously transcending denominational boundaries. The pan-Protestant nature of Ulster unionism was highlighted by the co-operation between the Church of Ireland and Presbyterian Church, especially at a local level in Ulster. The 1912 General Synod should be placed in the context of Irish Protestant opposition to home rule, providing a near mirror image of meetings held by the Presbyterian and Methodist Churches. The thaw in the relationship between the Presbyterian Church and the Church of Ireland probably aided co-operation between the Churches in opposing home rule. However, it is probable that the unionist campaign would have generated such pan-Protestant resistance even without already existing good relations. The threat of home rule subsumed denominational identities under the overarching unity brought by unionism. The fact that the Presbyterian origins of the 1912 Ulster Covenant was not an issue for the Church of Ireland in Ulster (or indeed for the Covenant's southern Anglican opponents) suggested Irish Anglicans were content to reside in the 'big tent' of Irish pan-Protestant opposition to home rule. At an internal governmental level, the Church of Ireland contributed to unionist opposition. Resolutions against *Ne Temere* and home rule coloured the relatively dull activity of select and general vestries, which were concerned primarily with managing the local church. The large number of these resolutions suggested the majority of the laity (unsurprisingly) were in agreement with the stand taken by their clergy in opposing home rule. Vestry resolutions also offered the laity an opportunity to affirm their opposition to home rule in what they perceived was a representative forum, a point attested to in many of the resolutions passed at meetings in 1911–12. The implicit assumption in their argument was that the structure of the Church of Ireland offered Irish unionists a 'vote' on home rule denied them by the Liberal government, who refused unionist demands for a general election. The representative function of general and select vestries mirrored how some Anglicans viewed the General Synod, which in 1912, at a corporate, national level, articulated the same anti-home rule arguments that were expressed by select and general vestries at a parish level. The earl of Desart believed the synod offered Protestants (and particularly southern Protestants) a 'voice' on home rule.[4] Indeed, for the unionist press, part of the value of synods (both diocesan and general) lay in how they were held to represent the views of Irish Protestantism towards home rule.

II

The strong identification of the various levels of Church government with unionism was seen as a justification for resisting home rule. Such endorsement was vocalised in sermons and speeches. The clergy, unsurprisingly, propounded a religious argument as the main (but not only) objection to Irish self-government. A contemporary observer, the nationalist commentator F.C. Ormsby, claimed that 'An Orange sermon will incline him [the unionist] to view Irish Unionists as a sort of modern Israelites warring against the hosts of Canaan for the possession of the Promised Land.'[5] Certainly, sermons and speeches provided a largely consistent narrative justifying opposition – and active resistance if necessary – to home rule. This narrative provided clearly defined enemies to Irish Protestants in the guise of, variously, Irish nationalists, Liberal party politicians, the papacy, and the Catholic Church in Ireland; equally, potential heroes were provided by the leaders of Irish – and Ulster – unionism, particularly Edward Carson. Hopes of salvation from home rule were sustained by a historicist interpretation of the Irish past, as the third home rule period was seen to fit seamlessly into earlier occasions of threats to Protestantism, such as the Siege of Derry and the Williamite war in Ireland. Unsurprisingly, clergymen looked further back, to the Bible, to find in many Old Testament characters (Moses, Joshua and Nehemiah were particular favourites) examples for Irish Protestants to follow if they hoped to defeat home rule. What lay behind such an at times cavalier interpretation of the Bible was a belief that the ultimate source of deliverance lay in the providential blessing of a God benevolent towards unionism, and, particularly from clergy based in Ulster, Ulster unionism.

By virtue of their position as 'spokesmen' of a Church, clergy and bishops were well placed to articulate a belief in the supposed malevolent influence the Catholic Church would exercise in a home rule Ireland. For the Church of Ireland, the alleged threat posed to Protestant civil and religious liberties was the main (although not the only) explanation for their determined opposition to home rule. When the ecclesiastical concern over *Ne Temere* coincided with the political threat of home rule in the form of the McCann case, little encouragement was needed for Protestants to confirm their long-standing suspicions of the Catholic Church. For many Protestants, home rule really would equal Rome Rule; Protestant liberties really would be placed in jeopardy by a parliament composed largely of Catholics; the Catholic Church really would appropriate Church of Ireland land and buildings. The anti-Catholic rhetoric of the Church of Ireland (and the clergy of other Protestant denominations) should not be viewed as a hysterical, irrational over-reaction, but as indicative of a desire to preserve intact liberties which were genuinely held to be under threat. Arguably, it is irrelevant if such fears were accurate, or justified – what mattered was the effect Protestant perceptions of the Catholic Church had on motivating and sustaining opposition to home rule.

However, it would be overly reductive to ascribe the Church of Ireland's opposition to home rule and its support for militant Ulster unionism solely to some deep-seated anti-Catholic sentiment given free rein by the introduction of the third Home Rule Bill. Legal (and theological) arguments based on the limits of obedience played an important role in justifying the Covenant. Also, the Church of Ireland did not exist in an Irish ecclesiastical vacuum. Its support for unionist militancy reflected a wider trend (shared by the Church of England) for paramilitary organisations; in addition, the deep-seated sense of imperial identity exhibited by the Church of Ireland was a fairly visible part of the cultural and political landscape in Britain in the early twentieth century, and was shared by sister churches (such as the Australian Anglican church) throughout the empire.

It is difficult to assess how far clerical rhetoric had a formative influence on unionist opinion and to what extent it served merely to reinforce already deeply held perceptions of the debilitating effects of home rule. At the most, the utility of clerical rhetoric may have lain in its ability to sustain opposition to home rule in the face of unfavourable parliamentary arithmetic; the imprimatur of the Church also extended a degree of respectability and legitimatisation to the often doubtful legality of unionist tactics. At the least, religiously motivated sermons and speeches provided partial evidence of the reasoning behind the widespread support offered to Irish unionism (and in Ulster, militant Ulster unionism) by large numbers of Church of Ireland clergy. Such involvement provided a practical outworking of a providential worldview in which God would reward faith and trust by preventing home rule. This worldview proved resilient in justifying involvement in the Great War, in which it was believed Britain would prove victorious if it placed its dependence upon God.

The difficulty in determining the formative effect of the Church of Ireland's involvement in Irish unionism is due largely to the fact that the Church's influence was exerted in the context of a complex two-way relationship. This was particularly evident in the case of the Church's participation in Ulster unionist resistance. On the one hand, it was the Ulster unionist leadership that set the political agenda: Ulster Day, the establishment of the UVF and the Larne gun-running were the creations of Carson, Craig and their lieutenants in Ulster. However, it is open to question whether these events would have represented such a potent demonstration of loyalist resistance to home rule without the patronage of the Church of Ireland. This support leant Ulster unionism a degree of respectability; in addition, clergy and bishops constructed a moral, 'Christian' defence for Ulster unionism against the barbs of opponents who claimed loyalist resistance represented reckless military posturing and illegality.

Indeed, an almost symbiotic relationship appeared to exist between the Church and unionism, and particularly Ulster unionism. The political leadership valued and perhaps even needed ecclesiastical endorsement if their stand against home rule was to prove successful – or at least sustainable. For the Church of Ireland, its strong articulation of an anti-home rule stance at various critical points – the 1910 elections, Ulster Day, the Larne gun-running – afforded it a position of prominence and influence in the political arena. In this respect, the Church of Ireland was little different from the Presbyterian Church. However, the Church of Ireland's role has been largely overlooked in accounts of the period, which is rather incongruous in light of its contribution to Ulster unionism. In terms of political influence, the involvement of the Church of Ireland in Ulster unionism casts some doubt on T.W. Moody's claim that the 'stronghold of Ulster Protestantism has always been the Presbyterian church, rooted in the Scottish reformation and containing close and continuous contact with Scotland'.[6] The organisational importance of Church of Ireland clergy eclipsed that of their Presbyterian counterparts: they outnumbered Presbyterians in positions of leadership in unionist clubs, while more Ulster Day services were held in Church of Ireland places of worship than any other Protestant Church. This prominent role was likely due to a number of factors. Church of Ireland patronage may have been more valuable than Presbyterian in how the Ulster unionist cause was perceived in England, providing a predominantly 'Anglican' population with evidence of the extent of opposition to home rule. D'Arcy's role as an apologist for Ulster unionist resistance, played out in the pages of English newspapers, lends some credence to this view. The Church of Ireland, due to its strength relative to the Presbyterian Church in western areas of Ulster, was able to provide an important leadership role 'on the ground', leading unionist clubs or assisting with the drilling of volunteers. In addition, the fact that D'Arcy (and to a lesser extent, Crozier) remained an Ulster-based bishop throughout the period provided a degree of consistency in the Church of Ireland's contribution to unionism. The Presbyterian Church, at a leadership level, may have lacked this consistency due to the limited term in office held by the moderator.

III

The increasing identification of the Church of Ireland in Ulster with Ulster unionism in 1912–14 affected the internal life of the Church. The Church of Ireland in Ulster was tied to a strategy of resisting home rule that moved slowly, but perceptibly, towards an acceptance of a partitionist settlement. Their patronage of the UVF confirmed episcopal and clerical support for the increasingly exclusivist line being adopted by Ulster unionism. Southern Anglicans, such as John Henry Bernard, who feared partition, were encouraged to seek a settlement with Redmond by the 'Imperial nationalism' certain sections of the Irish nationalist-Catholic community espoused at the outbreak of the Great War. While the Easter Rising was a visceral shock to southern Anglican opinion, it ultimately served to accelerate their desire for a settlement with the Irish Nationalist Party. Equally, for Ulster Anglicans, the Easter Rising and the war – in particular the Somme offensive – served to harden their opposition to home rule and by extension strengthen their support for partition, if it proved the best outcome that Ulster unionism could realistically obtain.

These increasingly divergent opinions were highlighted in the various resolutions issued by the House of Bishops in 1916–17 in response to the Lloyd George partition scheme; they found fullest expression, at an episcopal and high-political level in the Church in the private discourse surrounding the Irish Convention. Disagreements within the Church of Ireland over partition were also manifested during the 1918 general election in the contest for the Dublin University seat. Pro-partition members (or at least those prepared to accept partition) of the Church of Ireland championed William Jellett, a barrister, while those in favour of an all-Ireland settlement supported A.W. Samuels. The *Irish Churchman* praised Jellett for the 'fine part he played as a leader of the Southern Unionist protest against Lord Midleton's bungling'; on the other hand, the *Church of Ireland Gazette* noted how Jellett's position on partition (that it was acceptable under certain circumstances) was the 'least satisfactory' of the four candidates for Dublin University.[7] The relative disharmony of the 1918 general election was in stark contrast to the virtually unanimous display of support for Irish unionism adopted by the Church of Ireland during the 1910 general election campaigns.

The *Church of Ireland Gazette*, which throughout the period increasingly came to articulate the voice of southern unionism, explained why partition would be harmful for the Church of Ireland. An editorial outlining its opposition to the 1916 Lloyd George partition scheme claimed the Church of Ireland was a unifying force 'in this sharply divided country'. The 'unbiased observer' could not fail to notice that the Church of Ireland stood for a united Ireland: the primate was primate of *all* Ireland; Dublin was the centre of 'ecclesiastical machinery'; the General Synod was a 'great democratic assembly' drawing members from every county in Ireland. The Church's 'genius' was 'away from section and faction towards unity'. If partition would harm the Church of Ireland's unifying role in national life, the *Gazette* was also concerned that 'political alienation may issue in ecclesiastical aloofness', and that churchmen in the proposed excluded counties would see Dublin as being 'across a frontier'. Presbyterians, for whom Belfast was their 'Mecca', would not feel the inconvenience of partition: 'But because the Church of Ireland *is* the Church of Ireland, she stands to suffer most.'[8]

The *Gazette* expressed similar sentiments with greater force (and possibly desperation) in the run-up to the 1918 general election. Partition would degrade the Church of Ireland ('a national Church one and indivisible') 'into two shabby provincial sects'. The 'very life' of the Church of Ireland was inextricably linked to Ireland remaining united. While such unity was most easily preserved in the legislative union, if the union was 'abrogated' the Church of Ireland should favour 'some form of government, within the Empire, for a united Ireland'.[9]

Southern churchmen, such as Bernard, shared the *Gazette*'s abhorrence of partition. Its potentially harmful effect on Trinity College Dublin was one of Bernard's motivations in supporting an all-Ireland settlement. He feared partition would 'alienate Northerners who would thenceforward devote themselves to their own University in Belfast'. It would be a 'serious thing' for the members of Dublin University elected in the 1918 general election to 'commit themselves to the dismemberment of Ireland'. Such a policy would 'abandon the union quite definitely' and 'secure the interests of Belfast at the expense of Unionists in the South and West'.[10] Carson obviously had similar concerns – a few weeks before the election, he informed the provost of Trinity College Dublin (and Bernard) that he would not stand for Dublin University. 'Under existing circumstances', Carson felt that the university should be represented 'by a member who is not so closely connected with the Ulster position'.[11] Bernard also feared the rumoured establishment of a separate teacher training college for Ulster churchmen would erect another 'barrier' between Ulster and the rest of Ireland, noting that the Church of Ireland was too small to be split in half.[12]

The altruistic aspect of the Church of Ireland's opposition to partition – namely, that it would harm the Church's potential to act as a unifying force in Ireland – represented a degree of wishful thinking. Those within the Church who came to castigate partition initially shared their northern brethren's intense opposition to home rule, and, like Ulster churchmen, furnished their resistance with anti-Catholic arguments (such as Bernard's belief that the Catholic Church would lay claim to Church of Ireland buildings under home rule). Indeed, the very small degree of opposition to the 1912 General Synod resolutions was partly motivated by a belief that the synod's partisan nature would alienate the Church of Ireland from the Catholic Church. In addition, anti-partition forces in the Church reflected the sectionalised nature of Irish unionism – in the Irish Convention they articulated a position opposed by Ulster unionists and die-hard southern unionists. Therefore, it was perhaps naïve to expect that a 'united' Church of Ireland, exerting its influence in a 'united' Ireland, would establish peace and eliminate faction. Instead, it is likely one of the main explanations for the strong opposition to partition was a fear that the prophecies of Protestant persecution under home rule, preached in 1910–14, would come to fruition if southern Protestants were abandoned. Such fears were magnified by a belief that partition would rob southern Church members of the support of their more numerous northern counterparts.

Unsurprisingly, a different view of partition was propagated by northern

Church members. In Ulster, the majority of clergy followed the lead of 'secular' Ulster unionism and accepted partition as an escape route from home rule for all or part of the province. Within the Church, D'Arcy was the most visible and articulate representative of this position, proving a strong supporter of Ulster Day, the UVF, the Lloyd George scheme, and obstructive tactics at the Irish Convention. Clearly, D'Arcy also failed to share the year-zero opinion of partition held by the *Gazette* and a number of southern churchmen. He viewed the 1918 general election results as evidence of the strength of Ulster unionism, and claimed that if partition 'becomes necessary, we should now demand the whole of Ulster'.[13]

In Ulster, the southern Anglican view that partition meant abandonment by their northern brethren was rejected. James Stronge defended Ulster exclusion as it would leave the majority of Church of Ireland members exempt from the rule of a Dublin parliament, and therefore better able to assist their southern counterparts.[14] Another prominent layman, Hugh de Fellenburg Montgomery, took up the cudgels against the *Gazette*'s position on partition. He argued that if a Dublin parliament was established, it would be 'an immense advantage' for the Church of Ireland to have the major part of the northern province 'in the free atmosphere of direct Imperial British government', allowing churchmen in the excluded counties to assist their southern brethren. In any case, he believed it was 'gross selfishness' to insist that if there was to be home rule for any, there must be home rule for all.[15] In a further letter to the *Gazette*, Montgomery argued that southern unionist opposition to partition was a greater danger to the Church of Ireland than home rule. Resentment among northern Church members would harden if they suspected southern churchmen were 'plotting' to induce the government to force the 'north-east under a Home Rule yoke'.[16]

IV

The disagreements over partition revealed the Church's inability to maintain political influence when the all-Ireland nature of unionism was challenged. The Church's self-perception as an 'all-Ireland' church was both its strength and weakness politically. While the defeat of home rule *tout court* was pursued, the Church of Ireland provided a near mirror image of Irish unionism. Before Ulster Day, bishops and clergy were able to claim, with a degree of accuracy, that in opposing home rule they were representing not just the Church of Ireland, but Irish unionism. In 1912 the unanimous nature of the General Synod's opposition to home rule was seen as a potent demonstration of Church of Ireland, and more generally, Irish unionist, unity. However, the possibility of partition created competing views on an Irish settlement within the Church, meaning no distinctively 'Church of Ireland' political position could be established. The contrast with 1912 was evident at the 1916 General Synod when, in an attempt to avoid public disagreement, Crozier refused to allow debate on the House of Bishops' resolution against the Lloyd George partition scheme.

The culmination of Ulster unionist propaganda against home rule, Ulster Day, also marked the apotheosis of the Church of Ireland's role in Irish politics in the period. As the northern and southern components of Irish unionism grew further apart, the Church of Ireland's political influence waned, as personified by John Baptist Crozier. In 1912 he was asked by the Ulster Unionist Council to grant permission for the holding of Ulster Day religious services, whereas in 1917–18 he was largely ignored and marginalised by the delegates sent to the Irish Convention by the UUC. Crozier had never been favourable towards partition – his support for Ulster Day and the UVF was based on an assumption that such resistance would deter the government from introducing any form of home rule. In addition, Crozier, born in Cavan, was inclined to support partition only on the basis of temporary, nine-county exclusion. However, other churchmen faced similar pressures to Crozier yet remained staunch Ulster unionists. What set Crozier apart was his position as primate, which for him involved preserving the unity of the Church of Ireland. Crozier shared the southern Anglican belief that partition would be detrimental to the Church of Ireland, but was aware that members of the Church in Ulster were unwilling to accept an all-Ireland settlement if they could obtain six- or nine-county exclusion. This placed Crozier in a fairly impossible situation, having to balance the competing claims of Church members in Ulster with those in the rest of Ireland.

Individual churchmen maintained their positions of prominence – for example, D'Arcy remained as involved in Ulster unionism in 1918 as in 1912, while Bernard's continuing influence was revealed by the Irish Convention. However, their involvement was less as representatives of their church, and more as spokesmen (or leaders) of their respective partisan political positions. The issue of partition changed the Church of Ireland's relationship with Irish and Ulster unionism. In Ulster, the Church could still prove influential only if it was prepared to accept exclusion. Crozier's failure, until too late, to recognise this fact rendered him politically impotent at the Convention; equally, D'Arcy remained an insider due to his firm grasp of the hard-nosed pragmatism and political reality driving the Ulster unionist partitionist strategy. In the south, the Church of Ireland was divided between the conciliatory line favoured by Bernard and the die-hard stance of those who believed home rule could still be prevented. Ultimately, Bernard and D'Arcy had to subordinate their Church of Ireland identity to advance their respective political positions, neither of which were shared by large numbers of their fellow churchmen.

If the Church of Ireland's relationship with Irish unionism altered during the third Home Rule Bill period, Church members holding nationalist sentiments were increasingly marginalised due to the decline of Redmondite nationalism. The Irish Guild of the Church (Cumann Gaodhalach na h-Eaglaise) provided a case study of the effect Sinn Féin and Irish republicanism had on the more benign Irish nationalism exhibited by a small percentage of Church of Ireland members. The Irish Guild of the Church was formed in 1914 as a pressure group to promote the Gaelic revival within the Church. It aimed to 'preserve' the Church of Ireland's Celtic heritage and form a 'bond of union' for Irish-speaking members of the Church; it also sought to collect suitable Gaelic hymns for use in public worship.[17] The cultural nationalism of the Guild built on earlier expressions of support for the Gaelic League from largely southern-based clergymen, such as James Owen Hannay.[18] The Guild attracted interest and membership from a fairly eclectic range of Irish Protestants – Roger Casement sent his apologies for non-attendance to the Guild's opening meeting, while Douglas Hyde attended a meeting in October 1914.[19] A number of bishops, among them B.J. Plunkett and Sterling Berry (signatories of the Logue Manifesto), were office holders.[20]

Plunkett resigned as president of the Guild in June 1916 after disagreeing with its relatively half-hearted resolution of condemnation against the Easter Rising. The resolution stated that as a 'strictly non-political body', the Guild deplored the Rising and desired 'to make it plain that it [had] no connection whatever with it'.[21] However, Plunkett reversed his decision to resign after the strengthening of the terms of the resolution, which came to affirm loyalty to 'his Majesty the King' and to desire 'the establishment of law and order and the restoration of peace and goodwill among the people of Ireland'.[22] However, the resolution was rescinded at the annual meeting of the Guild in May 1918, causing Berry, Plunkett, the bishop of Limerick and the dean of St Patrick's to resign.[23] The *Gazette* believed that by rescinding the 1916 resolution, the Guild had terminated all its 'useful and legitimate activities'; by identifying with Irish republicanism, it had adopted an attitude 'inconsistent' with the teaching of the Church of Ireland.[24] The treasurer of the Guild later wrote to the *Gazette* claiming the 1918 annual meeting had been packed with a body of Dublin-based opponents to the union who had succeeded, in a poorly attended meeting, in having the 1916 resolution withdrawn.[25] However, the 1918 annual meeting did not represent some new move towards Irish republicanism – the dispute over the Easter Rising suggested internal tensions already existed, while in 1917 Berry and Plunkett had claimed the policy of the Guild was becoming 'more and more that of the extreme Republican party in Ireland'.[26]

The dispute within the Irish Guild of the Church suggested the vision of Irish unity preached by Berry and Plunkett in the aftermath of the Easter Rising, and formally outlined (in their opinion) by the Logue Manifesto, was incapable of realisation. The hopes of Berry and Plunkett, and the majority of pro-home rule Church of Ireland members, were based on a positive assessment of the Irish Nationalist Party, a view reinforced by Redmond's 'Imperial nationalist' response to the war. The IPP's collapse in the face of Sinn Féin after the Easter Rising and the ill-fated Irish Convention signalled the death knell for the moderate nationalist view propounded by various members of the Church of Ireland. The Irish Guild of the Church demonstrated how all but the most maverick figures in the Church of Ireland would reject the shift in Irish politics from moderate nationalism to republicanism.

The Church of Ireland's political influence by 1918 was in stark contrast to that of the Catholic Church, which was able to capitalise on the widespread opposition to conscription and play a prominent role in the resistance to the application of the Military Service Bill to Ireland. However, due to the deep divisiveness of the partition issue, there was no over-arching issue (even conscription) that could bring unity between the differing factions of Irish unionism. This left the Church of Ireland, as an 'all-Ireland' Church, with little opportunity to play a leading role in Irish politics – it could no longer speak with any authority or unanimity for Irish unionism.

V

Ultimately, the Church of Ireland did not split despite the fact Ireland was 'dismembered'. Organisationally, the Church of Ireland remained unchanged under partition: the General Synod continued to meet in Dublin; the Representative Church Body remained based in Dublin; the majority of clergy were trained in Dublin; and many clergy had little difficulty in serving what became joint parishes located on either side of the border. Clergy and bishops also continued to move between the northern and southern provinces. D'Arcy best personified this trend: despite being a firm supporter of partition, he was not prepared to take refuge behind the walls of the Protestant citadel of Northern Ireland for the rest of his career. In 1919 he became archbishop of Dublin, a position he held briefly until his elevation to Armagh in 1920.

There may be a number of reasons for this continued institutional unity. Most importantly perhaps, the Church remained united as it was of no benefit to its members, north or south, for it to be divided. The financial aid flowing from southern dioceses to Belfast from 1910 provided evidence of the mutual advantage unity could bring to northern and southern sections of the Church. Belfast obviously benefited from such generosity, but it is apparent the Church of Ireland in the south identified advantages of its own. Shortly after its determined opposition to the 1916 Lloyd George partition scheme, the *Gazette* urged Anglicans in the south and west of Ireland to support the Church in Belfast. The future of the Church of Ireland, it argued, lay in Belfast, with its rapidly increasing number of adherents. However, the *Gazette* feared the Church was 'rapidly losing the future' due to a lack of clergy able to serve there. Assistance was justified on the grounds that 'we are the Church of Ireland, and all Ireland is our parish'.[27] A similar concern was demonstrated by Sterling Berry, shortly after his participation in the Logue Manifesto dispute. Speaking at the Killaloe diocesan synod, Berry hoped that, whatever happened politically, there would be no partition of the Church of Ireland. Therefore, he urged clerical members of the synod to volunteer to serve in Ulster, in order to rectify the shortage of clergy. His appeal was motivated by a desire to avoid 'narrowness' in Church life and look beyond diocesan boundaries.[28]

This concern for Belfast undoubtedly reflected a pragmatic desire to provide assistance for perhaps the one success story, numerically speaking, in the Church of Ireland in the early twentieth century. However, perhaps a deeper, spiritual unity was revealed. A perceived status as the 'body of Christ' may have held the Church together despite the deep and irreconcilable differences over politics. If the disagreements in the Church over partition had followed theological lines, perhaps a split would have been more likely. However, low, high and middle-of-the-road churchmen were united in their opposition to home rule, meaning the Church's involvement in Irish politics was largely free of theological significance beyond the confines of a Protestant–Catholic dichotomy.

The importance of Archbishop Crozier should not be overlooked in any explanation of the Church of Ireland's continuing unity. As Primate of 'All-Ireland', Crozier represented an institutional unity absent from 'secular' Irish unionism. He consciously avoided endorsing either partition or an all-Ireland settlement, despite pressure from D'Arcy and Bernard to support their respective political positions. Crozier appeared indecisive in relation to an Irish settlement at various times in the period. He was unsure of the wisdom of the increasing militancy of Ulster unionism during 1913–14; he recognised the difficulty the Lloyd George partition scheme could cause for the Church of Ireland, and so prevented discussion of it at the General Synod in 1916; during the Convention, he avoided identifying with either unionist delegation. However, Crozier's prevarication may have served to preserve the unity of both the House of Bishops and the Church of Ireland, by avoiding the controversy that would have followed if he, as primate, had supported one side or the other. Crozier (like all unionist bishops and clergy) had an ecclesiastical and political loyalty. He was obviously an enthusiastic unionist and supported the Church being highly involved in the political arena. However, in choosing his Church as the ultimate focus of his devotion, Crozier demonstrated his intention to represent the membership community of the Church of Ireland ahead of articulating a particular political position that could have left certain sections feeling isolated.

VI

At the end of his speech at the Irish Convention advocating a federal plan, Archbishop Crozier, with a scriptural flourish, expressed his hope for an 'all-Ireland' settlement: 'More than once during the past eight months the vision appeared to me of a coming time when "Ephraim will not envy Judah, and Judah will not vex Ephraim".'[29] Crozier was to be disappointed. The general election of 1918 confirmed the change in the Irish political landscape caused largely by events catalysed by the First World War. Republicanism replaced moderate nationalism as the dominant electoral force in Ireland, while the vitality of 'six-county' Ulster unionism was reinforced, making some settlement based on the division of the island appear inevitable.

Partition left the Church of Ireland in a political no-man's-land, unable to speak with a clear, unanimous voice on either Ulster or southern unionism. This suggests the history of the Church of Ireland's political influence in the third Home Rule Bill period was one of decline. At times the Church was a prime agent in the organisation and justification of unionist opposition to home rule. However, the desire of its bishops and clergy to reflect – rather than reform – Irish unionism meant the Church reinforced the divisions in Irish politics, both between unionism and nationalism and within Irish unionism itself. This mimetic role was the Church of Ireland's strength when Irish unionism was united, and its weakness, as it came to mirror the tensions caused by the possibility of partition. However, while the period saw the fracturing of Irish unionism and the virtual disappearance of its southern component, the Church of Ireland maintained its institutional integrity. Judah may have vexed Ephraim, but, through a mixture of internal factors, luck – or providence – and the unexpected political awareness of its primate, the Church of Ireland survived the period intact, to minister in the newly divided Promised Land of the Irish Free State and Northern Ireland.

NOTES

1. *Irish Churchman*, 20 September 1912.
2. *Church of Ireland Gazette*, 22 November 1918.
3. *Newtownards Chronicle*, 24 January 1914.
4. *Church of IrelandGazette*, 19 April 1912.
5. F.C. Ormsby, 'Irish Unionism,' *Irish Review*, October 1912, p.400.
6. T.W. Moody, 'The social history of modern Ulster', in T.W. Moody and J.C. Beckett (eds), *Ulster since 1800* (London, 1958), p.231, quoted in R.F.G. Holmes, 'Ulster Presbyterianism and Irish Nationalism', *Studies in Church History*, vol. 18 (1982), p.535.
7. *Irish Churchman*, 5 December 1918; *Church of Ireland Gazette*, 13 December 1918.
8. *Church of IrelandGazette*, 16 June 1916.
9. Ibid., 22 November 1918.
10. John Henry Bernard to A.W. Samuels, 13 November 1918 (British Library, J.H. Bernard papers, Add. Ms 52783/32).
11. Edward Carson to the provost of TCD, 21 November 1918 (ibid., Add. Ms 52783/38); Carson to Bernard, 21 November 1918 (ibid., Add. Ms 52783/37).
12. *Church of IrelandGazette*, 22 November 1918.
13. Charles Frederick D'Arcy to Hugh de Fellenburg Montgomery, 31 December 1918 (Public Record Office of Northern Ireland (PRONI), Montgomery papers, D/627/434/137).

CONCLUSION

14. *Church of Ireland Gazette*, 29 November 1918.
15. Ibid., 20 December 1918.
16. Ibid., 3 January 1919.
17. Ibid., 15 May 1914.
18. See R.B. McDowell, *The Church of Ireland, 1869–1969* (London, 1975), pp.101–2.
19. Minute book of the Irish Guild of the Church, 29 April 1914; 21 October 1914 (Representative Church Body (RCB) Library, 131).
20. Ibid., 29 April 1914.
21. Ibid., 1 June 1916; Plunkett announced his resignation in a letter to a meeting of the executive committee, held 13 June 1916.
22. Ibid., 20 June 1916.
23. Ibid., 14 May 1918; the minutes noted that following the withdrawal of Plunkett and Berry, 'Prof French read an interesting paper on the Galation Celts.'
24. *Church of Ireland Gazette*, 17 May 1918.
25. Ibid., 31 May 1918.
26. Minute book of the Irish Guild of the Church, 12 December 1917 (RCB Library, RCB 131).
27. *Church of Ireland Gazette*, 22 September 1916.
28. Ibid., 3 August 1917.
29. Speech by Crozier at Convention, 14 March 1918 (Trinity College Dublin, Convention papers, Mss 2986–7/159).

Appendix
Archbishops and Bishops of the Church of Ireland, 1910–20

Armagh Province

	Appointed	Termination of office
Archbishops of Armagh		
William Alexander	25 Feb. 1896	res. 1 Feb. 1911.
John Baptist Crozier	2 Feb. 1911	11 Apr. 1920
Bishops of Tuam		
James O'Sullivan	15 May 1890	res. Feb 1913
Benjamin John Plunkett	10 May 1913	trs. Meath 15 Oct. 1919
Bishops of Clogher		
Maurice Day	25 Jan. 1908	27 May 1923
Bishops of Derry and Raphoe		
George A. Chadwick	25 Mar. 1896	res. 31 Jan. 1916
Joseph Irvine Peacocke	25 Apr. 1916	res. 31 Dec. 1944
Bishops of Down and Connor and Dromore		
John Baptist Crozier	26 Sept. 1907	trs. Armagh 2 Feb. 1911
Charles Frederick D'Arcy	29 Mar. 1911	trs. Dublin 15 Oct. 1919
Charles T.P. Grierson	28 Oct. 1919	res. 30 Nov. 1934
Bishops of Kilmore		
Alfred George Elliot	17 Oct. 1897	28 Sept. 1915
William Richard Moore	30 Nov. 1915	23 Feb. 1930

Dublin Province

Archbishops of Dublin		
John Ferguson Peacocke	19 May 1897	res. 3 Sept. 1915
John Henry Bernard	7 Oct. 1915	res. 30 June 1919
Charles Frederick D'Arcy	15 Oct. 1919	trs. Armagh 17 June 1920

Bishops of Cashel

Henry Stewart O'Hara	24 Feb. 1900	res. 31 Mar. 1919

Bishops of Cork

William Edward Meade	6 Jan. 1894	12 Oct. 1912
Charles Benjamin Dowse	23 Dec. 1912	res. 15 Sept. 1933

Bishops of Killaloe

Mervyn Archdall	2 Feb. 1897	res. 31 Mar. 1912
Charles Benjamin Dowse	11 June 1912	trs. Cork 23 Dec. 1912
Thomas Sterling Berry	25 Mar. 1913	res. 6 Mar. 1924

Bishops of Limerick

Raymond D'Audemar Orpen	2 Apr. 1907	res. 31 Dec. 1920

Bishops of Meath and Kildare

James Bennett Keene	17 Oct. 1897	5 Aug. 1919
Hon. Benjamin John Plunkett	15 Oct. 1919	res. 31 Mar. 1925

Bishops of Ossory and Ferns

Charles Frederick D'Arcy	5 Nov. 1907	trs. Down 29 Mar. 1911
John Henry Bernard	25 July 1911	trs. Dublin 7 Oct. 1915
John A. Fitzgerald Gregg	28 Dec. 1915	trs. Dublin 10 Sept. 1920

Source: N.C. Fleming and A. O'Day, *Modern Irish History since 1800* (London, 2005), pp.436–43

Bibliography

PRIMARY SOURCES

Private papers
<u>British Library, London:</u>
J.H. Bernard papers, Add. Mss 52781–4

<u>House of Lords Library, London:</u>
Lloyd George papers, D/14

<u>Lambeth Palace Library, London:</u>
Davidson papers, vols 389–90

<u>National Archives, Kew:</u>
Confidential reports to Dublin Castle, CO/904/27
Midleton papers, PRO/30/67/33

<u>National Library Ireland, Dublin:</u>
Hannay papers, Ms 8271

<u>Plunkett Foundation, Oxford:</u>
Plunkett papers, Arm.

<u>Public Record Office of Northern Ireland, Belfast:</u>
Carson papers, D/1507 taken from MIC/665
Sir Charles Falls papers, D/1390/19/1
Fermanagh UVF papers, D/1402
Lady Londonderry papers, D/2846/2 and D/2847/1
Montgomery papers, D/627
O'Neill papers, D/1238
Peacocke papers, MIC/87
Seaforde UVF papers, D/1263
Spender papers, D/1295
Lady Spender papers, D/1633
Ulster Unionist Council papers, D/1327

<u>Trinity College, Dublin:</u>
Convention papers, Mss 2986–7
Donoughmore papers, Don/K/40
J.H. Bernard papers, Ms 2388
J.O. Hannay papers, Ms 3455
J.O. Hannay papers, Ms 3436/PC 7

Church records
<u>Public Record Office of Northern Ireland, Belfast:</u>
Armoy, preacher book, MIC/1/334/E/2–3
Belleek, vestry minute book, MIC/1/270/D/1
Camus Juxta, vestry minute book, MIC/1/307/D/3
Culdaff, vestry minute book, MIC/1/278/D/4
Donagheady, vestry minute book, MIC/1/35/1
Down, vestry minute book, CR/33/DB/2
Drumclamph, vestry minute book, MIC/1/304/D/1
Kilbroney, vestry minute book, MIC/1/88
Kilrea, vestry minute book, MIC/1/55
Killeevan, vestry minute book, MIC/1/154/C/1
Killinchy, preacher book, CR/1/16F/6
Knockbreda, vestry minute book, CR/1/24D/3
Knockbreda, preacher book, CR/1/24G/6
Lisburn Cathedral, vestry minute book, CR/1/35/D/4
Lower Moville and St Columba's, vestry minute book, MIC/1/138/D/1
Muckno, vestry minute book, MIC/151/D/2
St Comgall's, Bangor, vestry minute book, CR/1/87/D/3
St Patrick's, Ballymena, preacher book, CR/1/78/E/5
St Thomas', vestry minute book, CR/1/36/D/4
Trinity (Belfast), CR/1/3/5/2
Upper Falls, vestry minute book, CR/1/69/D/2

<u>Representative Church Body Library, Dublin:</u>
Bray quarterly calendar
Donnybrook parish magazine, P. 246. 25
Howth parish magazine, P. 373. 25
Irish Guild of the Church papers, RCB 131
Mariners' Church parish magazine, P. 368. 25. 1
Minutes of the House of Bishops
Minutes of the Standing Committee of the General Synod
St Ann's parish magazine, P. 344. 25
St Bartholomew's parish magazine, P. 64. 25. 1
St Fin Barre's general vestry minute book, p.497. 5. 5
St Matthias' vestry minute book, p.44. 5. 4
St Peter's parish magazine, p.45. 16. 10
St Stephen's vestry minute book, p.46. 5. 2
Taney annual reports, p.609. 21. 3

<u>Private possession:</u>
All Saints', parish magazine
Holywood, vestry minute book
Lisburn Cathedral, parish magazine
Mary Magdalene, Belfast, vestry minute book
Mary Magdalene, Belfast, parish magazine
St Columba's, Belfast, report and accounts, 1915
St Jude's, Belfast, vestry minute book
St Mark's, Dundela, parish magazine
Willowfield, Belfast, preacher book
Willowfield, Belfast, vestry minute book

Newspapers and periodicals:

Ballymena Observer
Belfast Newsletter
Belfast Telegraph
Belfast Weekly Telegraph
Church of Ireland Gazette
County Down Spectator
Daily Mail
Daily Telegraph
Derry Journal
Down Recorder
Fermanagh Times
Freeman's Journal
Irish Church Directory
Irish Church Quarterly
Irish Churchman
Irish Ecclesiastical Gazette
Irish Times
Journal of the General Synod
Lisburn Standard
Lurgan Mail
Newtownards Chronicle
Northern Constitution
Northern Whig
The Times
Ulster Echo
Ulster Gazette and Armagh Standard
Ulster Guardian
The Warden

PRINTED PRIMARY SOURCES

George Birmingham, *The Red Hand of Ulster* (London, 1912)
W. St John Brodrick (Lord Midleton), *Records and Reactions, 1856–1939* (London, 1939)
Charles Frederick D'Arcy, *Adventures of a Bishop* (London, 1934)
Cyril Falls, *The History of the 36th Ulster Division* (Belfast, 1922)
Stephen Gwynn, *John Redmond's Last Years* (London, 1919)
Herbert Hensley Henson, *Retrospective of an Unimportant Life: vol. I, 1863–1920* (Oxford, 1942)
Richard George Salmon King, *Ulster's Protest: Her Industrial, Political, Imperial Reasons for Refusing to Submit to Home Rule. An Appeal to Great Britain* (Derry, 1913)
Richard George Salmon King, *Ulster's Refusal to Submit to a Roman Catholic Parliament, Stated and Justified* (Derry, 1914)
John Frederick MacNeice, *Carrickfergus and its Contacts: Some Chapters in the History of Ulster* (Carrickfergus, 1928)
Ronald McNeill, *Ulster's Stand for Union* (London, 1922)
Henry E. Patton, *Fifty Years of Disestablishment: A Sketch* (Dublin, 1922)

J. Irvine Peacocke, *Peacocke of Derry and Raphoe: An Autobiographical Sketch* (Dublin, n.d.)

Sir Horace Plunkett (*et al.*), *Report of the Proceedings of the Irish Convention, 1918* (London, 1918)

Simon Rosenbaum (ed.), *Against Home Rule: The Case for the Union* (London, 1912)

Oonagh Walsh (ed.), *An Englishwoman in Belfast: Rosamund Stephen's Record of the Great War* (Cork, 2000)

SECONDARY SOURCES

Books

Alan Acheson, *A History of the Church of Ireland, 1691–1996* (Dublin, 1997)

Donald Harman Akenson, *God's Peoples: Covenant and Land in South Africa, Israel and Ulster* (Ithaca, 1992)

Jonathon Bardon, *A History of Ulster* (Belfast, 2001)

Toby Barnard and William G. Neely (eds), *The Clergy of the Church of Ireland, 1000–2000: Messengers, Watchmen and Stewards* (Dublin, 2006)

Brian Barton, *Brookeborough: The Making of a Prime Minister* (Belfast, 1988)

George Kennedy Allen Bell, *Randall Davidson: Archbishop of Canterbury, vol. I* (Oxford, 1935)

Paul Bew, *Ideology and the Irish Question: Ulster Unionism and Irish Nationalism, 1912–1916* (Oxford, 1994)

Paul Bew, *Ireland: The Politics of Enmity, 1789–2006* (Oxford, 2007)

D. George Boyce, *The Irish Question and British Politics, 1868–1986* (London, 1988)

D. George Boyce and Alan O'Day (eds), *Defenders of the Union: A Survey of British and Irish Unionism since 1801* (London, 2001)

D. George Boyce and Alan O'Day (eds), *Ireland in Transition, 1867–1921* (London, 2004)

D. George Boyce and Alan O'Day (eds), *The Ulster Crisis 1885–1921* (London, 2006)

Patrick Buckland, *Irish Unionism I: The Anglo-Irish and the New Ireland, 1885–1922* (Dublin, 1972)

Patrick Buckland, *Irish Unionism II: Ulster Unionism and the Origins of Northern Ireland, 1886–1922* (Dublin, 1973)

Michael Burleigh, *Earthly Powers: Religion and Politics in Europe from the French Revolution to the Great War* (London, 2005)

J.L.B. Deane, *Church of Ireland Handbook: A Guide to the Organisation of the Church* (Dublin, 1962)

Christopher Fauske, *'Side by Side in a Small Country': Bishop John Frederick MacNeice and Ireland* (Dublin, 2004)

John Fitzsimons Harbinson, *The Ulster Unionist Party 1882–1973: Its Development and Organisation* (Belfast, 1973)

Alan Ford, James McGuire and Kenneth Milne (eds), *As by Law Established: The Church of Ireland since the Reformation* (Dublin, 1995)

Raymond Gillespie and William G. Neely (eds), *The Laity and the Church of Ireland, 1000–2000: All Sorts and Conditions* (Dublin, 2002)

David Hempton, *Religion and Political Culture in Britain and Ireland: From the Glorious Revolution to the Decline of the Empire* (Cambridge, 1996)

Thomas Hennessey, *Dividing Ireland: World War One and Partition* (London, 1998)

Arlie J. Hoover, *God, Germany and Britain in the Great War: A Study of Clerical Nationalism* (New York, 1989)

Michael Hurley (ed.), *Irish Anglicanism: 1869–1969* (Dublin, 1970)

Kenneth Hylson-Smith, *The Churches in England from Elizabeth I to Elizabeth II, vol. III, 1833–1998* (London, 1998)

Alvin Jackson, *The Ulster Party: Irish Unionists in the House of Commons, 1884–1911* (Oxford, 1989)

Alvin Jackson, *Sir Edward Carson* (Dublin, 1993)

Alvin Jackson, *Ireland 1798–1998: Politics and War* (Oxford, 1999)

Alvin Jackson, *Home Rule: An Irish History, 1800–2000* (London, 2003)

Keith Jeffery, *Ireland and the Great War* (Cambridge, 2000)

Keith Jeffery (ed.), *'An Irish Empire'? Aspects of Ireland and the British Empire* (Manchester, 1996)

Thomas Johnston, John Robinson and Robert Jackson, *A History of the Church of Ireland* (Dublin, 1953)

Sophia King and Seán McMahon (eds), *Hope and History: Eyewitness Accounts of Life in Twentieth-Century Ulster* (Belfast, 1996)

Joseph Lee, *Ireland 1912–1985* (Cambridge, 1989)

Breandán Mac Giolla Choille, *Intelligence Notes, 1913–1916* (Dublin, 1966)

Albert Marrin, *The Last Crusade: The Church of England in the First World War* (Durham, North Carolina, 1974)

Robert Brendan McDowell, *The Irish Convention, 1917–18* (London, 1970)

Robert Brendan McDowell, *The Church of Ireland, 1869–1969* (London, 1975)

Alan Megahey, *The Irish Protestant Churches in the Twentieth Century* (London, 2000)

David W. Miller, *Church, State and Nation in Ireland, 1898–1921* (Dublin, 1973)

Kenneth Milne (ed.), *A Church of Ireland Bibliography* (Dublin, 2005)

Robert Henry Murray, *Archbishop Bernard: Professor, Prelate, and Provost* (London, 1931)

Daithí Ó Corráin, *Rendering to God and Caesar: The Irish Churches and the Two States in Ireland, 1949–73* (Manchester, 2006)

Alan O'Day, *Irish Home Rule: 1867–1921* (Manchester, 1998)

Cornelius O'Leary and Patrick Maume, *Controversial Issues in Anglo-Irish Relations, 1910–1921* (Dublin, 2004)

Walter Alison Phillips (ed.), *History of the Church of Ireland from the Earliest Times to the Present Day*, 3 vols (Oxford, 1933)

Raymond Refausse, *Church of Ireland Records* (2nd edition, Dublin, 2006)

George Seaver, *John Allen Fitzgerald Gregg: Archbishop* (Dublin, 1963)

Hugh Shearman, *Not an Inch: A Study of Northern Ireland and Lord Craigavon* (London, 1942)

Harry Smith, *Heal Not Lightly* (Chichester, 2006)

Anthony Terence Quincey Stewart, *The Ulster Crisis: Resistance to Home Rule 1912–1914* (London, 1967)

Marcus Tanner, *Ireland's Holy Wars: The Struggle for a Nation's Soul, 1500–2000* (New Haven, 2001)

Brian Taylor, *The Life and Writings of James Owen Hannay (George A. Birmingham), 1865–1950* (New York, 1995)

Charles Townshend, *Political Violence in Ireland: Government and Resistance since 1848* (Oxford, 1983)

Charles Townshend, *Ireland: The Twentieth Century* (London, 1998)

Charles Townshend, *Easter 1916* (London, 2005)

Graham Walker, *A History of the Ulster Unionist Party: Protest, Pragmatism, and Pessimism* (Manchester, 2004)

Trevor West and Horace Plunkett, *Co-operation and Politics: An Irish Biography* (London, 1986)

Jérôme aan de Wiel, *The Catholic Church in Ireland: 1914–1918* (Dublin, 2003)

N.J.D. White, *John Henry Bernard, Archbishop of Dublin: Provost of Trinity College, Dublin. A Short Memoir* (Dublin, 1928)

Alan Wilkinson, *The Church of England and the First World War* (London, 1978)

John Wolffe, *God and Greater Britain: Religion and National Life in Britain and Ireland, 1843–1945* (London, 1994)

Articles and chapters

Tim Bowman, 'The Ulster Volunteer Force and the formation of the 36th (Ulster) division', *Irish Historical Studies*, 32, 128 (November 2001), pp.498–518

Tim Bowman, 'The Ulster Volunteer Force, 1910–1920: new perspectives', in Boyce and O'Day (eds), *The Ulster Crisis*, pp.247–58

D. George Boyce, 'British opinion, Ireland and the war, 1916–1918', *Historical Journal*, 17, 3 (1974), pp.575–93

Patrick Collinson, 'The vertical and the horizontal in religious history: internal and external integration of the subject,' in Ford, McGuire and Milne (eds), *As by Law Established*, pp.15–32

Marie-Claire Considere-Charon, 'The Church of Ireland: continuity and change', *Studies: An Irish Quarterly Review*, 87, 346 (Summer 1998), pp.107–16

Jim English, 'Empire Day in Britain, 1904–1958', *Historical Journal*, 49, 1 (2006), pp.247–76

David Fitzpatrick, 'The logic of collective sacrifice: Ireland and the British army, 1914–1918', *Historical Journal*, 38, 4 (December 1995), pp.1017–30

Neil Fleming, 'Old and new unionism: the seventh Marquess of Londonderry, 1906–21', in Boyce and O'Day, *Ireland in Transition*, pp.223–40

Alan Ford, 'Standing one's ground: Religion, polemic and Irish history since the Reformation', in Ford, McGuire and Milne (eds), *As by Law Established*, pp.1–14

Andrew Gailey, 'King Carson: an essay on the invention of leadership', *Irish Historical Studies*, 30 (1996), pp.66–87

Peter Gray, 'National humiliation and the Great Hunger: fast and famine in 1847', *Irish Historical Studies*, 30, 126 (November 2000) pp.193–216

Brad S. Gregory, 'The other confessional history: on secular bias in the study of religion', *History and Theory*, 45 (December 2006)

Finley Holmes, 'Ulster Presbyterianism and Irish Nationalism', *Studies in Church History*, 18 (1982), pp.535–55

Finley Holmes, 'Ulster will fight and Ulster will be right: the Protestant churches and Ulster's resistance to Home Rule, 1912–14', *Studies in Church History*, 20 (1983), pp.321–35

David H. Hume, 'Empire Day in Ireland, 1896–1962', in Jeffery (ed.), *'An Irish Empire'?*, pp.149–68

Alvin Jackson, 'Unionist myths, 1912–1985', *Past and Present*, no. 136 (1992), pp.164–85

Alvin Jackson, 'Irish Unionists and the Empire, 1880–1920: classes and masses', in Jeffery (ed.), *'An Irish Empire'?*, pp.123–48

Greta Jones, 'Eugenics in Ireland: the Belfast Eugenics Society, 1911–1915,' *Irish Historical Studies*, 28 (1992) pp.81–95

Raymond M. Lee, 'Intermarriage, conflict and social control in Ireland: the decree "Ne Temere"', *Economic and Social Review*, 17, 1 (October 1985)

Martin Maguire, 'The Church of Ireland and the problem of the Protestant working class of Dublin, 1870s–1930s', in Ford, McGuire and Milne (eds), *As by Law Established*, pp.195–203

Martin Maguire, '"Our people": the Church of Ireland and the culture of community in Dublin since disestablishment', in Gillespie and Neely (eds), *The Laity and the Church of Ireland*, pp.277–303

Johnston McMaster, review of *Heal Not Lightly*, *Search*, 30, 1 (Spring 2007), pp.77–8

Alan Megahey, 'God will defend the right,' in Boyce and O'Day (eds), *Defenders of the Union*, pp.159–76

Alan Megahey, 'William Connor Magee, the Church of England and the Church of Ireland', in Barnard and Neely (eds), *The Clergy of the Church of Ireland*, pp.186–98

Kenneth Milne, '1870–1992', in Milne (ed.), *A Church of Ireland Bibliography*, pp.41–50

John A. Moses, 'Australian Anglican leaders and the Great War, 1914–1918: the "Prussian Menace", conscription, and national solidarity', *Journal of Religious History*, 25, 3 (October 2001), pp.306–23

T.P. O'Neill, 'Political life, 1870–1921', in Hurley (ed.), *Irish Anglicanism*, pp.101–9

Jeremy Smith, 'Federalism, devolution and partition: Sir Edward Carson and the search for a compromise on the third Home Rule bill, 1913–14', *Irish Historical Studies*, 35, 14 (2007), pp.496–518

Graham Walker, 'The Irish Presbyterian anti-Home Rule convention of 1912', *Studies: An Irish Quarterly Review*, 86, 341 (Spring 1997), pp.71–7

Rev. C.A. Webster, 'The Church since Disestablishment,' in Phillips (ed.), *History of the Church of Ireland*, vol. iii

John Whyte, 'Political life in the South', in Hurley (ed.), *Irish Anglicanism*, pp.143–53

Robert Withycombe, 'Australian Anglicans and imperial identity, 1900–1914', *Journal of Religious History*, 25, 3 (October 2001), pp.286–305

Unpublished dissertations

Michael T. Foy, 'The Ulster Volunteer Force: its domestic development and political importance in the period 1913–1920' (Queen's University Belfast, unpublished Ph.D. thesis, 1986)

David McConnell, 'The Protestant Churches and the origin of the Northern Ireland state' (Queen's University Belfast, unpublished Ph.D. thesis, 1998)

Alan Megahey, 'The Irish Protestant churches and social and political issues, 1870–1914' (Queen's University Belfast, unpublished Ph.D. thesis, 1969)

Index

The Glory of Being Britons
Civic Unionism in Nineteenth-Century Belfast

John Bew

At a moment when British Prime Minister Gordon Brown has excluded Ireland from his version of modern Britishness, John Bew's book could not be more timely. Covering a period of almost ninety years, Bew demonstrates how a strongly held British national identity took hold in nineteenth-century Belfast, a town which was once regarded as the centre of republicanism and rebellion in Ireland. Starting with the impact of the French Revolution – a cause of huge celebration in Belfast - this book describes how political and civic culture in the town became deeply immersed in the imagined community of the British nation after the Act of Union of 1801, allowing the author to provide a new perspective on the roots of Ulster's opposition to Home Rule.

What caused this shift from 'Liberty, Equality, and Fraternity' to 'God save the Queen'? While entirely aware of the sectarian division in Ulster,. Bew places these developments in the wider context of the Westminster political system and debates about the United Kingdom's 'place in the world', thus providing a more balanced and sophisticated view of the politics of nineteenth-century Belfast, arguing that it was not simply dominated by the struggle between Orange and Green. The book breaks new ground in examining how the formative 'nation-building' episodes in Britain – such as war, parliamentary reform, and social, economic and scientific advancement – played out in the unique context of Belfast and the surrounding area. Ultimately, however, it also explains how the exponents of this civic unionism struggled to make their voices heard as Britain and Ireland entered the age of mass democracy and traditional modes of identification began to reassert themselves, even before the Home Rule crisis began.

2008   272 pages
978 0 7165 2974 3   cloth €39.95/ £45.00 / $59.95

Seán MacEntee

A Political Life

Tom Feeney

This is the first biographical work of one of the chief policymakers to have served the independent Irish state. It is also the only scholarly biography of a senior Fianna Fáil minister other than Sean Lemass. Seán MacEntee was in many ways a unique political personality. He was the most senior politician in the independent Irish state to have been born in what became Northern Ireland. Moreover, he was a fiercely independent thinker who left a voluminous collection of private papers. This capacious collection reflects MacEntee's insatiable interest in all aspects of government policy, not merely those for which he bore ultimate responsibility. The collection complements the official government files in the National Archives which, when viewed in toto, convey the full force of ministerial and departmental thinking and provide a comprehensive record of public policymaking from the 1930s to the 1960s.

2008   272 pages   illus
978 0 7165 2912 5   cloth   €39.95 / £45.00 / $59.95

Faith and Patronage
The Political Career of Flaithrí Ó Maolchonaire,
c. 1560–1629

Benjamin Hazard
Foreword by John McCafferty

The Franciscan friar Flaithrí Ó Maolchonaire was a man of many parts: Gaelic scholar and educator, special envoy and consummate politician with deep religious convictions. Hazard has written a fascinating and engaging study of this flawed yet brilliant man and his times. Ó Maolchonaire left Ireland in the 1590s after Tudor state-building policies had spread from the Pale into regions previously controlled by his family's powerful Gaelic allies. He studied at the University of Salamanca, leaving him ideally placed to act as diplomatic agent between the Ulster earls and the Spanish crown 15 years later.

He first gained renown when Spain intervened in Ireland's Nine Years War after which Ó Maolchonaire used his influence to find employment for battle-hardened Irish veterans in the Spanish armed forces. With the favour this gained for him at the Spanish court he established St. Anthony's College at the University of Leuven, thereby providing the foundations for a new network of Irish Franciscan colleges throughout Europe.

His desire to see the restoration of Catholicism and the Ulster earls in Ireland made his religious and political aims indivisible. With all his efforts directed towards this objective, we see both his genius and his hubristic aversion to compromise. Anglo-Irish Catholics wished to reach an accommodation with Whitehall and Ó Maolchonaire's resistance to this aim demonstrates the internal divisions inherent to Irish politics. The serious student of Irish history must study this period, and Ó Maolchonaire in particular, to gain insight into what followed.

November 2009 288 pages illus
978 0 7165 3048 0 cloth €35.00 / £45.00 / $64.95